OLD TESTAMENT ETHICS

WALDEMAR JANZEN

OLD TESTAMENT ETHICS

A *Paradigmatic Approach*

WESTMINSTER/JOHN KNOX PRESS

Louisville, Kentucky

Cover design by Susan E. Jackson

Book design by Drew Stevens

First edition
Published by Westminster/John Knox Press
Louisville, Kentucky

This book is printed on acid-free paper that meets the American National Standards Institute Z39.48 standard. ∞

PRINTED IN THE UNITED STATES OF AMERICA
9 8 7 6 5 4 3 2 1

Library of Congress Cataloging-in-Publication Data

Janzen, Waldemar.
    Old Testament ethics : a paradigmatic approach / Waldemar Janzen.— 1st ed.
       p.   cm.
    Includes bibliographical references and indexes.
    ISBN 0-664-25410-1 (alk. paper)

    1. Ethics in the Bible.   2. Bible. O.T.—Theology.   I. Title.
BS1199.E8J29   1993
241.5—dc20   93-32885

To my esteemed colleagues
past and present
on the faculty of the
Canadian Mennonite Bible College
Winnipeg, Canada

CONTENTS

3. PRINCIPLE AND LAW   55

INTRODUCTION

This book speaks to the church. It addresses Christians who have the Old Testament before them in its entirety and accept it as part of their canon. As such, they consider it to be relevant and authoritative for themselves, at least to some degree, not only in the realm of theological doctrine but also in the realm of ethics.

When such Christians search for a way to appropriate the Old Testament's guidance for the ethics of the church, they face a major problem in the multiplicity of Old Testament genres. Where should they begin to listen? Jewish tradition has heard the Old Testament, or Hebrew Bible, first and foremost as law. Many Christians, perhaps despairing of the multiplicity of genres and the sheer volume and complexity of the Old Testament, have attempted to limit God's requirements for the good life to the Ten Commandments. Others have reduced the Old Testament's ethical message to a general call for justice. But what of the many stories modeling God-pleasing behavior? Or the wisdom writings? Or the preaching of the prophets? It is my goal to provide Christians with a model for grasping the Old Testament's ethical message in a comprehensive way, thereby avoiding a reductionist concentration on any one genre, like law, or any one selection of texts, like the Ten Commandments or the prophetic calls for justice.

In this quest, I will argue, it is better to begin with the genre of story than with that of law, as is done so often not only in Judaism but also in Christian and in religiously detached academic treatments of Old

1

Testament ethics. Story is the literary genre that, next to actual cultic practice, was most important in the transmission of theological-ethical instruction in ancient Israel itself. The central mode of transmitting biblical faith was recital. When the Israelite child asked his or her parents for an interpretation of their religious and ethical practices, the father was to reply by telling a story (Deut. 6:20–25). The Old Testament as a whole, in all its diversity, is in a sense a story. Even its legal collections, including the Ten Commandments, have been incorporated into that story in the final canonical text. They no longer function as self-contained law codes, as they once did, but have become sermons heard by Israel in a particular story context, whether at Mount Sinai, as part of the proclamation of God's covenant (Exodus 20–Numbers 10), or on the Plains of Moab, where Moses exhorts the people to a new life in the new land that they are about to enter (Deuteronomy 12–26). In our quest for the Old Testament's ethical message, then, we stay closest to its own voice if we begin our search by listening to stories modeling the God-pleasing life.

We will do this in chapter 1 by analyzing five such stories, each of which claims in its own way to model right ethical behavior. And yet, these five stories are neither parallel nor repetitive. Each assumes that its hearers or readers assess its model action by a different inner yardstick or ideal. Such a hearer or reader is expected by the narrator to recognize in the model action of each story's protagonist the upholding of an ideal, a different ideal in each case. For example, in our second story selection, Phinehas acts rightly before God by *preserving the holiness* of Israel and its sanctuary. His action is to be judged and approved of by the reader as an action governed by the pursuit of the holy life. Abigail, on the other hand, in our third story selection, models right behavior by *acting wisely*. Her behavior is to be judged as exemplary by the canons of Israel's wisdom. Such diversity of yardsticks or ideals by which actions are to be judged raises the question concerning a comprehensive and overarching yardstick. In other words, does the Old Testament story as a whole not expect of its readers that its ethics be judged by a primary model or ideal, or "paradigm," as I will call it? I will argue that the different paradigms of the good life (like the holy life or the wise life) implied in our five selected stories indeed do not represent five different understandings or paradigms of what it means to live rightly before God. I will demonstrate, instead, that they are welded together into a comprehensive ethic by the fact that one of these—the "familial paradigm"—represents the comprehensive end of all Old Testament ethics. We will be introduced to the familial paradigm by means of the Abraham story (Genesis 13), which constitutes our first selection.

On the other hand, the remaining four paradigms—the priestly, wisdom, royal, and prophetic paradigms—are not independent and separate ethical ideals in the Old Testament's total story. Instead, they are united because they are subordinate to the familial paradigm and work together to uphold the latter. This preeminent paradigm will be developed, with the help of further model stories, in chapter 2.

At this point, one may well expect a justification for selecting one ethical paradigm as preeminent, relegating the others to a subordinate and supportive role. I invite my readers to accept as a working hypothesis the proposal of chapters 1 and 2, namely, that the familial paradigm represents the primary ideal of the Old Testament's ethic. Further chapters will then demonstrate that the remaining four paradigms are indeed not parallel and independent inner images of the good life, but promote and support the familial paradigm as their ultimate end. That demonstration will deal with the legal genres in chapter 3 and will pay special attention to the significance of the Decalogue for Old Testament ethics in chapter 4. Chapters 5 and 6 will then develop a fuller picture of the four supportive paradigms, based on texts from various genres. Finally, chapter 7 will sketch briefly the continuities between the Old Testament's ethics and the ethics of the New Testament.

In conclusion, a word must be added concerning my use of selected Old Testament texts. As stated earlier, the intended reader is primarily the Christian who confronts the Old Testament in its entirety as part of the Christian canon. Such a reader is able to recognize theological-literary patterns and relationships that were not available to Israelites themselves at any given time in their history. In other words, my approach will be synchronic, and a version of canonical criticism.[1]

In this perspective, the starting point need not be a text or set of texts enjoying some preeminent authority on the subject of our quest. We need not search out the oldest stratum, as a historical-critical approach would dictate, or a text enjoying a central position, either in the Old Testament itself or in its Christian interpretation. I have chosen ethical model *stories* as the entry point, for reasons explained above, but that choice also is not absolutely necessary. The reason for this openness lies in the assumption of the canonical approach chosen, namely, that an Old Testament theology is generated when any text is brought into dialogue with other texts. Such a dialogue will draw in further texts as conversation partners, beginning with texts thematically related closely to the initial text(s). Because the whole canon is understood, by those who accept it as canon, to be a compatible chorus of theological voices (though not without diversity), a full-fledged biblical theology would eventually draw the whole biblical story into the discussion.[2] Where one draws the line short of that will largely be determined by external limits such as research time or book size. I have chosen to base my proposal of an ethical paradigm pattern on relatively few texts carefully chosen for their thematic relevance. They are, however, not at all unique or exhaustive in supporting the paradigmatic pattern based on them.

I sense a special kinship between my book and two others in the sparsely treated field of Old Testament ethics. One of these is an older publication, the other very recent. Many years ago I read James Muilenburg's *The Way of Israel: Biblical Faith and Ethics* (1961) with great appreciation.[3] It was only when my present book was almost finished in a final draft, however, that I opened Muilenburg's slim volume again—and was amazed. There I found, not an earlier version of my proposal, but a pointer in the same direction. Muilenburg's comprehensive characterization of Israel's ethics, his sensitivity to the different genres with narrative at the head, his highlighting Old Testament ethics as a family ethos, his sketching of different perspectives on the good life—these and other features find immediate resonance in my own approach. One might suggest, without attempting to be too precise, that Muilenburg's use of "the way" (*derek*) almost corresponds to my use of "paradigm." Although nothing in the present work was consciously drawn from Muilenburg's, I acknowledge joyfully, and with a sense of having been affirmed, the company of that great teacher.

Kinship of a different kind links my study with the recent work of Bruce C. Birch, *Let Justice Roll Down: The Old Testament, Ethics, and the Christian Life* (1991).[4] Once again, my own book was essentially completed when I first saw Birch's volume. His presuppositions and his aims, as spelled out in Part One of his book, are almost identical to mine. His attempt to open the Old Testament as an ethical resource to the church; his canonical approach; his recourse to the Old Testament's many genres, yet within a narrative framework, are but the main features compatible with my own work. On the other hand, Birch and I follow very different routes from our common starting points to our common goals. Although a brief comparison between our proposals will be offered in chapter 3, I regret that the

4

timing of our publications made an ongoing dialogue throughout my text impracticable.

It is a pleasant duty to express my gratitude to those who have encouraged, enriched, and facilitated the writing of this book. My colleagues, Professors Gerald Gerbrandt (Old Testament), Harry Huebner (Ethics), David Schroeder (New Testament), and Gordon Zerbe (New Testament) have been especially helpful and encouraging partners in dialogue. Professor Elmer A. Martens, of Fresno, California, used an early draft of this work in a seminary course and has persistently encouraged publication. Professor Walter Brueggemann has encouraged me and advocated publication at several important points. To these and others who cannot all be named here I want to express my deep gratitude. I would add that I alone bear responsibility for the views and the shortcomings in this book.

The staff and students of the European Mennonite Bible School Bienenberg, of Liestal, Switzerland, where the major part of this manuscript was written, in pleasant surroundings, were a supportive community for my wife and me during a sabbatical leave. Professor Ernst Jenni, Basel, opened the library of the theological faculty to me and extended gracious hospitality. Jeffries M. Hamilton, my Westminster/John Knox Press editor, helped in many ways to make this a better work. Heidi Harms, Jim Suderman, and especially Chris Wiebe lent me their expertise in computer word processing, a field in which I am a mere beginner. My daughter Hildi and my son Edwin prepared the indexes.

Mary, my wife, shared the joys and frustrations of a writing project that extended through many years. Even more important, however, she has lived out for me an understanding of family faithfulness (*hesed*) that provided ongoing encouragement to keep searching for its roots in scripture.

Winnipeg, Canada   Waldemar Janzen
May 1993

Notes

1. The specialist in the field will readily recognize my indebtedness to the work of Brevard S. Childs. I assume throughout that the paradigmatic pattern discerned in this study is a theological-ethical construct visible to those of us who have the completed canon before us. Nowhere do I intend to suggest that historical Israel consciously accepted and lived by

this pattern. On the other hand, these paradigms derive from Israel's historical experience. It is clear also that, in less conscious and fully developed form, these paradigms did guide Israel or Israelite groups and individuals in living out God's revealed will. Therefore, a certain dialectical relationship between the completed canon and the history of Israel that led to it will mark our discussion throughout.

2. "Biblical theology" is used here advisedly, with the understanding that the approach taken in this book precludes a separation of ethics from theology; see Brevard S. Childs, "The Ethics of the Old Testament" and "The Theological Context of Old Testament Ethics," in *Biblical Theology of the Old and New Testaments: Theological Reflection on the Christian Bible* (Minneapolis: Fortress Press, 1992), 673–85, esp. 676f.

3. James Muilenburg, *The Way of Israel: Biblical Faith and Ethics* (New York: Harper & Brothers, 1961).

4. Bruce C. Birch, *Let Justice Roll Down: The Old Testament, Ethics, and the Christian Life* (Louisville, Ky.: Westminster/John Knox Press, 1991).

CHAPTER 1

ETHICAL MODEL STORIES

The Old Testament's Ethical Impact

Stories of Saints and Sinners

Most Christians first meet the Old Testament in the form of stories read or heard. These stories tell of events, but perhaps more impressively, of characters who act. Before long, the hearers or readers of these stories sense a distinct ethical appeal, even if one's Sunday school teacher or one's grandmother does not append a moral. Children are drawn to figures like Abraham, Joseph, Moses, David, or Ruth, not so much consciously convinced that they themselves ought to imitate these figures, but as generally aware that these figures are "good" and that siding with them somehow lays claim to the worthwhile side of life. By contrast, there are figures like Cain, Pharaoh, or perhaps Saul who invite rejection.

On immediate and open encounter, the Bible is perceived as stories filled with saints and sinners, heroes and villains. In this respect, it may not differ much from other literature, except that such other rewards of hearing or reading as suspense or surprising turns of plot recede in favor of the ethical sorting-out. The eventual reward in reading about Abraham, Moses, or David is perceived to lie less in "surprises" such as the report that Abraham and Sarah have a child after all, that Moses manages to overcome Pharaoh's resistance, or that David defeats Goliath. Rather, the satisfaction that remains with the reader or hearer is like that of a friendship concluded. He or she has now made the acquaintance of Abraham, and that in itself is worthwhile, for Abraham is good. It is an ethical-relational satisfaction that remains.

However, it may not remain for long. The perception that the Bible offers "good company" (or warning counterexamples) may soon be confused, even for a child, by ambiguous figures like Jacob or Aaron. These clearly belong to God's side of the story, yet they show such glaring shortcomings that it seems dubious whether one should allow them into the company of mental friends.

When the Saints Also Become Sinners

As soon as a Bible reader becomes more systematic, attempting perhaps to read it from cover to cover, grave doubt is thrown even on the figures earlier perceived as models. Abraham's lies (Gen. 12:10–20; 20:1–18), Moses' rashness and disobedience (Ex. 32:19; Num. 20:7–12), and David's acts of murder and adultery (2 Samuel 11) are enough to put into question the ethical adequacy of even the greatest Old Testament figures, and with them the Old Testament itself.

At this point, our hypothetical reader may well reject the ethical relevance of the Old Testament, consoled by the thought that the model of Jesus remains for him or her untarnished. In fact, this apparent failure of the Old Testament may be taken to serve the purpose of demonstrating, through its own inadequacy, the need for an ethic that is "higher." Here the popular distinction between law and gospel offers itself. Can the Christian not rejoice in leaving behind the unmanageable demands of the law and turn to the freedom of an ethic of love as taught and demonstrated by Jesus?

This road is not the only one open to the disappointed reader of the Old Testament. At least two others have frequently been taken. The favorite of nineteenth-century liberalism refocuses the search for ethical models from the historical literature to the prophetic. Abraham and David belonged to the ethically ambiguous early stages of Israel's history, according to this view. These served merely to lead up to a critique culminating in the ethical monotheism of the classical prophets, beginning with Amos. In them, so it was held, the Old Testament appeals to us legitimately in ethical matters. It is they who link up directly with the high ethic of Jesus and the Sermon on the Mount, a linking that eclipses the intervening period of legalistic Judaism.

A third road, preferred in more recent times, is associated with the term *salvation history*. It pursues a red thread of divine leading that runs through the centuries, from the earliest beginnings to the climax in Jesus Christ, from where it continues as the story of the church. In this history, Abraham and David, to pursue our main examples, but also Jacob, Pharaoh, Saul, and the whole breadth of characters populating the Old Testament, do not have individual significance as models or countermodels; they function as the varieties of raw material that God shapes and uses to achieve his ends. These ends may then be summarized as the kingdom or rule of God, characterized in conceptual terms such as love, justice, and peace (shalom).

Yet They Did Right

It is not my purpose to critique the approaches just sketched or to deny the significant insights contained, to a larger or smaller degree, in each. Instead, I want to proceed from an observation and a question. The observation, originally introspective on my part, tells me that somehow that first ethical appeal held out by the naive reader's early encounters with Abraham, David, and others does not want to leave us altogether. When we read the stories, the conviction of their ethical power and relevance asserts itself afresh. Even clergy, theologically trained in the alternatives just described, will use these biblical characters as models in their sermons time and again, a little more cautiously perhaps than the theologically less sophisticated and with a little less of a good conscience.

This observation poses the question whether something has not gone wrong in the initial rejection of the Old Testament figures once they were perceived as ethically ambiguous. Does the tenacity with which they claim ethical relevance perhaps point to a loss sustained by the believing community when that relevance is no longer acknowledged? I will argue that such a loss has indeed occurred and will attempt to refocus important aspects of our ethical perception of the Old Testament. In order to do so, I invite you to consider certain texts that convey the impression of offering models of right behavior.

A Familial Model Story: Genesis 13

Abraham's Right Act

Abraham and Lot are very rich, "so that the land could not support both of them dwelling together" (v. 6). The result is strife between their competing herdsmen (v. 7). This is the consequence of otherwise positive circumstances; no blame attaches to either Abraham or Lot. The strife, however, is considered by Abraham to be undesirable, not on general human grounds, but for the specific reason that "we are kinsmen" (Hebrew lit. "brothers," v. 8). His solution is geographical separation, and to facilitate this he makes a gracious offer: "If you take the left hand, then I will go to the right; or if you take the right hand, then I will go to the left" (v. 9). Lot chooses the fertile Jordan valley, leaving the hill country to Abraham. Thus the conflict is resolved and a peaceful relationship between them assured.[1] Even a quick reading suggests that Abraham acts in an exemplary fashion. His nonassertive and peaceful disposition makes him willing to yield the choice to Lot, even at the cost of personal disadvantage. In other words, verse 9 becomes the essence of the story's ethical message. Such a "Christlike" readiness for self-denial is welcomed by the Christian reader, but it is also perceived as exceptional. Refusal of self-interest marks neither the rest of the Abraham stories nor the Old Testament as a whole. Its occurrence in this story must, therefore, be perceived as atypical, perhaps one of those previews of New Testament ideals experienced here and there in the Old Testament, long before their full fruition in the life and message of Jesus Christ.

We noted, however, that Abraham himself states his motivation differently. He wishes to avoid strife with Lot, "for we are kinsmen" (v. 8). In other words, the aim of Abraham's action, and therewith of the story, is the restoration of harmony (shalom)[2] within the confines of a kinship group.[3] Abraham's meek and unselfish offer is the means to that end, a means chosen in this particular set of circumstances, but not necessarily characteristic of Abraham's life otherwise nor meant to be exemplary for later readers of the story. This does not mean that there might not arise circumstances again in which similar meekness might be called for. The aim of the story—namely, kinship shalom—is regarded as an "ethical good" throughout the Old Testament, that is, to live ethically as a member of the extended family, the clan, and the tribe. We will develop the concept of paradigm, and specifically this "familial paradigm," more fully in chapter 2, but for now we must return to the Abraham story once more.

Wider Contexts

Our analysis has up to now limited itself to the search for the answer to the question, In what sense is Abraham portrayed here as a model of right action? In its present context, however, the story has other functions as well. When interpreted within the story cycle about Abraham (Genesis 12–25), it becomes part of the theme of the man of faith who enters upon an unknown future at God's beckoning (12:1–3), believes in God's unlikely promise of a son to be born in his and Sarah's old age (15:1–6), and is ready to obey God to the extent of sacrificing that son and thus undoing the very future promised by God (ch. 22). In this context of self-abandoning trust in God, Abraham's risking his chances to possess the land—another promise of God—in our story (13:1–18) acquires a new significance in portraying the man of faith. And in this context it is indeed his self-effacing offer to Lot (v. 9) that becomes central. Only to such an Abraham willing to let the best land go can God promise the length and breadth of the land as a gift (vs. 14–18).[4]

We cannot stop even here. Our story belongs to a yet wider context consisting of the Tetrateuch (Genesis–Numbers), particularly to the theme of promise extending through it, and in a sense throughout the Old Testament. That promise is first given to Abraham in Gen. 12:1–3. There God calls him to set out into the unknown, assured that God would give him many descendants and a new homeland. When read in this context, it is the land choice that surfaces in our story. Unselfishly, Abraham yields his land interests to Lot in his effort to restore family shalom. But in so doing, he unwittingly retains the land destined by God for his descendants (vs. 14–18), whereas Lot's self-serving choice embroils him in the ill-fated future of Sodom and Gomorrah (v. 13).

It is necessary to pursue these two wider contexts to make two points. First, it is important to observe the narrative context within which the Old Testament places its ethical models. A story presenting an exemplary action is not a self-contained whole yielding an encapsuled and timeless ethical principle. Instead, the exemplary action emerges from a situation shaped by a preceding story and in turn contributes to the ongoing movement of that story.

Second, Genesis 13 exemplifies how theology and ethics cannot be separated from each other in the Old Testament. Both theological themes, such as God's promise, and ethical themes, such as Abraham's model behavior, are found in the same text. We cannot say that one story is ethical in content, whereas another is theological. Nor can we say that a right theology results in a right ethic. Instead, the two are aspects of the same text, which in turn is part of an ongoing narrative. The narrative that led to the conflict between Abraham's and Lot's shepherds begins with God's call to Abraham (Gen. 12:1–3) and Abraham's response in faith. In the course of following God's call into a new land, Abraham naturally lives by the ethical standards known to him, one of them being the concern to maintain peace within the extended family. This virtue is not linked specifically to the will or command of God here; we can assume that it was widespread in the ancient world. Nevertheless, it motivates Abraham to make an offer to Lot that moves God's specific plan for Abraham closer to its fulfillment, that is, the possession of the land of Canaan, unwittingly accepted here by Abraham as second best. Thus theology and ethics intertwine, not only in this Old Testament narrative but also in others. Although our attention in the present work is given primarily to the ethical content of the texts considered, we must not isolate that content from the theological-ethical narrative that contains it.

We will need to develop more fully the familial paradigm, that is, the ideal of family shalom that motivates Abraham here and is present throughout the Old Testament. Before we do that, however, we will turn to four other stories, stories that give evidence of a priestly paradigm, a wisdom paradigm, a royal paradigm, and a prophetic paradigm.

A Priestly Model Story: Numbers 25

In sharp contrast to the much-loved Sunday school story about meek and selfless Abraham, few accounts in the Old Testament repulse the Christian reader as strongly as the story to which we now turn. Yet it shares with the Abraham story the claim of modeling exemplary behavior. In fact, such a claim is made most explicitly, whereas the Abraham story merely implied it.

We begin again with a problem. Barely approaching the Promised Land, Israel is already embracing idol worship by playing the harlot with the daughters of Moab, sacrificing to their gods, and yoking itself to the Baal of Peor (vs. 1–3). As a result, Israel incurs the anger of the Lord (vs. 3–4). The Lord charges Moses to execute the guilty (v. 4) and also to harass the Midianites, who are apparently co-guilty with the Moabites in tempting Israel (vs. 16–18). Finally, a plague on account of the events of Peor is also mentioned (vs. 8–9, 18).

Into this story is set another that throws the events into sharp focus. A certain Israelite brings a Midianite woman into his family, taking her into the "inner room" (of the tent of meeting?), presumably to engage in a religiously understood sexual act with her, as was common in the fertility cult of Baal.[5] He does this with special brazenness, "in the sight of Moses and in the sight of the whole congregation of the people of Israel, while they were weeping at the door of the tent of meeting" (v. 6). Outraged by this, "Phinehas the son of Eleazar, son of Aaron the priest" (vs. 7, 11) follows them and thrusts his spear through both of them. His motivation is implied in his twice-stated careful identification as being of priestly line. He is therefore under special obligation to preserve the holiness of Israel's sanctuary, which symbolizes the holiness of Israel, a people set aside for God.[6]

Two consequences are reported. First, "the plague was stayed from the people of Israel" (v. 8), as stated by a pronouncement of the Lord (v. 11):

> Phinehas the son of Eleazar, son of Aaron the priest, has turned back my wrath from the people of Israel, in that he was jealous with my jealousy among them, so that I did not consume the people of Israel in my jealousy.

Second, Phinehas is highly praised and rewarded (vs. 12–13):

> Therefore say, "Behold, I give to him my covenant of peace; and it shall be to him, and to his descendants after him, the covenant of a perpetual priesthood, because he was jealous for his God, and made atonement for the people of Israel."

The modeling aspect is clear. Phinehas has acted as an exemplary priest. Therefore the office of priesthood is assured to him and his descendants.[7]

Christians reading this story tend to focus their attention on the violence of Phinehas's act. They are quick to characterize it as one of those crude remnants of primitive Old Testament religion fortunately overcome by the model of Christ's love in the gentler context of the New Testament. Upon closer study, however, we note that Phinehas is not put forward as a model because of his spear wielding. It is made very clear that his exemplary qualities are twofold: "he was jealous [= zealous] for his God, and made atonement for the people of Israel" (v. 13).[8] These are the qualities marking the ideal priest and, in a wider sense, every member of God's worshiping people. They are the qualities of Jesus as he cleansed the Temple[9] and as he gave himself on the cross.

Thus the story of Phinehas draws from, and contributes to, a "priestly paradigm," which we will need to discuss in greater detail. Phinehas's violence is as little essential for the exercise of priestly zeal as Abraham's peacefulness is for the maintenance of family shalom. We could also proceed to study, as in the case of the Abraham story, how this story modeling right behavior is embedded in wider narrative contexts and how it blends into wider theological themes. These will be taken up in chapter 5. Now we will proceed to a third story, a story giving evidence of a "wisdom paradigm" in the Old Testament.

A Wisdom Model Story: 1 Samuel 25

Again the story starts with a conflict situation. David, pursued by Saul, leads a fugitive's life in the wilderness of Paran, surrounded by the men who have joined him. They have protected the flocks of Nabal, a rich estate owner, but when David sends messengers to ask for a share on the occasion of sheep shearing, Nabal refuses and insults David.[10] The latter vows to kill every male of Nabal's household in revenge.

Nabal's wife, Abigail, "a woman of good understanding[11] and beautiful" (v. 3) hears of the matter. To avert evil from Nabal's and her household, she goes out to meet David and his men with rich gifts. More important even, she addresses David in a wise and well-formulated speech. She appeals to him to ignore Nabal, appropriately named the fool he is (for *nābāl* means "fool" in Hebrew);[12] asks David to accept now the gifts she would have provided immediately had she known his request; and reminds him to thank God for restraining him (through her action) from the bloodguilt that he might well have incurred through unbridled vengeance.[13] David complies, Nabal's house is spared, but Nabal still loses his life as a result of the jolt to his heart or brain when Abigail tells him of what has transpired. Eventually, Abigail becomes David's wife.

A modern reader may well side with Nabal, who insists on his property rights, and may perhaps consider David an extortioner. The story, however, leaves no doubt that Nabal has acted foolishly and that Abigail's conduct demonstrates an exemplary course of behavior. We will easily recognize her actions as clever and diplomatic, but the story goes beyond that. She is portrayed not only as pursuing enlightened self-interest, but as modeling a wise, and therefore ethical, course of action. Abigail has to choose between compliance or defiance. Compliance would preserve life and most of Nabal's and her property, though it would cost something. Defiance would bring death to Nabal and his men. It would also heap bloodguilt on David, destined to be "prince over Israel" (v. 30), a farsighted vision attributed to Abigail by the storyteller. She is choosing, therefore, not only between self-preservation and disaster, but between life and death in light of the wider counsel of God.[14] It is precisely such a choice of life over death, made possible by wise recourse to life experience as well as intelligence, that the wisdom teachers never tire of promoting with evangelistic zeal (cf. Proverbs 1–9). Thus our story does not merely constitute an anecdotal tale of wise behavior, but gives evidence of sharing in a far-reaching "wisdom paradigm."

Once again, an ethical model in story form is couched in a narrative context prepared by the earlier story of David and in turn propels the narrative into a future intimately linked to God's (theological) purposes with God's people and the world. We will leave further elaboration of these themes for later. Let us move now to a story governed by, and contributing to, the Old Testament's "royal paradigm."

A Royal Model Story: 1 Samuel 24[15]

Here again, as in the Abraham story, we are dealing with a Sunday school favorite. The conflict is provided by Saul's envious pursuit of David. When Saul enters a cave unaccompanied, David and his men, hiding in the back, face the sudden opportunity to kill their enemy. But David restrains his men, who see this as God's very gift of victory to him (v. 4). Instead, David stealthily snips a piece from Saul's robe. Later he uses it as evidence when he addresses the king from a safe distance and assures him of his loyalty, calling upon God to judge between them. Saul is reconciled and even acknowledges David's greater righteousness and his destiny to become king.

The exemplary character of David's course of action is evident throughout the story. It could easily be seen as focusing on his sparing his enemy, a good act acknowledged in the story (vs. 17, 19). However, the motive of David is twice characterized as rooted in his respect for the king as "the Lord's anointed" (vs. 6, 10). As a consequence, David states—again twice—that "my hand shall not be against you" (vs. 12, 13). He himself characterizes his self-restraint as a conscious decision to do the right thing when he sets his action

15

against the background of a proverb showing the way not taken: " 'Out of the wicked comes forth wickedness'; but my hand shall not be against you" (v. 13). Saul also acknowledges that David's restraint is not simply an expedient decision to achieve a particular end, but proceeds from a quality of character. Saul says, "You are more righteous than I; for you have repaid me good, whereas I have repaid you evil" (v. 17).

We must ask, then, in what sense David did what was good. We may well be tempted to see his exemplary action in repaying good for evil, an ethical principle that could be a model for anyone. But just as Abraham did not always and under all circumstances refrain from self-interest (see our discussion of Genesis 13), David certainly did not always spare his enemies or return good for evil to them. Again, his model behavior pertains to the right attitude and action called for toward "the Lord's anointed." David demonstrates how any Israelite should regard the king, namely, as one called to office by God, whom the king represents.

David's exemplary action, however, has an even deeper dimension. In the view of the biblical narrator, David's men are right when they remind David of God's promise to give his enemy into his hand, a promise now fulfilled.[16] They become David's tempters, however, when they imply that David should take history into his own hands by effecting the realization of that promise.[17] David's greatest claim to ethical modeling here (and elsewhere, e.g., 2 Sam. 15:24–26) is his refusal to diminish the sovereignty of God through his own autonomous action (vs. 6, 10, 12, 15).[18] It is this, more than anything else, that made David a proper candidate for kingship, for it was the question of subjection to the Lord by which Israel's kings were tested.

Saul, on the other hand, offers an antimodel. As we will see in the more detailed study of the "royal paradigm" (chapter 6), one of the king's chief duties was to guarantee justice in his realm. Saul, by contrast, pursues a subject who is righteous, that is, innocent in the matter held against him. David should have had recourse to Saul in case of injustice, but instead, he experiences injustice from the one who should have been his source of justice.[19] Consequently, he is driven to the last resort open to the oppressed, the direct approach to God. Twice he appeals, "May the LORD judge between me and you, . . ." (vs. 12, 15).

Thus justice is stood on its head; instead of the king bringing justice to his subject, the subject acts justly toward the king. It is clear that the roles were better reversed, a fact acknowledged by Saul when he predicts, "And now, behold, I know that you shall surely be king" (v. 20). But again, as in the case of David, there is here a deeper dimension than even the maintenance of justice, namely, subjection to the sovereign leading of God. By acknowledging God's will for David to become king, without submitting to that will, Saul gives evidence of his determination to act autonomously in his own self-interest. Thereby he himself disqualifies himself as Israel's king.

Again it is clear that our story reaches back and extends forward. It is shaped theologically and contributes to further theologically significant events. Ethically right (or wrong) action is interwoven into the historico-theological flow of Israel's story and feeds into its further development, rather than yielding a universal, contextless principle of sparing of one's enemy. However, the fact that David spares the Lord's anointed under these circumstances draws on, and contributes to, that inner image of king and subject that we will develop further under the name of "royal paradigm." But before we turn to an analysis of the four paradigms to which the four stories discussed so far have pointed, we must add a fifth and final story, pointing to a "prophetic paradigm."

A Prophetic Model Story: 1 Kings 21[20]

Clashing Stories

The suggestion of a prophetic paradigm may lead us to expect a story in which a prophet will act in exemplary fashion. Our story will not disappoint us, but it will also demonstrate that the prophetic model must be set apart from the others. Each of the previous four stories pointed to a certain realm of life within which right (or wrong) could be done, as measured by expectations that were rooted, for Israel, in that realm. The realms, or social-religious contexts, were those of kinship, priesthood, neighborly interaction, and royal rule. For each, a certain virtue was appropriate: promotion of harmony (shalom), zeal for holiness, wisdom for preserving life, and the quest for justice under God's sovereignty, respectively. Every Israelite was both object and agent of ethical (or unethical) behavior in each of these.

It is impossible, however, to delineate a comparable realm of

Israelite life within which an Israelite was expected to be the object or agent of right prophetic activity. The prophet in Israel was not surrounded by his or her own peculiar sphere of activity, but entered into the spheres already discussed. But before we develop this further, we must look at the story of Naboth's vineyard (1 Kings 21).

We note immediately that the conflict that opens the story does not involve a prophet. It is a clash between King Ahab's wish to acquire Naboth's vineyard, which is adjacent to the king's residence in Jezreel, and Naboth's refusal to comply. The king's request proceeds from a casual everyday whim, "that I may have it [the vineyard] for a vegetable garden, because it is near my house" (v. 2). Whether Ahab knows that his request is improper, for an Israelite is not to sell his hereditary plot of land (cf. Leviticus 25), is not stated in the story. Perhaps Ahab is not fully aware of that before Naboth's reply draws attention to it.

The refusal of Naboth to sell or exchange his land proceeds from well-considered theologico-ethical reflection. "The LORD forbid that I should give you the inheritance of my fathers" (v. 3).[21] He speaks from within the realm of the Israelite paradigm, or ideal, of familial ethics. To that paradigm belonged not only kinship shalom but also continuity of land ownership, understood as an "inheritance" from God going back to God's gift of the land to the people rescued from Egypt and preserved in the wilderness (see chapter 2). The conflict between Ahab and Naboth could have been resolved if the king, reminded by Naboth, had acknowledged the ethical legitimacy of Naboth's refusal. He appears to have done so in part, for the story describes him as sulking, but not as initiating further action to obtain Naboth's vineyard. So far, the story suggests that Naboth is acting in exemplary fashion within the familial paradigm, whereas Ahab has not yet violated openly the Israelite royal paradigm to which he is heir.

The conflict is sustained and aggravated by the entrance of Jezebel, daughter of the Canaanite king of Tyre (v. 5). She presupposes a different royal paradigm, a paradigm of absolute kingship expressed in self-serving power.[22] Her challenge to Ahab's acquiescence is the scornful "Do you now govern Israel?" (v. 7).[23] Her preference would, no doubt, have been direct expropriation of Naboth's property. Her arrangement of false witnesses and a mock trial to gain her end must be seen as diplomatic concessions to Israel's traditions. Ahab's guilt in the matter is silent complicity. As a result, a course of action is taken that violates both Israel's familial and Israel's royal paradigm by resorting to a Canaanite royal paradigm.

The Role of the Prophet

It is only now that a prophet, Elijah, enters the story. He does not appear on the scene in the course of his normal and proper prophetic activity but because God catapults him into a story not his own. His appearance initiates a new conflict, and in a sense, a new story: prophet confronts king. Although new in the present circumstances, this conflict has a prehistory, as Ahab's address indicates: "Have you found me, O my enemy?" (v. 20). The condemnation of Ahab and the terse pronouncement of God's verdict as given to him earlier (vs. 17–19)[24] follow in somewhat expanded language (vs. 20–24). They are directed at Ahab, giving only marginal attention to the non-Israelite queen (v. 23).[25]

We note further that the action of Ahab is condemned in absolute ethical terms: "because you have sold yourself to do what is evil in the sight of the LORD" (v. 20, cf. v. 25), "you have made Israel to sin" (v. 22). The verdict, in typical prophetic reversal of imagery, resorts to the same term: "Behold, I will bring evil upon you" (v. 21).

Throughout the confrontation, Elijah acts in ways totally appropriate to a prophet. He has received a word from the Lord and delivers it to its intended addressee, no matter what the risk to his own person may be. There the story could have ended. That it goes on to talk of Ahab's repentance and a new word of the Lord to Elijah granting a reduction of sentence to Ahab shows that a full picture of prophetic activity must not limit itself to prophecy of judgment.[26]

Thus a prophet acts properly as a prophet when he brings God's word to bear on the actions of persons (or groups) so as to judge (positively or negatively) such actions in terms of their own proper ethical paradigms, rather than according to a distinctive prophetic paradigm. In other words, Elijah judges Ahab because he has acted as an Israelite king should not act. In other instances, a prophet may judge a priestly action in terms of the priestly paradigm, a familial action in terms of the familial paradigm, or an everyday action in terms of a wisdom paradigm. In so applying to various contexts the measure of their appropriate paradigms, however, the prophets eventually create their own paradigm, the paradigm of a true prophet.

Stories Shape Paradigms

In conclusion, it is necessary to repeat that we have interpreted model stories; we have not characterized persons that could be considered comprehensive models. Abraham, Phinehas, Abigail, David, and Elijah are not perfect people held up to us for comprehensive imitation. That is precisely where our understanding of the Old Testament's ethical message fails us so often in our childhood. We make saints out of biblical characters, only to experience later that these saints come crashing down. Instead, we have looked at stories of persons who are exemplary in certain very specific actions and who are held up to us as models only with respect to these actions.

I have suggested further, however, that these model aspects, when combined with other stories and texts, issue into certain paradigms that stand personlike before the inner eye. At this point, we might be tempted to read our model stories, focus on the aspect they model, translate that aspect into an abstract principle (like self-denial, dedication to God, quest for justice, etc.), and consider this the ethical yield of our search. In that way, however, we would lose the narrative nature of Old Testament ethics. What comes to us in vivid stories of people would be reduced to abstract principles. We will later consider the place of principles, but for now it may suffice to say that such reductionism represents a great loss (see chapter 2).

Instead of sacrificing the vivid characters and actions of our stories, we will try to combine their model aspects into larger, more comprehensive characters and patterns of the kind that stood before Israel's eyes and shaped Israel ethically. In other words, we will search for Israel's inner image of a loyal family member, of a dedicated worshiper, of a wise manager of daily life, of a just ruler, and of an obedient proclaimer of the prophetic word.

Notes

1. Some scholars see this story as reflecting corporate tribal relationships and territorial claims. Claus Westermann disputes this, claiming that we have here a "quarrel narrative" (cf. Genesis 21 and 26, among others) "each detail of which accords with the era and life-style of the patriarchs" (*Genesis 12–36: A Commentary,* trans. John J. Scullion, S.J. [Minneapolis: Augsburg Publishing House, 1985], 173). Quarrels among shepherds

over pasture and wells were symptoms that a nomadic group had reached a size requiring separation.

2. Shalom, nonitalicized, will be used henceforth in its English meaning, "well-being" (*Webster's Third New International Dictionary,* 1961), but with awareness of the fact that "[b]oth in current discussion and in the Bible itself, it bears tremendous freight—the freight of a dream of God that resists all our tendencies to division, hostility, fear, drivenness, and misery." (Walter Brueggemann, *Living Toward a Vision: Biblical Reflections on Shalom* [2d ed.; New York: United Church Press, 1982], 16).

3. Cf. Westermann, *Genesis 12–36,* 176f. Abraham's peaceful proposal may well reflect traditional semilegal procedure in such quarrel situations. It may belong to the speech form called *Schlichtungsvorschläge* (reconciliation proposals) frequently practiced by nomadic kinship groups in place of settlement through war, a means characteristic of the larger tribal conflicts of later times; cf. Hans Jochen Boecker, *Redeformen des Rechtslebens im Alten Testament* (2d expanded ed.: Neukirchen-Vluyn: Neukirchener Verlag, 1970), 117–21; and Westermann, *Genesis 12–36.* Seen in this light, Abraham "did right" in keeping with socio-legal traditions. The "canonical reader" of our story, however, will be more conscious of Abraham's character as shaped by the story context than by his ancient social context.

4. The contrast between Abraham's faithful trust in God's promise reflected in this story and his fearful attempt at self-protection seen in the preceding story (12:10–20) is striking; cf. Walter Brueggemann, *Genesis,* Interpretation (Atlanta: John Knox Press, 1982), 125–34; Westermann, *Genesis 12–36,* 181.

5. Both mixed marriage and contamination of the sanctuary are in view. *Haqqubbâ* (RSV: "inner room") occurs only here. No such room is mentioned in any of the descriptions of Israel's tent-tabernacle. Possibly it was an addition or separate tent shrine to accommodate non-Israelite practices; cf. Philip J. Budd, *Numbers,* Word Biblical Commentary 5 (Waco, Tex.: Word Books, 1984), 280. Martin Noth suggests "wedding room" (*Numbers, A Commentary,* trans. James D. Martin, Old Testament Library [Philadelphia: Westminster Press, 1968], 198). Whatever the precise meaning, a desecration of the sanctuary is involved.

6. Commentators are not certain as to whether Phinehas's action is to be seen as evoked by the intermarriage or by the entrance of the pair into the "inner room." The two should not be separated, however. In Priestly perspective—and verses 6–18 are generally attributed to P—mixed marriage was a desecration of God's holy people Israel. The pollution of the sanctuary through the introduction of alien religious practices, so often the result of mixed marriage, only epitomizes such desecration.

7. That the story may well have served at one time to legitimate the

promotion of a specific Levitical group in Israel (i.e., the descendants of
Phinehas) to the priesthood or even to provide the high priest (see Budd,
Numbers, 278f., for a survey of opinions) is of historical interest but need
not concern us here.

8. It is said twice (vs. 11, 13) of Phinehas that he "was jealous" (or
"zealous," Hebrew root *qn'*) with "my [God's] jealousy" (*qin'ātî*, root
qn'). That he is jealous (*qannā'*, root *qn'*) is a prominent attribute of
God, not with respect to violence, but to zeal. According to Budd
(*Numbers*, 279): "Phinehas is the epitome of watchful zeal at the Temple
gate." For a study of the widespread interest in Phinehas, to the end of
the first century A.D., see William Klassen, "Jesus and Phinehas: A
Rejected Role Model," *SBL Seminar Papers* (1986), 490–500. Although
Phinehas was exploited by some to legitimize zealot violence, other
traditions, among them Philo and rabbinic sources, highlighted
Phinehas's zeal in the form of noble courage (cf. also Sirach 45:23–24)
and his readiness to sacrifice himself (for his zealous act was punishable
by law). If Psalm 106:28–31 is dependent on Numbers 25, as Noth thinks
(*Numbers*, 196f.), it would also instance the modeling of Phinehas
without highlighting his violence. It is possible, however, that this
passage antecedes Num. 25:6–18 (P); cf. Budd, *Numbers*, 277f.

9. The story occurs in all four Gospels, but John (2:17) motivates Jesus'
action explicitly by his zeal, quoting Psalm 69:9: "Zeal (*zēlos* = *qin'â*) for
thy house will consume me."

10. The enigmatic opening of verse 6 (RSV: "And thus you shall salute him")
is corrected by some in the direction of the Vulgate, and on the
assumption that MT *lḥy* is a corruption of "my brother(s)," to read "Say
thus to my brother"; thus Ralph W. Klein, *I Samuel*, Word Biblical
Commentary 10 (Waco, Tex.: Word Books, 1983), 243, 245, and Hans
Wilhelm Hertzberg, *I and II Samuel: A Commentary*, trans. J. S.
Bowden, The Old Testament Library (Philadelphia: Westminster Press,
1964), 199. (For a survey of text-critical possibilities, see P. Kyle
McCarter, Jr., *I Samuel: A New Translation with Introduction, Notes and
Commentary*, Anchor Bible 8 [Garden City, N.Y.: Doubleday & Co.,
1980], 392). If this were correct, the conflict between David and Nabal
would be given an important framework. David would then address
Nabal as a kinsman ("brother," as Abraham calls Lot in Gen. 13:8). No
doubt, this would be meant broadly, in the sense of "fellow Israelite,"
but it would assume a kinship context, marked by shalom (cf. the
threefold use of it in v. 6), for the dealings between them. Nabal,
however, rejects that and calls David an unknown runaway servant (v.
10). Abigail's action could then be seen, like Abraham's in Genesis 13, as
intended to restore kinship shalom, using wisdom as a means to that end.
The attention given to this possibility here anticipates our discussion of
the subservience of the wisdom paradigm (and all others) to the familial

paradigm. But our conclusions must remain tentative. David's designation of himself as "your son David" (v. 8), on the other hand, carries no kinship implications, but expresses humility and deference (cf. 1 Sam. 24:16; 26:17, 21, and McCarter, *I Samuel,* 397. Cf. also note 13, below).

11. Hebrew *ṭôbat-śekel.* Abigail is not accorded formal status as a "wise woman" (*'iššâ ḥăkāmâ*; cf. the wise woman from Tekoa, 2 Sam. 14:2); she simply acts with good sense. However, Jon Levenson has shown the close linkage in vocabulary and thought between our story and Old Testament wisdom thinking, to the extent of calling Nabal and Abigail "personifications of certain character types common in Israelite wisdom literature," bringing our story "close to the world of moral allegory" ("1 Samuel 25 as Literature and as History," *Catholic Biblical Quarterly* 40, no. 1 [January 1978]: 11–28, esp. 22). According to McCarter (*I Samuel,* 401), this story could be seen as "a story about the education of a future king. David is like the young man to whom much of the Book of Proverbs is addressed, who finds himself in contact with both the proverbial 'fool' (*nābāl . . .*) and the proverbial 'stalwart woman' (*'ēšet ḥayil*; see Prov. 31:10)," the latter teaching him self-control and the prevention of bloodguilt.

12. Compare verse 25 ("Nabal is his name, and folly is with him") with Isa. 32:5–8 (esp. v. 6); the sin referred to in that passage is the sin of Nabal. Levenson ("1 Samuel 25," 14) suggests that Abigail applies an old proverb. This emphasizes the closeness of our story to formal wisdom once again.

13. Hertzberg (*I and II Samuel,* 203) recalls briefly the similarity between Abigail's bringing of gifts to appease David with Jacob's similar action to appease Esau (Gen. 32:14–22). It is of interest here, in light of our further argumentation, that the latter story is concerned with the restoration of kinship shalom.

14. Hertzberg (*I and II Samuel,* 204) points out that Abigail's statement "the LORD will certainly make my lord [David] a sure house" (v. 28) clearly anticipates the dynastic promise through Nathan in 2 Samuel 7. We note how an ethical model story functions within a wider theological frame of reference. The darker side of David's future, on the other hand, is foreshadowed, according to Levenson ("1 Samuel 25," 23f.), by a revelation of those character traits of David that will manifest their full destructiveness in his affair with Bathsheba (2 Samuel 11), where no voice of wisdom intercedes to avert adultery and death. We note that it is family shalom again that is ultimately at stake.

15. The relationship of this story to chapter 26 has received much attention. Interpreters have argued for the dependence of either chapter on the other or for an underlying common source; see McCarter, *I Samuel,* 386f., n. 1, and Klein, *I Samuel,* 237. Klein's detailed comparison in two parallel columns (p. 236f.) shows a remarkable similarity. The essential

duplication of those motifs relevant to our analysis underlines the importance of David's and Saul's actions as modeling and countermodeling behavior, respectively.

16. This is true even though no precise promise of the kind cited here is extant. David's anointing through Samuel (1 Sam. 16:12–13), Jonathan's confidence that David would escape Saul and eventually become king (23:17), and a divine oracle assuring him of victory over the Philistines (23:4) substantially support this promise.

17. In 26:8, Abishai fulfills the same tempting role; see Hertzberg, *I and II Samuel,* 196, 209.

18. In chapter 25, it is the wise action of Abigail that saves David from this same temptation and makes room for God's vengeance (see esp. vs. 32–34, 38–39).

19. In 26:19–20, David even now pleads with the king for justice.

20. Several commentators hold verses 20–29 to be a series of secondary additions; cf. John Gray, *I and II Kings, A Commentary,* Old Testament Library (2d ed., rev.; Philadelphia: Westminster Press, 1970), 435f. Simon DeVries argues for the inclusion of verses 27–29 in the original story, considering them a "regal self-judgment genre" characteristic of similar stories (*I Kings,* Word Biblical Commentary 12 [Waco, Tex.: Word Books, 1985], 255f.). Our reading is based on the story's canonical shape. Such a reading perceives it, above all, as a story portraying the abuse of royal power and the judgment of such abuse by God, through his prophet. (Thus also DeVries, *I Kings,* 258). Hypotheses as to earlier and rather different historical functions of the story are irrelevant to our purpose. DeVries (256) suggests, for example, that the story was originally composed as propaganda from the time of the Jehu dynasty, to justify Jehu's bloody acts against Ahab's family at Jezreel (2 Kings 9; cf. Hos. 1:4) by blaming Jezebel for Ahab's aberrations. On this, see below, n. 26.

21. DeVries's translation (*I Kings,* 252) makes Naboth's theological reasons for his refusal even more explicit: "It is forbidden me by Yahweh to give you the inheritance of my forefathers."

22. Whether this characterization of Jezebel's understanding of kingship is a historically correct picture of Canaanite or Tyrian kingship is less important than the fact that the Deuteronomistic Historian saw the kingship of the surrounding nations in this way (1 Sam. 8:11–17). It seems likely, however, that there was at least some historical basis for this understanding. According to John Gray, (*The Canaanites* [London: Thames & Hudson, 1964], 111), the king in Ugarit, "as feudal head of the state had absolute rights to all the assets of the realm." Gray sees Solomon as introducing this same "economic absolutism" into Israel (ibid.). Similarly, I. Mendelsohn has argued that 1 Sam. 8:11–17 reflects correctly the nature of Canaanite kingship before Samuel's time; see "Samuel's

Denunciation of Kingship in the Light of the Akkadian Documents from Ugarit," *Bulletin of the American Schools of Oriental Research* 143 (1956): 17–22.

23. Gray (*I and II Kings,* 437, with Greek) translates: "Now is it you who exercises royal authority over Israel?" For problems and possibilities of translation, see ibid., 439. The central thrust of the question is not affected by these problems, however.

24. Formally, verses 18–19 offer a perfect model, *in nuce,* of prophetic judgment speech as found in preliterary form, later continued and developed in classical literary prophecy; see Claus Westermann, *Basic Forms of Prophetic Speech,* trans. H. C. White (Philadelphia: Westminster Press, 1967), 129–36; cf. also Klaus Koch, *The Prophets, vol. 1: The Assyrian Period,* trans. M. Kohl (Philadelphia: Fortress Press, 1983), 19–23.

25. The claim of DeVries (*I Kings,* 256) that 1 Kings 21 is a propagandistic story to justify Jehu's violence against the house of Ahab by shifting blame for Ahab's aberrations onto Jezebel is weakened considerably by the fact that the prophetic oracle of Elijah is directed squarely at Ahab, whereas only two (secondary?) references (vs. 23 and 25) draw Jezebel peripherally into its orbit.

26. See above, n. 20, and reference there to DeVries's characterization of verses 27–29 as a regal self-judgment genre. Elsewhere, DeVries (*I Kings,* 258) calls verse 29 "paradoxically, an oracle of salvation for Ahab, but also an oracle of judgment for his son."

THE FAMILIAL
PARADIGM

The Meaning and Function of Paradigm

Paradigm Defined

The bulk of this chapter will be devoted to the fuller exposition of the familial paradigm suggested by the Abraham story discussed in chapter 1. However, it is necessary to develop further what I understand by "paradigm" in this connection. Christopher J. H. Wright's definition offers a good starting point: "A paradigm is something used as a model or example for other cases where a basic principle remains unchanged, though details differ."[1] He states further that "a paradigm is not so much imitated as applied."[2] This definition is useful, but a few more accents need to be set for our purpose.

It is important to remember that the five stories considered in the preceding chapter offered model dimensions of behavior, but in no case did we find their main characters (Abraham, Phinehas, etc.) to be models or paradigms as such. Thus the readiness of Abraham to promote family shalom at the cost of personal disadvantage (Genesis 13) is exemplary, although Abraham as a person is not always so. The story, therefore, does not call its readers to an emulation of Abraham, not even in Wright's sense, that is, of applying rather than imitating.

If the story is challenging its readers ethically without offering Abraham as a paradigm, we might conclude that the challenge lies in a maxim emerging from it, such as "Place the (extended) family's interests before your own." However, biblical Israelites did not carry with them a stock of maxims or principles, but mental images of model persons. Such inner images had wholeness and embodied the rich and multifaceted qualities of exemplary behavior appropriate to a given sphere of life. In other words, before the Israelites' inner eye stood a vivid, lifelike yet ideal family member, worshiper, wise person, king, or prophet. The familial ideal or paradigm figure was not Abraham, but the figure of Abraham contributed certain aspects to that paradigm through stories such as Genesis 13. Similarly, the paradigmatic wisdom figure was not identical with Abigail, Job, Joseph, or the woman of Proverbs 31:10–31. Instead, it was a composite image shaped from aspects of the stories of all these and others. Such a personal paradigm is not created by abstracting a principle from a story like Genesis 13 and then reclothing it with lifelike features. On the contrary, ethical model stories flow together directly to form such a paradigm before the mental eye, as the pieces of a jigsaw puzzle fit together to yield a picture.

Moreover, such a composite paradigm becomes effective in shaping people ethically through its complete and direct impact; it need not be reduced first to a set of abstract principles that must be retranslated into life. For example, a sage may have told a young man setting out on a journey, "Remember all I taught you!" This was a reminder to live wisely or, in our terminology, to follow the wisdom paradigm. To do so, the young man need not recall each proverb or exhortation heard from his teacher and then apply them in situations encountered on his journey. He carried with him, imprinted on his character, the sum total of instruction received. As he would meet with new situations, he would "act in character," that is, wisely. The sage's parting words were not a reminder to recall stored intellectual content; rather, they functioned as a sort of encouragement: "Be what you have become!"

With respect to this immediate and total impact of an acquired inner image or paradigm, my understanding departs somewhat from Wright's definition quoted above. For Wright, a "basic principle" that remains unchanged forms the link between the paradigm and the new situation to which it is applied. That is certainly true of grammatical models, from which the concept of paradigm is usually borrowed.[3] For our purposes, however, paradigm will be understood as a personally and holistically conceived image of a model (e.g., a wise person, good king) that imprints itself immediately and nonconceptually on the characters and actions of those who hold it.

Paradigm Versus Law and Principle

Such a process of paradigm shaping and paradigm effectiveness, far from being an exotic dynamic unearthed here for faraway ancient Israel, is a common daily occurrence. Every North American, for example, has internalized the image of a "good driver." That paradigm does not coincide fully with one's mom, dad, driving instructor, uncle X, or anyone else. It is composed, in an immediate and nonconceptualized way, by the impact of the observed driving habits of all of these and others. Further, its effectiveness in shaping a driver who holds it in mind is again a total and nonintellectualized one. We could exemplify such paradigms in other areas, such as "good neighbor," "loyal citizen," "honest businessman," and so forth.

If this process of internalizing paradigms and experiencing their person-shaping effectiveness is so common, it may be asked why so much effort needs to be expended here in asserting its existence and clarifying its operation in ancient Israel. The answer is that such a mode of paradigmatic shaping of Israel's ethic has been obscured by the dominance of two other modes. Generally, the ethical message of the Old Testament has been equated with the proclamation and observance of law. Israel is assumed to have been a people guided ethically by law. As a result, the question of the Old Testament's ethical relevance for Christians has almost always immediately turned into the question as to whether Old Testament law is still binding. The answer is usually the quick rejoinder that this law has been superseded in its ethical claims by the paradigm, or model, of Jesus Christ.[4] Such a contrasting of law (Old Testament) and paradigm (Jesus Christ) is, however, improper. Instead, Old Testament Israel was also shaped and guided ethically not primarily by law, but by paradigm. The question for Christians is what those Old Testament paradigms were, whether they still speak, and how they relate to the paradigm of Jesus Christ.

This is in no way to diminish the significance of law. The importance and function of law will be considered in chapter 3. What is questioned here is the widespread neglect of the role of paradigm in Old Testament ethics due to improper views of law. Continuing our example from driving, the fact that a good driver in our society is usually the product of a paradigm of the "good driver" does not diminish the importance of legislation. On the other hand, everyone knows that the imprint of a composite paradigm of the "good driver" produces good drivers, which the reading of legislation concerning traffic on the highways does not.

The second mode of seeing Old Testament ethics that obscures awareness of the otherwise common paradigm-shaping process is the Western attraction to principles. The ethical impact of an Old Testament story is all too often reduced to a principle, such as selflessness, humility, truthfulness, liberality, or compassion.

In an attempt to be more true to Hebrew modes of thought and expression, principles are sometimes expressed in Hebrew terms, such as *sĕdāqâ* (righteousness), *mišpāṭ* (justice), *ḥesed* (loving-kindness, covenant loyalty), *'ĕmet* (faithfulness, truth), *šālôm* (peace, harmony, wholeness), and others. Such abstractions are then carefully qualified as to their precise Hebrew connotations, as contrasted with their approximate English translations. It is assumed that the ethical yield of stories, encapsuled in such terms, can be transferred to other situations, biblical or modern, and reincarnated in the lives of groups and individuals. The ultimate reduction consists of seeing all stories of ethically exemplary behavior, but also all laws, as symptomatic expressions of the principle of love.[5]

Just as in the case of law, it is far from my intent to detract from the significance of principles, whether in modern Western or ancient Hebrew garb. Principles possess their own legitimate functions, as will be discussed below.[6] But their use to encapsule the ethical yield of a story, or even a law, is a reductionistic process that results in considerable loss. This use could be compared to the retention of a choral performance in a musical score. The score, though helpful, fails to capture the essence of the performance. The transmission of story (or law) by composite paradigm, on the other hand, could be compared to a live recording of the performance. A recording allows later hearers to relive the original experience in all its musical vitality.

Paradigms in Canonical Context

The five stories discussed in chapter 1 were selected for the clarity with which they illustrate my thesis. All of them clearly present a person who behaves in an exemplary way without the assumption that he or she should be considered a perfect model. In fact, many of them we would not want to hold up as ethical models in every respect. All of them, therefore, pose the question concerning the nature of their ethical claim on us. No attempt was made, on the other hand, to locate these stories historically as to date or setting, or to relate them to each other according to literary-critical, form-critical, or other criteria.[7] They were simply used as pointers to the five paradigms posited.

A full treatment of these paradigms would require us to consider, according to historical period and socio-geographical setting, every story or other text in the Old Testament contributing to the composition of the five paradigms. This would demonstrate, among other things, that these paradigms were not static but kept changing from time to time, and perhaps from one region or social setting to another. Thus we must not assume that the familial paradigm was identical in the minds of early seminomadic Israelites, of those living in villages during the monarchy, and of the exiles in Babylon. In other words, our search for these holistic mental images is not a search for universal ethical constants lying beyond the timebound stories of Abraham or Phinehas and remaining unchanged throughout all time, or at least all Old Testament time.[8] Instead, I am trying to give proper weight to *one* instrument, besides law and principle, of shaping Israel in her ethical development. It is my contention that this much-neglected instrument—namely, the paradigm—is in certain ways of prior ethical importance to those of law and principle.

Again, just as it is a misguided effort to reduce Old Testament ethics to a timeless set of laws or principles, it would be equally misguided to attempt to find a timeless set of paradigms. Just as the laws reached a certain completion and final authority for Israel, however, and in its wake, for Judaism and Christianity, so we can also search for those paradigms that emerge from ethical model stories and other relevant texts within the bounds of the completed Old Testament canon.[9] We must remember, however, that such a comprehensively based, "final" set of our five paradigms was not available to the participants in Israel's history before canonization, just as those participants could not resort to "Old Testament law" but only to certain laws and law codifications. With these clarifications in mind, I want to expand the discussion of one paradigm posited in chapter 1, the "familial paradigm." In doing so, I must restrict myself to a limited selection of texts showing both variety and unity in the paradigm that they helped to shape, without documenting detailed historical development or socio-geographical diversity.

Paradigm, Character, and Story

Story, Character, and Ethical Decision

Stanley Hauerwas has argued convincingly that ethics ought not begin with the consideration of situations that call for an ethical decision, for such situations of ethical quandary would not have come about if the participants had not been persons of particular character, shaped by their particular stories.[10] "The 'situations' we confront are such only because we are first a certain kind of people."[11] The truth of this claim is readily seen when we consider, for example, the conflict between Ahab and Naboth (1 Kings 21). At face value, it is a conflict over real estate that might raise the question concerning general ethical principles of private property in light of government rights of purchase or expropriation. An ethical conflict situation would not have arisen at all if either one of two conditions had existed. If Ahab and Naboth had both been shaped in their ethics by Israel's story of relating to the land, Ahab would never have made his request. If, on the other hand, both had been shaped by Canaanite history, with its assumption of absolute kingship, Naboth would never have considered refusing the king's request. No ethical quandary would have existed.

Such a quandary comes about because Naboth has been shaped by Israel's history, whereas Ahab hovers at its edges. This makes it imperative for Naboth to challenge Ahab's action in light of the story to which Ahab gives at least nominal allegiance. It is Jezebel, acting completely within her story, in whose eyes it is Naboth who acts outside that story and must be coerced to conform to its norms. Thus the ethical decision demanded in the story is not the result of an isolated "quandary situation," but of two different stories and the characters shaped by them. To quote Hauerwas again, "[T]he kind of quandaries we confront depend on the kind of people we are and the way we have learned to construe the world through our language, habits, and feelings."[12] If this is so, our five stories of chapter 1, each presenting an ethical quandary and its resolution, raise the question concerning the stories that lie behind each and have shaped their characters in such ways as to lead to the quandaries they express. Because we want to address the familial paradigm first, we begin by asking what story lay behind Abraham's great concern for family shalom in Genesis 13.

The Story Context of Genesis 13

In our effort to develop the "familial paradigm," we must revisit briefly the Abraham story of Genesis 13 discussed more fully in chapter 1. Why did Abraham act selflessly to preserve family shalom? We can safely assume that, historically, a high valuation of family shalom was a legacy shared by Israel with the seminomadic as well as the settled populations of the ancient Near East. Indeed, the importance of the extended family network has only been eroded in recent centuries in the industrialized West.

As we are concerned with a study of biblical texts in their canonical Old Testament context, however, it is not enough to understand Abraham's action in general ancient Near Eastern or human terms. We cannot leave it as an isolated instance of instinctive human family preservation but must try to link it to the central themes of the longer narrative of which it is a part. The narrative unit in view is the Tetrateuch (Genesis–Numbers), but of special concern for our purpose is the section preceding our story, Genesis 1–12.[13]

It is a theological narrative, with God as the chief actor. In Genesis 1–12, humanity is created by God as a spreading network of families emanating from a parental pair (Adam and Eve). Human rebellion, or sin, threatens that kinship-structured humanity at various points. God's grace, however, preserves and restores it again and again. First in the story of Noah and family, and then again in the calling of Abraham and Sarah with their family, God initiates the restoration of humanity through the election of parental pairs as redemptive agents. The goal of God's activity is again expressed in kinship language: to bless "all the families of the earth" (12:3). Thus, when Abraham acts to preserve family shalom in Genesis 13, he does nothing less than act in keeping with the purpose and will of God.

It was acknowledged earlier that the concern for family shalom was not distinctive for Israel, but constituted a widespread ethos among ancient Near Eastern peoples and beyond them. This ethos, however, did take on distinctive literary-theological expressions in Israel that anchored it in the central purposes of God. I will argue below that the narrative theology of kinship exemplified by the early chapters of Genesis underlies not only the exemplary behavior of Abraham in Genesis 13. Some version of it forms the narrative background also of further stories and other texts that point to a familial paradigm, a paradigm ultimately rooted in God. First, however, it is necessary to clarify this story by drawing attention to a possible alternative.

The Ancient Near Eastern Alternative

Do not all societies understand humanity as a great family? Does not even our modern vocabulary testify to a universal human lineage when we refer to the "human family," the "brotherhood of man," and so forth? Whatever may be true of Western thinking, largely shaped by the Bible, this was not the only mode of understanding humanity in the ancient Near East. The central myths of the great cultural centers of Mesopotamia and Egypt, but also of the Canaanite people immediately adjacent to Israel, understood the emergence of humanity as the primeval establishment of a state. When the gods created the world from primordial chaos, they structured it as a state (Egypt or a Mesopotamian kingdom, respectively) reflecting the heavenly state.[14] Humankind was, first and foremost, a monarchy presided over by the king. In this, it mirrored the divine world in which Marduk (or Enlil) or Re, but also Canaanite Baal, had been enthroned either by himself, or by a venerable high god, or by the assembly of the gods.[15] This heavenly state was reflected in the earthly kingdoms. Such an understanding stands in sharp contrast to the familially structured humanity presented above. This royal model touched Israel in its royal paradigm. It was subordinated, however, to the overarching familial paradigm, as we will see in chapter 6.[16]

The ultimate paradigm of an upholder and restorer of family shalom, then, is God. Abraham, to the extent that he acts in exemplary manner in Genesis 13, provides a few strokes toward sketching the human image of this familial paradigm. Further strokes are added by other stories and texts, two of which will be considered now.

A Second Familial Paradigm Story: Ruth

The Paradigmatic Behavior of Ruth and Boaz

Prominent among texts displaying the familial paradigm is the book of Ruth. Its theological thrust has been interpreted variously, as has been its historical setting.[17] There can be little doubt, however, that both Ruth and Boaz behave in exemplary fashion. Their exemplary behavior is related to the preservation of a family that might otherwise have become extinct.[18] Elimelech, his wife Naomi, and their two sons are driven by famine to migrate to Moab, where the sons marry Moabite wives. When Elimelech and the two sons die, Naomi returns to her home in Bethlehem in Judah. One of her Moabite daughters-in-law stays in Moab, but the other, Ruth, declares her absolute loyalty to Naomi, her people, and her God (1:16f.). If she, too, had remained in Moab, the family of Elimelech would have ceased to be. Her loyalty, on the other hand, leaves open the possibility "that the name of the dead [Elimelech] may not be cut off from among his brethren and from the gate of his native place" (4:10).

This is only a possibility, however, and the model behavior of Ruth can advance Elimelech's cause only to this point. From here on it is the action of Boaz that leads to the desirable end. Being Ruth's kinsman, though only second in line of responsibility, he makes every effort that Elimelech's inheritance be redeemed and that his line be continued through a modified form of levirate marriage.[19] That he places his kinship obligations above his self-interest is shown by the behavior of the "next of kin," who refuses to assume these obligations, "lest I impair my own inheritance" (4:6). Thus the "right" behavior of Ruth and Boaz has worked together to ensure that the family line of Elimelech is not "cut off from among his brethren and from the gate of his native place" (4:10).[20]

Why have Ruth and Boaz acted in this way? Throughout the book we gain the impression that they do not merely make one or two right decisions each, but that they act in character. They are the kind of people "who would do that kind of thing." But character is shaped by story. What stories have formed such characters? For Ruth, the limited information available suggests that she demonstrates at its best the kind of filial piety to which a Moabite upbringing could lead. Accepting the duties of marriage with uttermost seriousness, she rejects the security of parents and home country (2:11)[21] in order to advance the meager prospects of her deceased husband's family. On this basis she is called "a woman of worth" by Boaz[22] (3:11; cf. 2:11–12).

Boaz's situation is somewhat different. He is characterized in various ways as an exemplary Israelite. In view of enormous differences among scholars in dating the book of Ruth,[23] it is impossible here to determine to what extent the story presupposes the laws and customs available to us in the Old Testament itself and how far it simply assumes views similar to these laws in early Israel. When we read this book in the context of the whole Old Testament canon, however, it is impossible not to construe many of Boaz's actions as expressions of virtues promoted in Israel's story.[24] His care for the stranger and the widow (e.g., Lev. 19:9–10; Deut. 24:19–22), his concern for the redeeming of a kinswoman's inheritance (e.g., Lev. 25:25), and his zealous observance of the (supposedly Israelite) levirate laws (e.g., Deut. 25:5–10) make him appear as an Israelite at his best.

It is of further importance that the contrast between Israelites and Moabites forms a persistent theme in the book. Ruth's action taken by itself, just like Abraham's in Genesis 13, could have taken place in many parts of the ancient Near East where family shalom was rated highly. In the book of Ruth as a whole, however, it becomes a part, not merely of preserving a family line, but of preserving a family line within Israel's framework of self-understanding. Together, Boaz and Ruth preserve a line that has behind it the story of Rachel and Leah, the wives of Israel's eponymous forefather Jacob/Israel, and their descendants (4:11–12). Unknown to the participants, but not to the storyteller, it is also the family line that will bring forth David, Israel's greatest king (4:17–21).[25]

The Story Context of Ruth

We located the story of Abraham (Genesis 13) in the theological narrative of Genesis 1–12 and beyond, which envisions a humanity created and structured by God into families. From that wider context emerged the concern for family shalom modeled by Abraham in Genesis 13. In the book of Ruth, we can understand the ethical modeling of Boaz by placing him into the more specific self-understanding of Israel as a kinship group held together by a common forefather, Jacob/Israel, and a common history extending to David.[26] Ruth's general kinship loyalty feeds supportively into the specific kinship loyalty defined by this narrative, a narrative in which she voluntarily becomes an actor. This narrative shapes an ethos in many ways akin to the general concern for family preservation, but bearing specifically Israelite features. Among these, the concern for the stranger who receives an inheritance is particularly prominent. One can hardly overlook the connection of this to the story of a people who were strangers in a foreign land (Egypt) but received an inheritance through the grace of Yahweh. Israel's familial paradigm goes beyond the general concern for the preservation of life, of a name, of a family line—though these remain prominent—to a special concern for the disadvantaged, the poor, and the needy.

A Third Familial Paradigm Story: Judges 19

Models and Countermodels of Hospitality

This concern for shalom within the specific kinship group that saw itself as the descendants of the twelve sons of Jacob/Israel is developed in several directions by the shocking but highly instructive story of the Levite and his concubine (Judges 19).[27] That story has a pronounced "all-Israel" horizon. It begins by locating its action "[i]n those days, when there was no king in Israel" (v. 1), assuming that events like those to be reported would not have occurred had there been a king.[28] In those days, a certain Levite, "sojourning in the remote parts of the hill country of Ephraim," had a concubine "from Bethlehem in Judah" (v. 1). The story will be far-flung in its geographical reach, embracing both Ephraim and Judah, North and South. These two parts of Israel often held together only tenuously, and eventually they were to break apart into separate kingdoms.

When the concubine "became angry" (v. 2) with the Levite and returned home to her father in Bethlehem, the Levite followed her "to speak kindly to her and bring her back" (v. 3). Apparently he succeeded, and they were ready to leave again. Thus far, the story may already convey some ideals of family shalom, but the storyteller proceeds to place the accent on the model behavior of the girl's father.[29] With an almost tedious repetition, the father urges the Levite to stay and enjoy his hospitality. There can be no doubt of the clear message that differences in Israel, even between North and South, can and should be bridged, and that a spirit of welcome as magnanimous as that shown by the concubine's father models the proper inter-Israelite ethos.

Guided by the expectation of such hospitality on his return journey, the Levite refuses to spend the night in non-Israelite Jebus (Jerusalem), saying to his servant, "We will not turn aside into the city of foreigners, who do not belong to the people of Israel; but we will pass on to Gibeah . . . which belongs to Benjamin" (vs. 12, 14). Gibeah, then, is deliberately chosen as an Israelite city, where hospitality could be expected, in contrast to Jebus, "the city of foreigners." But his expectations are sorely disappointed. "And he went in and sat down in the open square of the city; for no man took them into his house to spend the night" (v. 15, cf. v. 18). Finally an old man, himself a sojourner from the hill country of Ephraim, takes in the Levite, his concubine, and his servant. He provides for their cattle, washes the guests' feet, and gives them food and drink.

The contrast between the old man and the townspeople, "base fellows," is accentuated when the latter surround the house and demand the handing over of the guest, "that we may know him" (v. 22).[30] The old man offers his virgin daughter and the guest's concubine instead. The guest, however, pushes out his concubine to them, apparently refusing the offer of his host's daughter. They abuse her, so that she is found near death on the threshold of the house in the morning. The Levite takes her home to his place, cuts her body into twelve pieces, and sends these to the twelve tribes of Israel, presumably with an account of what has happened. This evokes a moral verdict from "all who saw it": "Such a thing has never happened or been seen from the day that the people of Israel came up out of the land of Egypt until this day" (v. 30).

The story is so repulsive and abhorrent to us that we may want to reject it immediately as a text with an ethical message. At first glance, it treats both the daughter and the concubine as objects readily available for abuse. It will take an extra effort on our part to hear the full meaning of this story in its context. As a start, we must recall that the Levite certainly cared deeply for his concubine, for he had undertaken a long and dangerous journey to win her back. If he, nevertheless, sacrifices her to the mob outside, he does so to protect his host's daughter. The host, for his part, holds to the highest ideals of hospitality. These require of him that he not withhold even what is dearest to him. The two men here outdo each other, as it were, in the greatness of the sacrifice they are ready to offer.[31]

A major problem remains for us. Could not the Levite have faced the danger himself? Probably, for although our text does not portray him as acting from callousness toward his concubine, it does also not intend to make him into a self-sacrificing saint. A further complication has to be considered, however. By offering himself to the mob's intended purpose, the Levite would have exposed himself to homosexual practice. This is elsewhere ranked an "abomination" deserving the death penalty (Lev. 20:13; cf. 18:22). Whether our Levite knew of such a law or not, we may assume that the biblical author of this story shares in similar views.

Finally, the whole incident is judged, in the text itself, to be a crime of unprecedented gravity (v. 30). It calls forth the wrath of the rest of Israel and leads to a punitive war against Gibeah and the Benjaminites (ch. 20).[32] This war itself involves phenomenal violence and injustice, but it does represent a condemnation of the events of chapter 19.

The Israelite Context of Hospitality

Thus this story models, by way of positive (the concubine's father and the old man) and negative (the men of Gibeah) example an expectation of solidarity in Israel that would issue in a mutual claim of Israelite on fellow Israelite.[33] Such a claim would express itself tangibly in the requesting and offering of hospitality. It is assumed in the servant's suggestion to seek hospitality in Jebus (v. 11) that the exchange of hospitality could also be expected between Israelites and non-Israelites, in keeping with our earlier observation that the familial paradigm of behavior is broadly human. The point of the story, therefore, is not to promote a sharp contrast between Israel and other peoples. Instead, Israel is to model in a special way what might also be recognized as good among people generally. The flagrant denial of this ideal is more heinous, however, within the context of the expected solidarity created by the story of Israel that "came up out of the land of Egypt" (v. 30).[34] Now, a story has not only a past but also a future, and we are to understand that the events described here show Israel on its way from its beginnings as a people just delivered from Egypt to a time when a king (19:1; 21:25) would restore the shalom so flagrantly broken here.

The Three Stories Compared

Let us look back on our analysis of three stories (Genesis 13, Ruth, Judges 19) pointing to a familial paradigm. Each of them makes the claim to portray behavior that is in some sense exemplary. We were able to show that the exemplary dimension in each was such, not by virtue of generally valid principles, nor by virtue of the observance of specific Old Testament laws.[35] It resulted, instead, from the expectations placed on the actors by their own understanding (or lack of understanding) of their kinship context. In the case of Abraham, the immediate kinship context was his uncle–nephew relationship to Lot. In the case of Ruth and Boaz, the kinship context was the household of Elimelech, of which three generations were immediately involved.

In the story of the Levite and his concubine, the kinship context was all Israel.

We saw, further, that each story was placed by its narrator, writer, or final editor into a larger story. For the incident of Abraham and Lot, the wider story context was the early story of Genesis, consisting of the account of creation, of the Fall, and of beginning redemption, initiated through a chosen family sent into the unknown with God's promise of many descendants and a new homeland in an open future. For the story of Ruth and Boaz, the outside parameters were narrowed somewhat to the memory of Rachel and Leah (the wives of Jacob/Israel) in the past, and the eventual birth of David in the future. For the story of the Levite and his concubine, the story horizons extended from the origins of a people at the exodus from Egypt to the intimated expectation that there might come a time when Israel would no longer lack a king.

The date of oral and/or written origin for each story in its present form has been debated with greatly varying results. For each, there are proponents of an early dating, possibly to the time of the early monarchy, and a late dating, generally to the period of the exile or later. If the earlier dating could be proved for each of the three stories, one could use them as evidence of a familial ideal existing in Israel at an early time in its history. It is not impossible, however, that the origins of the stories lay centuries apart, in which case it would be improper to draw on all of them to begin to reconstruct an Israelite familial paradigm belonging to one particular period. In any case, it is not the purpose of our canonical investigation to arrive at such a historical paradigm for any one period in Israel's history.

It is clear, on the other hand, that the narrators, authors, or editors of each of these stories deliberately located their stories in the time before Israel "had arrived"; more specifically, in the formative phase of Israel's canonical story that lay between the call of Abraham and the kingship of David. To the degree that this placement also represents historical fact, we could seek in these stories witnesses to a common familial paradigm in late second-millennium Israel. But this is not the object of the present study. On the contrary, it is of primary interest for our thesis that the narrator, author, or editor—possibly at work many centuries later—*located* his story in Israel's *early* history. In this way he ensured that Israelite hearers or readers of later times, and the post-Israelite religious communities claiming the Old Testament as canon, would look back to these (and other) stories as belonging to the era when God shaped a special people for his service. Such literary-theological activity would make it especially clear that these ethical model stories were told and placed, not primarily for whatever historical memories they contained, but precisely because of their modeling features. It need hardly be repeated that only certain features of these stories have exemplary character, rather than the stories or their actors in all they tell or do.

Components of the Familial Paradigm

Life

Let us summarize, then, those features of our stories that we have recognized as exemplary and as pointing to a familial paradigm in the Old Testament canon. Central to the familial paradigm is the preservation and continuation of life, understood simply as biological human existence, but including dimensions transcending such existence. In the book of Ruth this is clearest. The story begins with a threat, in the form of famine, to the life of Elimelech and his family. Elimelech dies, whether as a result of the famine or otherwise, and little is said about that. Every individual must die. The concern of the book is whether he will also "die" in a different sense; namely, whether his name, his family line, will come to an end or be preserved. All who contribute to its preservation, especially Ruth and Boaz, act in keeping with the highest ideal. Preservation of life, then, is not limited to the sustaining of individual life, important as that must always be. It extends to the future that gives meaning to present life, and that future, for Israel, was vouchsafed by the ongoing family line created through God's election of a people to serve his special purposes.

EXCURSUS: Individual and Society

This view of life appears to confront us with the vexed question of the priority of individual or society, and the subsequent question as to whose interests ought to prevail over the interests of the other. Such a quandary, however, is foreign to the Old Testament. In fact, I hope that an understanding of Old Testament ethics as an ethics of story and paradigm will automatically collapse the polarity between individual and group; and therewith, of personal ethics and social ethics. A quick review of our three familial model stories shows clearly that the exemplary action in each case led to the good (or ill) of those engaged in it and of future generations. Abraham preserved peace (for himself!) with Lot, but unwittingly avoided embroilment of his clan in the doom of Sodom and Gomorrah. Boaz and Ruth gained personally while they kept alive the house of Elimelech. The men of Gibeah were personally evil and brought evil upon their town and their tribe. It is firmly entrenched in the familial paradigm that individual ethically exemplary action is at the same time the best for the community whose story has shaped the character of the exemplary actor. The modern Western notion that right-living individuals (personal ethics) can contribute by their goodness to the creating and maintaining of oppressive or destructive social structures (social ethics) is foreign to this paradigm. Thus the prophets assume throughout that the social ills of Israel can be addressed by appealing to individual people to seek the right. In turn, the covenant-breaking direction of society will inevitably bring distress to its individual members.[36]

This linking of individual and communal welfare is further illustrated by the fact that individuals are often called upon to forgo self-interest, but rarely, if ever, to "sacrifice" their life for the welfare of the group. Joseph's story is a prime example. He suffers much for his family, "for God sent me before you to preserve life" (Gen. 45:5; cf. 50:20), but if he had died, his family would not have been preserved, either. I am not aware of any one in the Old Testament, save the Suffering Servant (Isaiah 53), who dies so that his family or people might live. Of course, many people died as the consequence of going to war on behalf of their people, yet their deaths were not glorified, but lamented. Their deaths were a diminishing of their people. The Old Testament has no cenotaphs for the war dead, and no glorification of martyrdom. In other words, the self-sacrifice of the individual for the good of his or her people is not sought or commanded, though it may be the result of necessity.[37] On the other hand, the lone survival of the individual does not appear as an ethical good, either. When Baruch asks for his personal preservation, Jeremiah chides him for disidentifying with his people (Jeremiah 45). Preservation of self or immediate family from an atomic cataclysm, in a mountain bunker, would hardly have appeared as "life" to an Israelite!

Thus life, as the highest value in the familial paradigm, is not the life of the individual preserved at any cost to the community, nor the life of the community demanding the self-sacrifice of the individual. The Old Testament assumes without argument that life for an individual is life in community.

Land

Preservation of life, understood as the life of the individual as it extends beyond personal existence to children and children's children, forms the pinnacle of the pyramid of values that make up the familial paradigm. It is linked immediately and concretely to the provision of land and its produce. The quarrel of Abraham's and Lot's herdsmen was over land. One or the other party might be crowded out of the land, and therewith out of its livelihood. To restore shalom meant to preserve life by apportioning land. The continuation of a name for Elimelech was closely tied to his inheritance; the whole story moved "to restore the name of the dead [Elimelech] to his inheritance" (Ruth 4:5).

Just as with life itself, the possession of land is contingent in Israel on God's promise and leading (Gen. 12:1–3, 7 and throughout the Old Testament). Landholding, for Israel, is based neither on aboriginal claims nor on military power; it is inheritance and rest (Deut. 12:9) granted by God's grace. It can be forfeited when considered a permanent possession managed in human autonomy from God. God alone is its owner, and human existence is properly existence as "strangers and sojourners" (Lev. 25:23). Trusting in God's grace, however, humans can live securely in that impermanent status, knowing that the hospitality of God alone offers the real security of home.[38]

In view of these perspectives on life and land in the context of the familial paradigm, the first task of right, ethical living is not active self-assertion, but trusting acceptance of God's hospitality. That an active dimension, the extension of hospitality, must then follow will be our next concern.[39]

Hospitality

Access to land and food does not only take the form of God-given possession. People do not live only by their own land and its produce or profit, but also by the graciously extended produce of the land of others, in time of need. Hospitality is an ethical component of the familial paradigm that is hard for modern Western readers to appreciate in its full weight and significance. It may help us to remember that travel, in the ancient world, was only undertaken for grave reasons, often negative in nature, such as flight from persecution or search for food and survival. Hospitality, under those circumstances, has little to do with modern tourism, but embraces the biblical equivalent to our policies regarding refugees, immigration, welfare, and social security. Hospitality appears prominently in Boaz's treatment of Ruth, and it forms the main theme for the ethical modeling (both positively and negatively) in the story of the Levite and his concubine. Numerous other biblical stories highlight this aspect of the familial model.[40]

It is also in its modeling of hospitality that the Old Testament's familial ideal provides a counterweight to the tendency of close-knit kinship groups to accent responsibilities toward the members of one's own group and reject the claims and needs of outsiders.[41] Hospitality is the extension of life to those for whose lives one is not held responsible through kinship obligations. In Israel, immediate and full responsibility for life existed within the extended family or "father's house."[42] Any life-sustaining service rendered to a member of one's own father's house would therefore not have been considered hospitality. Almost the same must have been true of the next larger kinship unit, the "clan," as its members lived next to each other in neighboring tents or houses. This last fact must in itself have made the extension of hospitality superfluous. Nevertheless, as the "protective organization,"[43] the clan must have offered food and shelter at times to members of a disadvantaged father's house. The hospitality extended to Ruth in her husband's hometown could be seen as an example.

The tribe must have been the main social context for the extension and reception of hospitality. Thus Abraham's servant (Genesis 24) and Jacob (Genesis 29) enjoy the spontaneous hospitality offered to all strangers, but are taken in with special attention when it is discovered that they belong to the kinship group.

Within Israel's twelve tribes, the same openness to the "brother" should also ideally prevail. The story of the Ephraimite Levite's reception by his Judahite father-in-law models this ideal. The expectation harbored by the Levite toward the Benjaminite men of Gibeah, and only less confidently toward the non-Israelite Jebusites, points to the same ideal. Of course, the events of the story show that the ideal did not always prevail in the all-Israel context. It would take a king to unify the tribes and ensure the right intercourse between them.

Hospitality, however, transcends the bounds of the kinship group. Elimelech apparently found it in Moab, and the Levite's servant expects it from the Jebusites. Abraham and Lot model it in exemplary fashion toward the strangers that visit them (Gen. 18:1–16 and 19:1–9), and Moses receives it at the hand of the Midianites (Ex. 2:15–22). Hospitality is that dimension of the familial paradigm which ensures that the pursuit of family shalom does not degenerate into in-group selfishness.[44]

It is in this context of hospitality also that a person acting in keeping with the familial paradigm may be called, not only to forgo self-interest, but also to suffer.[45] Boaz not only allows Ruth to glean after the reapers the grain that would be lost anyway; he makes special provision to give her of his own harvest (Ruth 2:14–16; cf. Deut. 24:19–22). The old man who offers hospitality to the Levite and his party goes so far as to offer his virgin daughter to the men of Gibeah in exchange for the safety of his guest (Judg. 19:23–24). The same is true of Lot (Gen. 19:6–8). Although their gesture is abhorrent to our sensibilities—as it probably was to those of the Israelites!—the intent is undoubtedly to express that no sacrifice is too high for a host in behalf of his guest. When the prophet Nathan tells David the parable of a rich man who was unwilling to take a lamb from his flock for his guest, but took instead the only lamb of his poor neighbor, David judges that man to be deserving of death (1 Sam. 12:1–6).

An Ethic Rooted in God's Story

So far, our inductive approach may have created the impression that the familial paradigm in the Old Testament is little more than the Israelite version of ancient Near Eastern societal norms and ideals. It may have appeared no different than such North American paradigms as "good neighbor" or "loyal citizen," composite ideals emerging from daily experience but devoid of theological content or roots. That is not so. It is true that the concern for continuity of life, for possession of land, and for hospitality can be found widely, both in the ancient Near East and beyond. We recall, however, that each of our three familial model incidents was set in the context of a story rooting it in Israel's own experience and theology, and shaping it in accordance with these.

To summarize, Abraham's concern for family shalom is a part of the Genesis story's portrayal of a humanity created in families. The familial structure is threatened repeatedly in the course of the story of human rebellion/sin. God's preservation of humanity repeatedly assumes the form of reconstituting kinship structures and initiating new possibilities through them. In the related and contrasting stories of the Tower of Babel (Gen. 11:1–9) and the call of Abraham (Gen. 12:1–3), we see particularly clearly how God rejects humanity's attempt to entrench its security in Mesopotamian royal-religious superstructures (the city and the [temple-]tower). He chooses, instead, a family line to become instrumental in his plans. This "elected" family is to live insecurely, by human standards, guided solely by the promise of God. Abraham's exemplary act toward Lot (Genesis 13), though immediately motivated by kinship claims, exhibits his willingness to shoulder the insecurity of living by promise. In doing so, he—without his knowledge—allows God to work out his plan of providing Abraham's descendants with land. In short, by forgoing his chance to grasp for the good land on his own, Abraham makes it possible for God to grant that land to his descendants as a gift, albeit centuries later. It becomes clear, then, that the kinship paradigm as lived out by Abraham (Genesis 13), far from being only a general human impulse, is rooted in and shaped profoundly by Israel's theology of God's creating, blessing, electing, and redeeming activity.

Further, but more briefly, we can make the same point for our other two familial model stories. The exemplary acts of Ruth and Boaz were shown to be part of God's story with his people, a story viewed here as it is led by God from the foremothers of Israel— Rachel and Leah—to Israel's greatest king, David. By responding to their kinship duties, Ruth and Boaz play their role in God's leading. And finally, the story of the Levite and his concubine presents its message of all-Israelite solidarity expressed through hospitality, within the horizons of Israel redeemed from Egyptian bondage. This Israel was expected to let itself be shaped in its hospitality ideal by that origin, but failed to do so until an anticipated king would actualize this ideal in the future.

We can therefore confidently claim that the familial paradigm, with its key facets of life, land, and hospitality, is more than a collection of ancient Near Eastern customs and popular ideals. It is the expression of an ethic evoked by, and in keeping with, Israel's theological story. It is linked in particular to such key features of that story as mark the primeval history (Genesis 1–11), the election and leading of Abraham, the beginnings of the twelve-tribe kinship model with Jacob/Israel, the exodus from Egypt, and the establishment of Davidic kingship.

The familial paradigm, developed around the conceptual triad of life-land-hospitality on the basis of three ethical model stories, could be expanded further by way of analysis of other stories, some of which have been referred to briefly. It is also reflected in many literary genres other than story. One of the more prominent of these is law. But before we consider the contribution of laws and law codes to the familial paradigm, we need to clarify the relationship of paradigm to principle and law.

Notes

1. Christopher J. H. Wright, *An Eye for an Eye: The Place of Old Testament Ethics Today* (Downers Grove, Ill.: InterVarsity Press, 1983), 43.
2. Ibid.
3. Thus Wright, ibid.
4. However, the continuing ethical validity of Old Testament law as law for Christians is also maintained by some Christian ethicists, especially those of a conservative stripe. An outstanding example is Walter C. Kaiser's *Toward Old Testament Ethics* (Grand Rapids: Zondervan Publishing House, 1983). Acknowledging the variety of ethically relevant Old Testament genres (p. 41) and the desirability of studying all of them (p. 56), Kaiser states: "What we need is a lodestone or a stance from which we can view the whole testament [*sic*]. We believe that point can be identified. The heart of Old Testament ethics is to be placed squarely on the explicit commands found mainly in the Pentateuch" (p. 42). His extensive volume (314 pages) is devoted, accordingly, to a study of Old Testament law, the Decalogue providing its organizing principle. Christian identifications of Old Testament ethics with law follow in the wake of rabbinic Judaism; for a concise statement of Jewish-Christian differences in this respect, see Dale Patrick, *Old Testament Law* (Atlanta: John Knox Press, 1985), 204f.
5. In both Testaments, love appears in prominent contexts as a comprehensive term embracing all human requirements and laws with respect to God and neighbor (e.g., Deut. 6:4–5; Lev. 19:18; Mark 12:28–34 and parallels; John 13:34–35; 1 Corinthians 13; Gal. 5:14). For a justification of the use of key terms as shorthand embracing story-based biblical truths, together with a differentiation of such shorthand use from reductionist principles rejected here and elsewhere in this book, see below. Love as adequate for generating Christian ethics is rejected here only in so far as it is understood as a universally available and self-interpreting principle. Patrick (*Old Testament Law,* 207–19) offers a helpful discussion of the relationship of love and law in New Testament

perspective; but due to his free recourse to principle as underlying law, he does not completely escape the danger of characterizing love as a self-interpreting principle that can be extracted from, and even juxta-posed to, biblical law. For further discussion of Patrick's position, see chapter 3. It would go beyond the scope of this study to determine whether my use of paradigm is compatible with paradigms as understood by Thomas S. Kuhn, *The Structure of Scientific Revolutions* (Chicago: University of Chicago Press, 1962). I have not derived my paradigmatic approach from Kuhn's theory, nor have I attempted to apply the latter. Historically, the paradigms described in my book may well have shaped the vision of certain segments of Israelite society in a manner that corresponds to Kuhn's characterization of scientific communities held together by shared paradigms. There may also have been shifts in paradigms of the good life in Israel, for example, from premonarchical times to the era of monarchy. The paradigmatic pattern developed in our study on the basis of the completed canon, however, appears to me to function differently. It shares—at least as seen from within the commu-nity of faith—in the "timeless" authority of the canon itself. A person standing outside of biblical faith may, of course, consider the biblical worldview as such to be a paradigm for understanding the world that determines the world vision of a particular group for a time. For such a person, the inadequacy of this paradigm may lead to a paradigm shift away from the canon. Such a shift would, of course, also affect the pattern of ethical paradigms described in our study.

6. See chapter 3.
7. I have used the term "ethical model stories" to embrace the common characteristics just described, but not to designate a distinct form or genre.
8. Here I find myself in substantial agreement with Stanley Hauerwas's characterization of Christian ethics as qualified ethics, defined by the story that shapes it; cf. *The Peaceable Kingdom: A Primer in Christian Ethics* (Notre Dame: University of Notre Dame Press, 1983), 17–34. The question of the story's claim to authority, especially in relation to the authority claim of other stories—a question frequently asked of Hauer-was and other narrative theologians/ethicists—cannot be addressed here.
9. The reader acquainted with the debate between Brevard S. Childs and James A. Sanders concerning the nature of canon and canonical criticism will detect here a certain preference for Childs's emphasis on the canon's final form, over Sanders's accent on an ongoing canonical process. However, it is my conviction that the two positions are less incompatible than is often believed, even by their chief proponents; cf. Timothy A. P. Reimer, "Canon as Product or Process? A Comparative Analysis of the Canonical Hermeneutics of Brevard S. Childs and James A. Sanders" (M.A. thesis, University of Manitoba, 1987). As long as Christians today

perceive themselves to share a common identity with the early Christian church that was brought into being by the biblical story, and in turn delimited that story by defining its canonical shape, they do better to understand their adaptation of that story to contemporary needs as interpretation (with Childs), rather than canonical reshaping (with Sanders). Stability and adaptation are inherent in both approaches, however. In this sense, a "final" canonical shape of the Old Testament's ethical paradigms is based here on a synchronically available canon.

10. Hauerwas, *The Peaceable Kingdom,* 116f.
11. Ibid.
12. Ibid. For the historico-theological background to this clash of stories, see Walter Brueggemann, *The Land: Place as Gift, Promise, and Challenge in Biblical Faith,* Overtures to Biblical Theology 1 (Philadelphia: Fortress Press, 1977), esp. 71–89. For Brueggemann's application of this development to 1 Kings 21, see ibid., 93–96.
13. In literary-critical perspective, Genesis 13 belongs to the J source of the Tetrateuch. A reading of our story in the literary context of that source, rather than the extant canonical text as a whole, would not alter the emphasis on the essential nature of human existence as an existence in families, as will emerge from our canonical reading. The presence of the familial motif in both the oldest (J) and the youngest (P) layer of the Tetrateuch, however, confirms that we are dealing here with an understanding of human existence that pervaded Israel's history.
14. Henri Frankfort, H. A. Frankfort, J. A. Wilson, Thorkild Jacobsen, *Before Philosophy: A Study of the Primitive Myths, Beliefs and Speculations of Egypt and Mesopotamia, Out of Which Grew the Religions and Philosophies of the Later World,* Pelican Books A 198 (Baltimore: Penguin Books, 1961 [1946], 71–102 (for Egypt), 137–65 (for Mesopotamia). For a discussion of the consequences of the reenactment of cosmic realities on earth for Mesopotamian ethics, see Walter Harrelson, "The Significance of Cosmology in the Ancient Near East," in *Translating and Understanding the Old Testament: Essays in Honor of Herbert Gordon May,* ed. Harry Thomas Frank and William L. Reed (Nashville: Abingdon Press, 1970), 237–52.
15. Cf. James B. Pritchard, ed., *Ancient Near Eastern Texts Relating to the Old Testament* (3d ed. with supp.; Princeton: Princeton University Press, 1969), 3f. (for Re), 69–72 (for Marduk-Enlil), 133–35 (for Baal). At least for Mesopotamia, however, the understanding of the heavenly state as ruled by a God-king was a later development, superseding an earlier understanding of the universe as a "primitive democracy" reflective of prekingship conditions in earliest Mesopotamia. Cf. Frankfort et al., *Before Philosophy,* 141ff.; and Thorkild Jacobsen, "Primitive Democracy in Ancient Mesopotamia," in *Toward the Image of Tammuz and Other Essays on Mesopotamian History and Culture,* ed. William L.

Moran, Harvard Semitic Series 21 (Cambridge, Mass.: Harvard University Press, 1970), 157–70.

16. Our contrasting of a family/kinship understanding of human existence with a state/kingdom understanding ought not be read simplistically. It is not assumed here that kinship structures embody a self-understanding of their members as literal blood relatives, nor that kingship societies and geographically based political power structures (states) are discontinuous. For a discussion of the complex interrelationships, see George Mendenhall, "Tribe and State in the Ancient World: The Nature of the Biblical Community," in *The Tenth Generation: The Origins of the Biblical Tradition* (Baltimore: Johns Hopkins University Press, 1973), 174–97. In spite of these complex interrelationships, however, there remains a striking contrast, so that Mendenhall can say that the twelve tribes of ancient Israel "appear to have been the largest social organization known in the latter half of ancient Near Eastern history which was not based upon a monopoly of force in a political state. Although tribal organizations tend to be ephemeral in comparison with political states and empires, nevertheless in important respects this period of ancient Israel's history remained normative for many centuries. It laid the foundations for a cultural continuity with a tenacity that outlived the supposedly much more efficient and indubitably more wealthy and powerful politically organized cultures of the ancient world" (ibid., 175).

17. Over against the earlier historical-critical scholars, who tended to see in Ruth a polemical tract against the narrow nationalism of Ezra-Nehemiah, several recent interpreters date the book to the early monarchical period; cf. Gillis Gerleman, *Ruth/Das Hohelied*, Biblischer Kommentar Altes Testament 18 (Neukirchen-Vluyn: Neukirchener Verlag, 1965), 10; R. M. Hals, *The Theology of the Book of Ruth*, Facet Books, Biblical Series 23 (Philadelphia: Fortress Press, 1969), 65–75; Edward F. Campbell, Jr., *Ruth: A New Translation with Introduction, Notes, and Commentary*, Anchor Bible 7 (Garden City, N.Y.: Doubleday & Co., 1975), 24.

18. Brevard S. Childs states succinctly that the story "was to show the ways of God in the life of one family" (*Introduction to the Old Testament as Scripture* [Philadelphia: Fortress Press, 1979], 565). This holds true whether one considers the linkage of Ruth's child to David (4:17b) to belong to the original story (with Campbell, *Ruth*, 15f.) or holds this linkage to be a secondary extension (though not alteration) of theme (with Childs, *Introduction*, 566). The concern for the preservation of the family in the book of Ruth is underscored by the generally recognized similarity of the book to the story of Tamar (mentioned explicitly in 4:12) in Genesis 38. Ruth 4:18–22 (based on 1 Chron. 2:9–15) is generally taken to be a secondary genealogical linkage already present in 4:17b. Gerleman's proposal (*Ruth*, 5–11) that the central function of Ruth is the legitimation of David's Moabite ancestry must be rejected; cf. Childs, *Introduction*, 566f.

19. Cf. the similar concern in the related story of Tamar, Genesis 38.
20. The modeling role of Ruth and Boaz is summarized well by Childs (*Introduction*, 567) when he states that they "emerge as models of the faithful religious life of Israel." Campbell (*Ruth*, 16, with reference to Bertman), points out a symmetry between 1:8–18 and 4:1–12, each focusing "upon responsibility inherent in ties of kinship," exercised by Ruth and Boaz, against the foil of Orpah and the next of kin, respectively.
21. Like Abraham; see below, n. 26.
22. Hebrew *'ēšet hayil,* lit. "woman of strength/wealth." Because Ruth's only asset here is her right attitude, we must understand the attribute in an ethical sense, as something like "strength/wealth of character." In this light, the reference to Boaz as "a man of wealth" (*hayil*) in the literal sense (2:1) may also have anticipating ethical overtones.
23. See above, n. 17.
24. Although all interpreters underscore the masterful artistry of the book, some regard it as pure fiction, whereas others find in it considerable historical memory. Campbell (*Ruth*, 9f.) offers a judicious assessment of various social, legal, and onomastic features of the book that lead him to see it as a story "historically plausible" in the context of late premonarchic Israel.
25. See above, n. 18.
26. Internal references locate the canonical story in "the days when the judges ruled" (1:1) and mark off its historical horizons by naming the mothers of Israel, "Rachel and Leah, who together built up the house of Israel" (4:11), in the past, and David, Israel's greatest king (4:17, 22), in the future. Beyond this explicit definition of context, however, Gerleman (*Ruth*, 10f.) points out a far-reaching and probably intended thematic parallelism between the story of Ruth and the patriarchal stories, involving such topics as emigration due to famine (Genesis 12 and 26), childlessness of the clan mother (Genesis 16f., etc.), and the purchase of a field (Genesis 23). He interprets this as a deliberate attempt in the book of Ruth to point to parallel prehistories, leading toward the Sinai covenant (patriarchal stories) and the Davidic covenant (Ruth), respectively. The location of Ruth in the canon also deserves note. Although most commentators consider its place among the Writings, according to the Hebrew canon, to be original, the Greek-Christian tradition of placing it after Judges is at least appropriate (cf. 1:1 and n. 24 above), and it may even be more ancient than is usually thought; cf. Campbell, *Ruth,* 34–36.
27. In the canonical text, chapter 19 belongs to the longer story of chapters 19–21. Hypotheses as to the compositional history of these chapters vary. According to J. Alberto Soggin, the story of the Levite and his concubine (ch. 19) was originally independent of the account of the Benjaminite war

(chs. 20–21), but the two were welded together firmly into a unit on the basis that certain things should not happen in Israel (19:30; 20:6b–7); *Judges, A Commentary,* trans. J. S. Bowden, Old Testament Library (Philadelphia: Westminster Press, 1981), 282, 300–301. Similarly, the assessments of the historicity of chapters 19–21 range widely with a general tendency to see older, historically based data poured into later literary molds. For our purpose, only the shape and message of the canonical text is important.

28. Thus Hans W. Hertzberg, *Die Bücher Josua, Richter und Ruth,* Das Alte Testament Deutsch 9 (2d ed.; Göttingen: Vandenhoeck & Ruprecht, 1959), 248, 255. According to Soggin (*Judges,* 280f.), this formula belongs to the earliest, pro-monarchical phase of Dtr. H. (Veijola's terminology). A contrasting tendency, found by Soggin in these chapters, which presents the institutions of the tribal league as competent to deal with the problems, is then ascribed to a late anti-monarchical redaction, Dtr. N. In view of the muddled situation and the questionable good achieved by this attempt of the league to uphold justice, the latter observation hardly commends itself. Even less convincing is Robert G. Boling's suggestion that a final exilic (?) editor gave the formula a positive reading meant as an encouragement to the exiles to do right before Yahweh, "without any sacral political apparatus to get in the way"; *Judges: Introduction, Translation and Commentary,* Anchor Bible 6A (Garden City, N.Y.: Doubleday & Co., 1975), 293. On the generally positive evaluation of kingship in the Deuteronomistic History, see Gerald E. Gerbrandt, *Kingship According to the Deuteronomistic History,* SBL Dissertation Series 87 (Atlanta: Scholars Press, 1986), and on chapters 17–21, with attention to the formula under discussion, pp. 134–38.

29. Cf. the hospitality of Abraham (Gen. 18:1–8) and Lot (Gen. 19:1–11), and n. 30 below. In her masterful and deeply disturbing "journey alongside the concubine" (p. 66), Phyllis Trible agrees that the theme of the story is hospitality. She points out, however, that the rules of hospitality highlighted in this chapter and in Genesis 19 (Lot's hospitality) protect only males. See *Texts of Terror: Literary-Feminist Readings of Biblical Narratives,* Overtures to Biblical Theology (Philadelphia: Fortress Press, 1984), 65–91, esp. 75.

30. Homosexuality is implied here, but not highlighted, in contrast to the similar incident in Gen. 19:1–11, a story that has influenced our text, according to many commentators; cf. Soggin, *Judges,* 282, 288.

31. Hertzberg (*Josua,* 252) calls the old man's action "a witness to a hospitality ready for greatest sacrifice" (*Zeugnis opferbereitester Gastfreundschaft*). To point this out is by no means to lessen the cruelty done to the concubine. Trible (*Texts of Terror,* 80f.) makes the stunning observation: "Of all the characters in scripture, she is the least. . . . She is

property, object, tool, and literary device. . . . Captured, betrayed, raped, tortured, murdered, dismembered, and scattered—this woman is the most sinned against."

32. Hertzberg (*Josua*, 259) emphasizes that the crime is a crime against Israel, and that the embeddedness of the Levite's story into the web of Israelite corporate responsibility is an important feature of chapters 19–21.

33. For a fine depiction of this hospitality, see Hertzberg, *Josua*, 251f. The modern reader wishes with sadness that this ideal of inclusiveness might have embraced the women in the story equally. Trible (*Texts of Terror*, 84f.) points out sensitively that the shapers of the canon placed the stories of Hannah (1 Samuel 1–2; in the Hebrew canon) and Ruth (in the Greek canon) next to Judges 19–21. In both texts, women are portrayed and treated in ways that contrast favorably with the concluding chapters of Judges.

34. Soggin (*Judges*, 301) aptly states: "The redactors therefore propose to their hearers and readers a very high ethical standard: certain things may happen among other peoples, but they must not come about in Israel."

35. In the case of Boaz and Ruth, of course, laws defined to some extent the shape of the actions expected. That their exemplary behavior did not consist merely of their obedience to these laws, however, is made clear by the fact that the next of kin, who refused to accept responsibility, also did so within the context of law.

36. In Ezekiel 18, the prophet holds out the promise of life as a consequence of individual right living. It becomes patently clear throughout the prophet's visions for the future (e.g., 37:1–14), however, that he looks forward to God's gracious restoration of life in community. The call to personal righteousness in chapter 18 must therefore be heard as an interim-ethic for a time when communal existence had become disrupted by external forces. See below, pp. 167–69.

37. Cf. the willingness of Tamar (Genesis 38), Esther (Esth. 4:10–17), and Daniel and his friends (Dan. 3:16–18; 6:10) to endanger their lives in order to remain faithful.

38. Walter Brueggemann's theological theme-study *The Land* (see above, n. 12) traces the complex and dialectical relationship between landlessness and landedness throughout the Old Testament story. Cf. also my article "Geography of Faith: A Christian Perspective on the Meaning of Places," *Studies in Religion/Sciences Religieuses* 3, no. 2 (1973): 166–82, reprinted in Janzen, *Still in the Image: Essays in Biblical Theology and Anthropology* (Newton, Kans.: Faith & Life Press, 1982), 137–57; and my article "Land," *Anchor Bible Dictionary*, ed. David Noel Freedman (New York: Doubleday & Co., 1992), 4:143–54.

39. To maintain this order—the readiness to receive and only then to give—is central to the biblical message. Thomas W. Ogletree has offered an

impressive study of Christian ethics under the aegis of hospitality to the stranger as the central metaphor for the moral life; *Hospitality to the Stranger: Dimensions of Moral Understanding* (Philadelphia: Fortress Press, 1985), esp. 1–9. According to Ogletree, "to be moral is to be hospitable to the stranger" (p. 1). Much of his perspective is germaine to mine, and I enthusiastically approve of his elevation of hospitality as an ethical category to an importance not usually granted to it by ethicists. Although he balances the call for hospitality to the stranger with the need to be ready to be a stranger, a receiver (p. 4), and acknowledges the vulnerable human pilgrim status under God's grace (p. 7), his accent, however, seems to me to fall, in the first instance, on hospitality as an active human initiative rather than a response. By contrast, I perceive the biblical understanding to begin with receiving hospitality, followed by extending it.

40. Some of the most prominent hospitality scenes are Gen. 18:1–16; 19:1–9; 24:15–33; 29:1–14; Ex. 2:15–22; Josh. 2:1–21; 1 Kings 17:8–16. The theme of hospitality in the New Testament has received extensive recent treatment in John Koenig, *New Testament Hospitality: Partnership with Strangers as Promise and Mission,* Overtures to Biblical Theology 17 (Philadelphia: Fortress Press, 1985); see p. 13, no. 11, for older literature. Although there is much literature on the stranger (*gēr*) in the Old Testament, I am not aware of any systematic treatment of hospitality in the Old Testament; nor is there an equivalent term in Hebrew.

41. Hospitality is characterized by Ogletree (*Hospitality,* 2f., and throughout) as an outgoing mode of existence that is always ready to embrace the strange(r) and thereby extend one's own horizon. Without denying this aspect, my emphasis here is on hospitality as the extension of life and land (home) to the other because of his or her need. In this light, hospitality is the other-directed side of the grace experienced as a sojourner with God.

42. For a discussion of Israel's kinship structure, see Roland de Vaux, *Ancient Israel,* vol. 1: *Social Institutions* (New York: McGraw-Hill, 1965), 7f.; and Norman K. Gottwald, *The Tribes of Yahweh: A Sociology of the Religion of Liberated Israel 1250–1050 B.C.E.* (Maryknoll, N.Y.: Orbis Books, 1979), 237–341. "Father's house" and "clan," as used in our text, translate the Hebrew *bêt 'āb* and *mišpāhâ,* respectively.

43. Gottwald, *The Tribes of Yahweh,* 257–67; and Christopher J. H. Wright, "Family," *Anchor Bible Dictionary,* 2:761–69.

44. A special dimension of hospitality is the treatment of the resident alien (*gēr*); cf. de Vaux, *Ancient Israel,* 1:74–76; Diether Kellermann, "*gûr,* etc.," *Theological Dictionary of the Old Testament,* ed. G. J. Botterweck and H. Ringgren, trans. John T. Willis (Grand Rapids: Wm. B. Eerdmans Publishing Co., 1975), 2:438–49; and Frank Anthony Spina, "Israelites as *gērîm,* 'Sojourners' in Social and Historical Context," in *The Word of the Lord Shall Go Forth: Essays in Honor of David Noel*

Freedman in Celebration of His Sixtieth Birthday, ed. Carol L. Meyers and M. O'Connor (Winona Lake, Ind.: Eisenbrauns, 1983), 321–35.

45. Ogletree mentions the "risk" and "danger" incurred in practicing hospitality (e.g., *Hospitality,* 6, 58). On the whole, however, he associates these with the unsettling impact of the strange(r) upon the world perceived as home by the host. Without denying that truth, I want to emphasize more concretely the suffering potentially incurred by hospitality through self-deprivation, exposure to danger, and so forth, in the course of meeting the needs of (rather than opening oneself to the world of) the stranger.

PRINCIPLE
AND LAW

Story and Principle

Life, Land, and Hospitality

The claim that the Old Testament's familial paradigm is characterized by its orientation toward life, land, and hospitality may suggest that
our search for a story-based ethic of paradigm has inevitably led to an
ethic of principle, in spite of all earlier protestations. Are not these
terms conceptual abstractions, just as selflessness, humility, and compassion, or as *ṣĕdāqâ, mišpāṭ,* and *ḥesed,* and ultimately, the principle of
love? It may appear so on the surface, but there is a difference.

My earlier rejection of principles as helpful in comprehending the
Old Testament's ethical message was directed at principles understood as universally available and more or less self-interpreting truths.
Such abstractions have tended to lead to two apparently diverse, but
ultimately identical approaches, each of them reductionist in its
effect. First, such a principle has often been seen as the real aim of a
story. Thus a Sunday school class studying the story of Ruth and Boaz
(Ruth 2) has not finished its task until the story has led to an abstract
maxim, such as "Help the needy!" At that point, no great loss is felt if
the pupils forget the story on their way home, as long as they hold on
tightly to the principle "Help the needy!" Of course, such a principle
might have been drawn also from a passage in Amos (e.g., 2:6–16),
from Jesus' story of the Good Samaritan (Luke 10:25–37), or from

many other biblical texts. It is clear that the story or text, in this approach, becomes exchangeable and secondary, a mere scaffold for establishing a principle that can then stand and be effective on its own.

The second approach to principles rejected here is the inverse of the first. In it the teacher or preacher begins with an abstract ethical aim, such as the decision to promote the principle "Help the needy!" He or she then considers a way of presentation, and in doing so, eventually rejects the story of the Good Samaritan as too common and the Amos text as too austere, deciding upon the story of Ruth and Boaz as a fresh and appealing way of "getting it [the principle] across." Once again, the biblical story or text has lost all intrinsic value and has become a mere teaching aid in communicating what has independent ethical validity, namely, the principle.

In contrast to these reductionist uses of principle, my employment of the terms *life, land,* and *hospitality* should be understood as shorthand for the stories themselves and should not be separated from them. Thus "life," in this context, is not a universal principle known and pursued in all cultures, but the life that our model stories portrayed. It is life structured in families, valuing family shalom above economic advantage to self, attached historically to ancestral land and shared freely—even at the cost of suffering—through the extension of hospitality. In other words, it is the life that can be grasped fully only as the stories and other texts shaping the familial paradigm are heard again and again.[1] Through the use of this general term as shorthand, the stories and texts from which it emerges, or that it calls to mind, are in no way reduced in significance. The ethical reality continues to reside in them, rather than in a general formulation abstracted from or illustrated by them.

Justice as Principle

Perhaps this can be illustrated best by considering the term "justice," so beloved by ethical activists in our time, especially when safeguarded by the adjective "social" against any suggestion of referring to personal or parochial values. Under the banner of social justice, it is widely held, the most diverse individuals and groups can safely collaborate, for they all share in a universal human value. Such an understanding marks "justice" as an abstract principle by virtue of the fact that it can never be experienced directly. What a person can experience under the name of justice are such things as an adequate wage, protection from thieves or from state brutality, or nondiscriminating access to promotion in a career. But what are the specifics that persons of diverse background and persuasion experience under the abstract term of justice? Are they the same?

I am writing this chapter on a sabbatical leave in Switzerland. At present, this country is experiencing a great influx of persons from the Middle East and elsewhere claiming asylum as political refugees. As a World War II refugee who found a new home in Canada, and as someone steeped in the Old Testament's story of a people guided by God from oppression in Egypt to a new homeland not theirs by birth, I am easily persuaded that justice means granting asylum to those requesting it. I must also be sensitive to the story of the Swiss, however. Having lived in their small country for centuries, they trace their national existence to the struggle of their ancestors to preserve their home rights against outsiders; in the thirteenth century, the Habsburg rulers. Having thrown off foreign domination and developed a distinctive mode of life marked by prosperity and peace (albeit fiercely guarded by military preparedness), many Swiss perceive it as unjust that large numbers of foreigners should enter their crowded little land, take their jobs, and transform the nature and composition of their society. Does justice mean granting asylum or tightening the borders? The answer is not self-evident. My story and the Swiss national story lead to different understandings of "justice" at this point. The apparently universal and self-explanatory concept of justice dissolves into diverse understandings evoked by diverse stories.[2]

For the ancient world, indeed for all societies, the same is true. One ancient example may suffice. The Code of Hammurabi, expressing the ethos of a sedentary, class-structured society with high valuation of private property, considers punishment of theft by bodily mutilation or execution to be proper administration of justice. In Israel, by contrast, bodily mutilation was almost never practiced to punish crime, and property crimes did not carry the death sentence.[3] Thus we conclude that "justice" as a principle is less than adequate to express the content of Old Testament ethics.

Law as Principle

Two Views of Laws

To reject the usefulness of principles, understood as generally valid and self-interpreting abstractions, has weighty implications for our understanding of the nature and function of law(s) in Old Testament ethics. A law can be seen as a particular brand of a generally valid self-interpreting principle. Old Testament laws, especially those of the apodictic kind, have often been seen as such principles; thus, "You shall not kill" or "Remember the sabbath day to keep it holy" have been regarded as self-contained and self-interpreting universal moral maxims that, if observed, form the moral backbone of any nation.[4] Countless wall plaques and other isolated reproductions of the Ten Commandments, usually without the story-related introduction of Ex. 20:1–2, testify to the self-contained and isolated authority claimed for them.

The occurrence of similar commands in the writings of other religions can then be taken to demonstrate their universal authority, possibly grounded in natural law or archetypal consciousness. This may then invite the assumption of the essential unity of all basic religious truth. That these kernels of truth are couched in greatly diverging religious literatures recedes in importance, just as we observed in the principle-centered approach to Old Testament ethics at the beginning of this chapter.

A very different understanding of such laws emerges when one sees them, in light of our preceding considerations, as shorthand formulations of ethical values and imperatives emerging from a particular story—Israel's story—and as continuing to be defined by that story. Then they can no longer be seen as self-contained universal maxims, nor can they be loosened from the story in which they are embedded. They no longer derive their validity and claim to authority from natural law or archetypal religio-ethical consciousness. Whatever authority they hold over us is rooted in our acceptance of the story that defines them.

Rabbinic and Rational Influences

How are we to judge between these two options, that is, between law as abstract principle and law as determined by story? The former exerts a double attraction for Christians. First, it is abetted by the interplay of rabbinic Judaism and early Christian hermeneutic. In rabbinic Judaism, the virtual identification of ethics with law (*halakah*) tended to give the commandments a status largely independent of their Pentateuchal story context.[5] Christians, since earliest times, have appropriated the story of the Old Testament as a story of promise pointing forward to, and finding its climax in, the life and ministry of Jesus Christ. They have generally, however, adopted rabbinic Judaism's identification of Old Testament ethics with law and have quickly rejected its relevance in favor of the ethical model of Jesus. A reading of passages like Luke 16:16 in isolation seems to lend support to this rejection. To the extent, however, that Christians have allowed the Old Testament to address them ethically at all, they have largely done so by granting exceptional status to certain laws and other texts in isolation. Among the laws, the Ten Commandments received pride of place, in part because of their explicit affirmation by Jesus and in part because of their supposed self-evident universal validity. Similar status was granted, though less widely and consistently, to certain prophetic words and certain proverbs. Seldom were any of these "ethically relevant" texts accepted on the basis of an authority residing in the story of Israel.

The acceptance of ethically relevant Old Testament texts in isolation, abetted by rabbinic Judaism's identification of ethics with laws, has found powerful support in the affinity of Western mentality for abstract thinking. This, of course, is a mentality very different from that of rabbinic Judaism. Whereas the latter stresses God's particular gift of Torah to a select and specific people, the former finds a stumbling block in precisely this particularity. Nevertheless, the two have combined to promote within the church a tendency to detach law from story and to see the authority of laws, to the extent that it was granted to them, in their self-contained isolation.[6] It will be the task of the remainder of this chapter to argue for an alternative, namely, a story-related understanding of law, on the basis of the Bible itself.

Law as Story

The Story Context of Old Testament Law

The first and most important observation with respect to the Old Testament's story-related understanding of law is the fact that all law codes in the Old Testament are embedded in Israel's story.[7] Most of them are presented as proclamations of God's will at Mount Sinai. Only the giving of the Deuteronomic Code (Deuteronomy 12–26) is located in the plains of Moab in the form of a farewell speech of Moses reminding Israel of the duties it had assumed at Mount Sinai. Each of the promulgations of law occurs, in the present canonical documents, at a specific time and place. It is directed at a specific group of hearers at a specific historical moment that has a before and after. Further-more, these bodies of law function as a basis for Israel's self-commitment to the God who has redeemed it from slavery in Egypt.[8] Such a commitment is to be evidenced by a new way of life, marked particularly by a distinctive stewardship of the land to be received.

This transmission of law codes in story contexts becomes especially significant when seen against the backdrop of Mesopotamian law. From that remarkably legal civilization[9] several law codes have been preserved, most prominent and best known among them the Code of Hammurabi.[10] All of them have come to us as self-contained docu-ments, inscribed on clay tablets or stone slabs. Although the Code of Hammurabi is introduced by a prologue, none of the codes are embedded in the story of the people they address, nor did they function as the bases of religious commitments analogous to the Sinai covenant. Their significance lay clearly in the realm of administration and reform of justice, even though there is some dispute concerning the precise nature of their function.[11]

The Judicial and Covenantal Function of Law

Modern scholars generally agree that certain Old Testament codes, in many ways resembling the Mesopotamian codes, functioned much like the latter in Israel's administration of justice before they were incorporated into the story of the Pentateuch. Like the Meso-potamian codes, they undoubtedly portrayed models of jurisprudence for the benefit of the elders who administered justice in the gate. They were probably intended also to set and/or correct certain directions in Israel's communal life. But if this had remained their essential significance in Israel, they might well have been forgotten as society changed, or preserved as archaeological relics only, like their Meso-potamian counterparts.

Instead, we may assume that their role transcended their strictly judicial function relatively early in Israel's history. The so-called motive clauses, very rarely if ever found in Mesopotamian laws, bear witness to this.[12] These are clauses giving reasons why a certain law should be observed, thus providing motivation for its observance. The parents commandment of the Decalogue may serve as an example:

> Honor your father and your mother, that your days may be long in the land which the LORD your God gives you. (Ex. 20:12)

The first clause states the law and would be sufficient to instruct an Israelite as to his or her duty. The second is the motive clause. It appeals to the reader's or hearer's insight and seeks inner assent. The Israelite addressed is not only to observe the law, but to become the kind of person who would want to do as the law says. Frequently, the motive clauses remind their Israelite addressees of their redemption from slavery in Egypt and exhort them to act as those rooted in that story. Thus the motive clauses add a pleading, preaching, persuading tone to the Old Testament's bodies of law, something quite unheard of in law codes generally.[13] If Erhard Gerstenberger were right in his claim that apodictic law originated in the ethos of the clan as taught by the elders, its hortatory, persuasive dimension, evidenced in the motive clauses, would receive a plausible life setting.[14] Of course, there is no reason to limit the instruction of the elders to apodictic laws; they may well have taught casuistic laws also, as the presence of motive clauses there gives reason to assume. Such instruction may have had its setting in the village circle where the men of the village gathered to exchange the news of the day, to tell the stories of old, and to rehearse traditional wisdom.[15]

However one may regard Gerstenberger's claim, it is certain that observance of law was to be motivated in Israel by the story of Israel's redemption. This is emphasized by the introduction to the Decalogue (Ex. 20:2; Deut. 5:6) and by the structure of the "small historical credos." The latter are summaries of Israel's faith, consisting of a rehearsal of the story of Israel's redemption, for the purpose of accounting for, or recommitting oneself to the observance of God's will as expressed in the laws (cf. Deut. 6:20–25; 26:1–11; Josh. 24:1–15). Dale Patrick describes the aim of such education by way of analogy to family life: "The family ethos should instill values and principles that the child learns to apply independently. When a child encounters temptation, he or she should know without a stated rule the kind of behavior expected."[16] Patrick, in his broad "collective" definition of law as "the order of justice and right to which individuals and groups should conform and which judicial authority should enforce," claims correctly that "explicit rules—laws—are only the tip of the iceberg of the phenomenon of Law."[17] I would prefer to refer to this broad range of values as ethos, to avoid the suggestion implicit in calling it (capitalized) Law that the essence of Old Testament ethics is legal. I would further propose that a significant component of the values to be internalized by an Israelite took the form of paradigms shaped in his or her mind by model stories, as suggested above in chapters 1 and 2.

We conclude, then, that even the codes of Old Testament law that at one time served judicial purposes were made to transcend these early in Israel's history as they were communicated in exhorting form to elicit assent, shape character, and renew commitment to the God who had saved his people. As a consequence, these laws were transmitted, not as separate legal collections, but as sequels to the story of redemption.[18]

It is interesting to note in this connection how little attention is given in the Old Testament to the actual administration of justice. Although "countless thousands"[19] of contracts and other materials pertaining to the practice of law have been unearthed in Mesopotamia, we have almost no such records in the Old Testament. Only incidentally do we learn something about Israelite court procedures (e.g., the mock trial of Naboth, 1 Kings 21; or the case against Jeremiah, Jeremiah 26) or hear of legal transactions (e.g., Ruth 4; Isa. 8:1–2; Jer. 32:6–15). On the other hand, Israel preserved in the prophetic writings an extensive and, in its scope, unique literature of "self-evaluation." In it, however, the issue is not so much the observance of laws as it is the faithfulness of the people to the God of their history. The observance, or more often, nonobservance, of laws does play a great role in this self-assessment, but is thoroughly subservient to the question of Israel's character shaped by her story.[20]

The Community-Shaping Function of Legal Series

That the concern of Old Testament law, at least in its canonical context, was not so much the adjudication of cases as the shaping and defining of character is further evidenced by its frequent arrangement in series. In such series, the accent is shifted from the single commandment to the total impact of all the commandments in the series. Each individual commandment contributes a stroke of the brush toward the painting of a person or people. As we read such commandments or laws together, there emerges before our inner eye a picture or paradigm that possesses a certain wholeness not unlike that of the paradigms.

Among these series, the Decalogue deserves a privileged position, of course. In its present place in Israel's story, it constitutes the central content of Israel's commitment to God in the context of covenant. The you/thou addressed in each of its commandments is primarily the head of the Israelite household, who is to ensure that he and his family respond to God, their covenant Suzerain, or overlord, with a new quality of life based on God's revealed will. In spite of its largely negative formulation, its total effect is a positive one; it creates the image of a covenant-keeping Israelite.[21]

Somewhat different in their impact are the other three series identified by Albrecht Alt as apodictic.[22] They are the death-sentence series, the so-called *môt-yûmāt*-laws (laws concluding with "shall be put to death"),[23] the curse series of Deut. 27:15–26, and the series prohibiting sexual intercourse between certain persons (Lev. 18:6–18). The combined effect of the laws in each case is to ward off dangers from the community. The community in focus is the extended family, whose positive central characteristics we have seen earlier on the basis of selected stories to be certain defined concerns for life, land, and hospitality. In other words, the specific laws enumerated do not constitute the level on which Israel's, much less the Old Testament's, ethical concern was focused. These individual laws are merely instrumental in achieving and/or safeguarding an ethos of communal life structured along kinship lines.

This is most evident in Lev. 18:7–17. Hans Jochen Boecker, following Karl Elliger, points out that the aim of these prohibitions is not designed to promote "a general moral ideal or universal idea of modesty. . . . They are designed rather to safeguard a given community. They deal with the problems of maintaining the health and purity of a family. The common life is not to lead to a sexual free-for-all."[24] In nomadic times, such families lived together in groupings of three or four generations. As Boecker points out further, this originally family-oriented series has been refocused, in its present context, on forbidden intercourse within certain degrees of relationship.[25] We must not neglect the wider context, however—that is, the Priestly Code—and ultimately the story line of the Pentateuch. Within these, the series contributes to the shaping of a people who live in awareness of Yahweh's ordering of creation, by observing the holy and the common, the clean and the unclean. At this point we take note of the fact that, very early in Israel's history, laws tended not to function as isolated, more or less self-interpreting principles of right and wrong, but as instruments for maintaining that same communal ethos that is portrayed in a more immediate way by the Old Testament's model stories of family shalom. Thus such laws contribute to the shaping of the familial paradigm, albeit less directly than the stories. We will not take time here to spell out the similar community-protecting function of the death sentence and curse series (Ex. 21:12–17; 22:19–20, and Deut. 27:15–26, respectively).

To summarize: I have argued against a reductionist use of principles—a use demoting Old Testament stories to an auxiliary function in establishing or illustrating ethical principles that can ultimately have a self-contained existence and authority. I have extended this argumentation to cover laws, for these are often interpreted as a particular form of abstract principle. I have drawn attention, instead, to the functioning of Old Testament laws, embedded without exception in story contexts, as instruments of shaping a kinship society with the same paradigmatic elements as we discovered earlier, and more immediately, in model stories.

The Primacy of Story Over Law

Law as Secondary Genre

In our study of law so far, there has emerged the claim that stories operate on an ethically prior or more primary level, whereas laws, even the comprehensively formulated apodictic laws, operate on a secondary or subservient level. This claim may seem particularly open to question when even the Ten Commandments, often regarded as the hard core of Old Testament ethics, are consigned to that secondary level. A justification is therefore in order and will be offered in chapter 4. Let it be said right away, however, that this apparent demotion of law, though unusual in studies of Old Testament ethics, is no novel pursuit and should not surprise ethicists.

It is general knowledge that law proceeds from, upholds, and enforces values that are prior to it. This is certainly true of laws in relation to their ultimate source, whether one thinks of that as the covenant will of God, as natural law embedded in the created order, as the will of the people, or simply as inherited culture. It is true also on the level of specific legal formulation. Values expressed in the form of laws have invariably been communicated earlier in other modes. W. Malcolm Clark says that "[b]y and large the genres [of law] are related to or arise from speech patterns or genres in other areas."[26] He cites Paul Bohannan as stating that "law may be regarded as a custom that has been restated in order to make it amenable to the activities of the legal institutions."[27] Here we find the motivation for the transformation of other genres into laws.

For our study it is important not only to take note of such a transformation leading to legal formulation of values, but also to inquire concerning the earlier genres that transmitted these values, and frequently continue to transmit them. If everything eventually codified as law was at one time handed down in other oral or literary forms, what may the latter have been? Erhard Gerstenberger's thesis becomes inviting at this point, namely, that many laws now formulated as prohibitions originated in popular ethos, for example, in the teaching of the village elders.[28] Such teaching can lay claim to both a temporal and a formal priority over codified law.[29]

How was such custom (Bohannan, Clark) or popular ethos (Gerstenberger) communicated before it became law? Surely a major avenue was story. Some of these stories must have been rehearsals of the great acts of God in the past, such as the election of Abraham, the exodus from Egypt, the covenant at Sinai, and the occupation of the land. Although these had their most important place of transmission in the cult, they were also proper subject matter for replying "[w]hen your son asks you in time to come" (Deut. 6:20–25). But the stories handed on in the village circle may also have included less central events.

> In those days, when there was no king in Israel, a certain Levite was sojourning in the remote parts of the hill country of Ephraim. (Judg. 19:1)

There followed a story upholding ethical values and contributing to a paradigmatic image of right living in Israel's kinship society, as we saw earlier.

Of course, the societal customs in Israel issued not only into laws, but also into proverbs and other wisdom genres, and possibly formed the basis of appeal for the preaching of at least some of the prophets.[30] Naturally, the priority claimed here for story over legal formulation has little direct bearing on the dating of any given story or law; it is a typological priority.

Common law, or precedent-based administration of justice, represents an intermediate step between story and law. It consists of remembering and retelling what happened in the past (= story) in order to guide the administration of justice in the present (= law). Jeremiah 26 may serve to illustrate. Jeremiah is arrested in the

Temple and accused of uttering seditious words worthy of death, by proclaiming God's threat to destroy the Temple. In the course of a quickly summoned court session headed by the princes, "certain of the elders of the land" (v. 17) arose and told the story of the prophet Micah. He had announced similar threats a century earlier and effected the repentance of King Hezekiah and the preservation of city and Temple.[31] The citation of this precedent preserved the life of Jeremiah. In other words, the telling of a story had upheld Israelite ways and led to a just decision in a legal case.

Legal codes, both in the ancient Near East and in Israel, are now widely considered to be "collections, or perhaps even revisions, of traditional case law."[32] E. A. Speiser, citing J. C. Miles, has called the Code of Hammurabi "a series of amendments to the common law of Babylon."[33] Both in Israel and in the ancient Near East, codes appear to have functioned as model illustrations for applying case law as well as for effecting reforms and setting new directions. They do not create new values for societies, but preserve, uphold, and sometimes reshape already existing values.[34]

The Interpretive Force of the Sinai Framework

We have seen the priority of other modes of transmitting values over legal formulations. But although this may be a correct anthropological description of the gradual emergence of legal codifications within a society governed by popular ethos and common law, is it not in head-on collision with Israel's canonical text? Does not the latter portray a grand law promulgation by God at Mount Sinai, albeit modified somewhat by the claim of Deuteronomy that the people heard only the Ten Words (the Decalogue), whereas the other laws were communicated to them through Moses (Deut. 5:5; Ex. 25:1; Lev. 1:1; 4:1; etc.)? Does not, according to the canonical text, a totally new covenant people have its beginning as it hears the will of Yahweh for the first time and commits itself to obedience to that will, expressed as law?

Such a view of the canonical portrayal, however, misses the meaning of the Sinai events in its assessment of what is new. By the very act of placing all of Israel's law, headed by the Decalogue, into the flow of the exodus story, the text itself asserts, as it were, that Israel's law could not be understood without a prior story. Even the collections and codes that must have had separate circulation in Israel at various times are now bereft of their separate existence. They were not to be interpreted according to their own original backgrounds and contexts, but were to be read now as giving expression to a reality that had emerged in the story now embracing them. In other words, the present location of Old Testament laws in the Sinai context must not be interpreted as emphasizing the newness of its promulgation. Instead, it aims at transferring these laws from their original contexts into a new story.

It is precisely in their subjection to the interpreting impact of this new story that we must see the new dimension of the law proclaimed at Sinai. That story began with creation, gained new impetus with Abraham, and reached its climax in those events that filled the newly proclaimed name of God, Yahweh (Exodus 3 and 6), with its lasting meaning:

> I am Yahweh your God, who brought you out of the land of Egypt, out of the house of bondage. (Ex. 20:2)

This brief characterization of Yahweh as savior is prefixed to the Ten Commandments as a reminder that they, and with them all the laws that follow, shall be understood as interpreted by the story that it summarizes. Further reminders of this abound in the Old Testament, prominently, in the so-called small historical credos (e.g., Deut. 6:20–25).

The new dimension of the law giving at Sinai must also not be sought in the content of the laws. Surely we cannot assume that Israel's ancestors, wherever they lived and whatever sociological structure they had, were free to kill, commit adultery, steal, and so forth, at will, before they received God's law at Sinai! With respect to certain laws, their early and widespread ancient Near Eastern existence can be demonstrated.[35] Such laws, and—we can safely assume—most of those for which equally clear evidence of ancient Near Eastern background is not available, had had a life as part of various and different stories among Israel's ancestors and beyond. But now they were to be transplanted into a new and overarching story that would function as their main interpreter henceforth. Interspersed motive clauses serve as additional reminders of this. The commandment to honor father and mother (Ex. 20:12), for example, states an essential requirement among all people living in kinship structures. Now, however, it is not only to be seen in the context of the ongoing existence of the clan, but also[36] in reference to God's promise of a land to Abraham, a land toward which Israel at Sinai was on the move. To give one more example, Israel is not to wrong or oppress a stranger, "for you were strangers in the land of Egypt" (Ex. 22:21). Often the phrase "I am Yahweh," placed with some abruptness into legal contexts at various points (e.g., Lev. 19:12), is enough of a reminder that these laws are not self-contained or self-interpreting, but are covered by the story that fills the name Yahweh with content. Thus the canonical text, including all laws in the law-giving of Sinai, presents in one grand panorama what must have taken place in Israel historically in the course of many centuries: the permeation of tribal, local, or widespread ancient Near Eastern values and laws by the distinctive theology revealed to Israel in the great acts of God in creation and salvation history.

Proposals for the Anchoring of Law

Laws and law codes, then, do not stand alone or possess inherent authority; they express the authority and the values of a community and, ultimately, of God. We have pointed out their story context in the Old Testament. In this section, we will consider the danger of dissolving the relevance of specific laws through a central principle, a danger illustrated in Emil Brunner's approach. I will argue for the need of a "middle level" that serves as the stable, ongoing, and relatively specific carrier of the Old Testament's ethos. Finally, we will look at three different proposals for such a middle level.

Emil Brunner: One Divine Imperative

So far, my argumentation has moved in one direction. I have rejected the view that laws can be understood in self-interpreting isolation (as individual laws or law codes), just as I rejected this possibility for principles earlier. I argued for the priority of story as carrying the community's values, values that were protected by common law and eventually crystallized, in some instances, into written laws and law codes. These in turn were transplanted, for Israel, into the overarching story of God's mighty acts.

If we accept this secondary, dependent function of Israel's laws, we may well be faced by a very different danger. Instead of seeing them as self-contained and self-interpreting "ethical morsels" to be observed piecemeal, we may swing to the opposite extreme and lump all of them together as expressions of one general ethical principle, such as covenant love for God.

Emil Brunner's great work on ethics offers a classical example. God's will for us, according to Brunner,[37] is completely and fully expressed in the First Commandment: "I am the Lord thy God, thou shalt have none other Gods but Me" [sic].[38] This is God's loving gift to us, and God requires solely and only that we respond in exclusive love that accepts the love he has extended.

> We are never bidden to do anything else. "Love is the fulfilling of the law" [Rom. 13:10]. From this point of view this obedience-of-faith-in-love alone is the "moral"; everything else—from the ethical point of view—is technique, that is, the search for, and the use of, means which make this love real.[39]

Love is the one and only divine imperative.[40] Somewhat abruptly, and with reference to Matt. 22:39, Brunner incorporates the love of neighbor in this central imperative as well. All other commandments, statutes, and ordinances are characterized as technique, that is, as means of implementing the love commandment. They illustrate, at a given time and under given circumstances, what it means to love. One must never turn to them, however, to determine in advance what decisions in specific matters God's central imperative will require in the future. These commandments, be they the Decalogue or the Sermon on the Mount, belong to God's historical revelation. In other words, if I understand Brunner correctly, they give evidence of what it meant in certain biblical contexts to fulfill the divine imperative. In particular, they are witnesses of the covenant and authentic interpretations of the central imperative; they are God-given illustrations.

What do we make of this all-encompassing focus on love and the consequent "demotion" of all laws to the level of instrumentality? Consistent with our central line of argumentation, it is easy to accept the "demotion" just referred to. Laws, as we have seen, are always secondary expressions of prior values flowing from other sources. I certainly also accept Brunner's thesis that all biblical ethics is ultimately rooted in God's self-revelation, which is gathered up for us in the divine name. Biblical ethics is ultimately to be understood as exclusive and obedient response to the one and only God who has revealed himself.

But can this self-manifestation and response of obedience be conceptualized adequately and helpfully as love? What kind of love?

How is this concept to be understood? If it gathers into itself the whole biblical story and is fully defined by it, I could accept it as shorthand in a manner similar to my interpretation of the function of the terms life, land, and hospitality.[41] Brunner's use of the phrase "historical revelation" suggests this.[42] Assuming such a function, I can come to terms with Brunner's formulation. There remains, however, an uneasy feeling that this function might be lost for many readers and that the love principle might be considered as a self-contained and self-authenticating ethical maxim that, once attained, no longer needs the story that gave rise to it.

The Need for a Middle Level

Granting, then, the rootedness of the love principle in, and its definition by, the story of God's revelation in scripture, I am faced with a second question. Is the love imperative the immediate source of the statutes, commandments, and ordinances, that is, of the multiplicity of specific injunctions found in scripture? One could first ask the question historically. Although a Western theological ethicist might find it possible to move from an abstractly formulated principle (even if rooted in and shaped by history) to the concrete specifics of daily life, can the same be assumed of ancient biblical people? Can we expect that an Israelite of old, or for that matter, an early follower of Jesus, could be referred to the love principle and then left to his or her own devices in matters of ethical living? Although the love commandment receives one of its most succinct and powerful formulations in Deut. 6:4–5, the inquisitive son of the same chapter (vs. 20–25), who wants to know "the meaning of the testimonies and the statutes and the ordinances," is not referred directly to the love commandment, but rather to Israel's story: "We were Pharaoh's slaves in Egypt . . ." (v. 21).

Luke 10:25–37 is also instructive here. Asked by a lawyer, "Teacher, what shall I do to inherit eternal life?" Jesus elicits from the lawyer's own lips the double love commandment. But the lawyer, not satisfied, continues with the question "And who is my neighbor?" Now, his motivation in this instance is judged negatively, namely, as "desiring to justify himself." Nevertheless, Jesus does not reply, "You know very well!" Instead, he tells the well-known story of the Good Samaritan. Should all those more positively motivated than that lawyer dismiss this story as a superfluous intrusion between the central love principle and its obvious consequences for daily life? Did

Jesus only accommodate himself to a negatively predisposed questioner? Or did he, by telling this story, acknowledge the legitimate need, at least in that case, of a "middle level" of ethical imagination? And if the necessity existed only because of the lawyer's inclination to self-justification, do we dare to place ourselves outside of that disposition? In positive terms, I believe that the ethical imagination of biblical people operated effectively on a "middle level," the level characterized earlier as that of paradigm. But this "middle level," on which ethics functions through the medium of story-shaped paradigm, is also neglected by Western Christian ethics only at the peril of great loss. Between the principle of loving our neighbor and the actual implementation of it in specific modern situations stands the lawyer's and our search for a concrete, neither abstract nor casuistic, image of neighbor. Who would want to deny that the story used by Jesus (together with others, such as that of the rich man and Lazarus, Luke 16:19–31) has been a most powerful impetus in Christian ethics?

Every all-too-rapid reduction of the multiplicity of ethical demands in daily life to a central principle is in grave danger of short-circuiting the biblical content of that principle and of leading to its isolation. This then throws open its transplanting to a different base of authority. Detached from its rootage in the biblical story and robbed of its interpretation and actualization in paradigmatic images, it soon seeks its authority in natural law, reason, or some other soil.

Dale Patrick: Unwritten Law

A particularly impressive attempt to distinguish between the multiplicity of Old Testament laws and the prior level of ethical values that informs them has been offered by Dale Patrick.[43] Patrick's proposal is developed in the context of a thorough study of Old Testament law. Rejecting, like Brunner, an understanding of the Old Testament's written laws and law codes as intended for casuistic application, he inquires concerning their ultimate source and their function. He concludes that in ancient Israel, "[t]he law which the judicial system enforced was an unwritten law woven into the fabric of society and discovered in the course of judicial deliberation."[44] Its gist was a sense or principle of "justice and right."[45] Beginning with Deuteronomy, and promoted especially by the Deuteronomistic school that emerged in Judah after the discovery of Deuteronomy, a new trend set in. The recourse to the unwritten law, centering in a sense of justice and right, diminished progressively in favor of an identification of God's will with the text of the written law.[46] This development led logically to canonization and eventually to the preoccupation of rabbinic Judaism with the multiplicity of laws.[47] Christianity, according to Patrick, directed by the impetus of Jesus and Paul but followed by most New Testament authors, returned to the unwritten law of the Old Testament but also transcended it: "The epitome of this unwritten Law is the commandment to love God and one's neighbor, which both fulfills and surpasses the sense of justice and right forming the basis of Old Testament divine law."[48]

Once again, as in the case of Brunner, it is easy to assent to Patrick's distinction between concrete judicial decisions and written laws and law codes on the one hand, and a prior realm of values that informs these, on the other. In addition, Patrick's finely nuanced picture of the development of this prior level of values from a communal sense of justice and right, and on to its reclamation by Jesus and the New Testament, now centering in the double commandment of love, is extremely appealing. And yet it raises once more the question evoked by Brunner. Are we again confronted with a prior source of value formulated in terms of (potentially abstract) principles expected to inform directly the multitude of ethical demands of daily life, without a "middle level" of paradigm? It is the claim of our study that this short-circuits an ethical reality in scripture. We can schematize our disagreement in the following diagram.

The diagrammatic presentation may have drawn attention to another point of difference between Patrick's and the present proposal. Patrick designates his prior level of values as unwritten law and its Old Testament focus as justice and right. This immediately gives Israel's ethos a legal stamp. Some of this may properly be ascribed to the focus of Patrick's study on law. I would prefer, however, to avoid legal terminology ("justice and right," "unwritten law") in describing the "middle level." It seems more helpful and less restricting to think of positive law as rooted in a communal sense—I use "paradigm" or inner image—of virtue or of the good life. Such formulations do not tie the middle level to any genre (such as law). It also allows for the fact that this "middle level" of ethos underlies not only the genres of law, but other ethically relevant genres (such as proverbs) as well.[49]

Christopher J. H. Wright: A Paradigm-Shaping Triangle

In the claim just stated, our study seems compatible in various respects with the work of Christopher J. H. Wright, although it also

Emil Brunner:

Positive / written
biblical laws

(Illustrative of technique of applying
love in biblical context)

Dale Patrick:

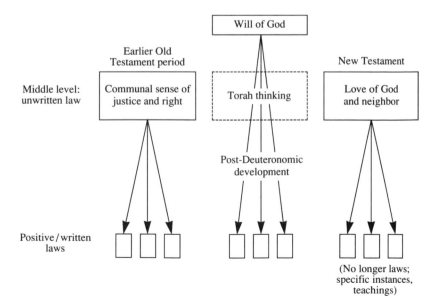

Earlier Old
Testament period

New Testament

Middle level:
unwritten law

Post-Deuteronomic
development

Positive / written
laws

(No longer laws;
specific instances,
teachings)

Waldemar Janzen:

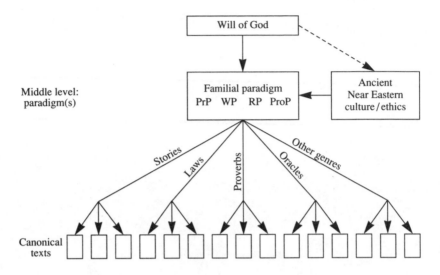

diverges from Wright in important ways.[50] Wright conceives of Old Testament ethics broadly, not limiting it to one genre or realm such as law, nor immediately relating it to an overarching principle such as justice or love. Instead, he takes seriously what we have called an unwritten "middle level" of ethical authority or value.[51] He employs the concept of paradigm for Israel: "[W]e are to take Israel's social shape and characteristics, her institutions, laws and ideals . . . as paradigmatic when we are engaged in the social ethical task."[52] This shape and these characteristics are determined, in turn, by two reference points: God and the land. Thus a triangular relationship results between God, Israel, and the land. This relationship is informed and defined by the Old Testament's story, from creation to eschatological expectation. From this story-shaped relationship of Israel to God and the land emerges the specifics of Israel's (paradigmatic) ethic, in economics, politics, justice, law, society and culture, and individual ethics.[53]

Among the paradigmatic aspects of Israel's ethic, Wright highlights the centrality of the family: "So all three realms, social, economic and theological, were closely bound together . . ., and all three had the family[54] as their focal point."[55] Wright stresses the centrality of social ethics in the Old Testament, giving only marginal attention to individual ethics in a brief final chapter.[56] His treatment, in that context, of "the wise man" and "the acceptable worshiper" recalls our wisdom and priestly paradigms, though limited to the personal realm.

Despite these many affinities between Wright's work and mine, there are major differences, both in approach and in substance. First, Wright presents his "middle level" of ethical values (the triangular interrelationship between Israel, God, and land) in a unified and summarized form. He does not take sufficient account (other than marginally with respect to individual ethics) of the fact that Israel's unwritten self-understanding was not monolithic, but multifaceted. In my view, this multifaceted self-understanding has found its Old Testament deposit in clusters of texts pointing to a variety of ethical paradigms. Although the familial is foremost of these, the priestly, sapiential, royal, and prophetic paradigms seem sufficiently distinct to warrant differential treatment.[57] Second, Wright distinguishes sharply between social and individual ethics, a separation that I hope to overcome through a greater emphasis on the ethical significance of character shaped by story. One problematic result of such a separation tends to be the marginalization of the wisdom literature as individual ethics.

Finally, there seems to be a tension, in Wright's schema, between the language of paradigm employed throughout, generally with reference to Israel, and the rather abrupt introduction of the concept of principle or "middle axiom" as underlying any particular law. Such principles are equated with, but apparently not limited to, the commandments of the Decalogue. Are we to posit a layer of principles between the story-shaped paradigm of Israel (in relation to God and land) and the specifics in which that paradigm expressed itself in each of Wright's "themes" in Old Testament ethics (economics, politics, etc.)?[58] Or do these principles or middle axioms merely apply to the theme of "Law and the legal system," where they are introduced? In other words, are they merely terms for more comprehensive legal formulations, as compared with the "small galaxies of supporting laws, exhortation and motivation which surround them"?[59]

These objections not withstanding, there is considerable substantial compatibility between Wright's analysis and my own. In particular, Wright is committed, as I am, to a broad definition of the range of genres that convey the Old Testament's ethos.

Bruce C. Birch: Covenant Community and Decalogue

As I stated in the Introduction, Birch's recent work stands particularly close to my own in its presuppositions and its goals.[60] It seems appropriate, therefore, to compare our approaches generally before we look at Birch's way of anchoring laws in broader authoritative contexts. Of course, only a few points of compatibility in our works can be highlighted here.

Birch's approach takes account of the multiplicity of genres in the Old Testament, according special importance to narrative. It is based on a canonical reading of the Old Testament. And it seeks to make the Old Testament relevant for the ethics of the church. All these aspects of Birch's work, and others, are almost identical with my presuppositions and my goal.

As to the way from the starting points to the goal, however, Birch and I diverge significantly. In contrast to my developing a pattern of paradigms, Birch allows the flow of the Old Testament's story to guide him. Thus the main section of his book ("Part Two: The Old Testament Story as Moral Resource") begins with "Creator and Creation" and proceeds through the themes of exodus, covenant, kingship, and the prophets to "Exile and Return." A final chapter, "Wisdom and Morality," stands apart from the course of the story.

As to content, Birch and I also share very similar views. There is very little in Birch's book with which I disagree. But again, we structure our presentations very differently. Both of us agree that biblical theology and biblical ethics cannot and should not be separated. It appears to me, however, that Birch leans more toward the theological spectrum of this continuum, and I more to the ethical. In his chapter "Prophetic Confrontation," for example, Birch gives extensive discussion to God as the source of the prophetic word, to the covenant as context, and to the calling and authority of the prophet. He does eventually discuss the addressees of the prophetic word and the specific content addressed to them, in the relatively brief subsection "The Prophetic Indictment." My approach, on the other hand, assumes the divine origin and theological context. Although referring to it throughout, I focus on the ethical worlds addressed by the prophets, that is, the royal, priestly, and wisdom realms. Each of these is critiqued by the prophets in terms of its own paradigm and recalled to it. If each would return to its own inner image of the good life, I point out, they would come together in a life marked by the same vision, namely, that of the familial paradigm.

A final point of comparison pertains to our distinctive ways of seeking relevance for Christians today. Birch freely relates his insights to us and our time throughout his book. On the other hand, he does not link the Old Testament to the New in any systematic way. There are a few references to the New Testament, and the brief epilogue affirms the need for preserving the continuity of the canon and of biblical communities of faith. By contrast, my book makes few explicit applications to present-day Christian life, although I hope that Christian readers will readily find an immediate relevance. On the other hand, I attempt in my final chapter to relate the paradigmatic pattern of the Old Testament to a similar pattern discernible in the life and teachings of Jesus.

Birch's and my approaches are—I believe—both compatible and complementary. They start at the same place and seek to serve the same end. Birch stays closer to the biblical story, whereas I move further in the direction of systematizing Old Testament ethics.[61] Both approaches have distinctive strengths and weaknesses, and each—so I hope—will meet the needs of specific readers in specific tasks and contexts.

In keeping with his total approach, Birch sees specific laws and law codes as emerging from Israel's story with God.

> The narrative context makes clear that for Israel all law receives its authority from the belief that it has been divinely revealed as a part of the solemn covenant established by God with Israel and agreed to by Israel at Sinai.[62]

Far from advocating a detailed application of the various laws to later times, however, Birch places emphasis on the role of the covenant community. This community is not static, but exhibits a dynamic, ongoing life with God. The law codes reflect this dynamic in their historical development.

For Birch, the anchoring ground, or middle level, for all the laws and law codes seems to be the Decalogue.

> Standing prior to all other law codes, the Decalogue appears not so much as a legal code itself as the foundational principles of the covenant on which subsequent legal codes may be based.[63]

He sees many of the other laws as lending greater specificity to the principles laid down in the Decalogue. In spite of the general compatibility of our works, we diverge at this point. I will propose a different role for the Decalogue in chapter 4.

The Multiplicity of Genres and the Unity of Old Testament Ethics

Birch and Larry L. Rasmussen have pointed out that it is precisely the diversity of ethically relevant genres that makes the use of the Bible in Christian ethics so difficult.[64] How can one draw on stories, parables, proverbs, laws, sermons, and liturgies for their respective contributions to a biblical ethos without a discouragingly complex task of differentiation and nuancing? How can one give proper weight to the differing functions, authority claims, and historico-sociological contexts of each genre and yet lay hold on the ethos of the Old Testament as a whole? How can one do this in sufficiently focused yet content-filled form to be immediately useful for Christian ethical discourse?[65] Some abandon the attempt altogether[66] and consider the Old Testament's ethos as belonging to the domain of the historian.[67] Others select one-sidedly one genre, or even a selection within one genre, as an ethical canon within the canon.[68] Still others attempt, as we have just seen, the formulation of an overarching unity and center by means of a principle, like justice or love. Although this appears on the surface to be diametrically opposed to capitulation before the diversity of genres and historical nuances, the result is the same. For such a central principle, though claiming to comprehend that diversity, effectively abandons any attempt to take seriously the substance contained in the multiplicity of genres.[69]

It is the intention of the present study to steer a central course by discerning certain paradigms, in particular the familial paradigm, developed in chapter 2 on the basis of selections from one genre (story). It will have to be shown, below, that such genres as law, wisdom, prophecy, and possibly others, also contribute to build up, uphold, and promote the central familial paradigm. It will have to be demonstrated also that the multiplicity of genres functions together to shape subsidiary and supportive paradigms, among them especially four: the priestly, the wisdom, the royal, and the prophetic.[70] Each of these paradigms meets the following criteria: (1) It images life in response to God's self-revelation with a concreteness and specificity not mediated by a central principle like justice or love. (2) It represents that "middle level" of values that generates and informs the "positive" expressions of Old Testament ethics, such as laws, proverbs, prophetic oracles, and so forth. (3) Precisely because of the function just described, a reconstruction of these paradigms amounts to finding a common denominator for these "positive" ethical expressions. To reconstruct such paradigms, then, does not only serve our historical understanding of how ethical dynamics functioned in ancient Israel. It also holds promise for laying hold of the Old Testament canon's ethical substance and momentum in a sufficiently comprehensive yet concrete form to be manageable and useful in Christian ethical discourse.

Summary

This chapter has attempted to clarify the nature and function of principles, and in particular that subcategory of principles called laws, in relation to paradigms as developed in chapters 1 and 2. We have seen that a certain self-conscious use of the key terms *life, land,* and *hospitality,* as characterized in chapter 1, can help as a kind of shorthand without displacing the stories from which they emerge. On the whole, however, the recourse to principles in an attempt to grasp the Old Testament's ethos comprehensively has a stubborn inclination toward making these principles self-contained and self-explanatory, on the basis of natural law or some other source of authority. We have further seen how laws, being a particular category of principles, must also be guarded against the tendency to absolutize them and thus detach them from the prior values that generate them. We observed how the Old Testament's laws and law codes in particular are firmly embedded in Israel's story account of her faith and interpreted by the framework of meaning inherent in that story. Finally, we tried to indicate briefly how laws, instead of functioning immediately as the chief locus of Old Testament ethics, must be seen as functioning together with other ethically relevant genres to evoke paradigms in Israel's and our ethical imagination. Such paradigms have a potential for making Old Testament ethics palpable and usable on a "middle level," between general principles like justice or love on the one hand, and the multiplicity of positive ethically relevant genres on the other. This promise of usefulness for Christians will be developed further in chapter 7. Now it is imperative to demonstrate that the Old Testament's laws indeed spring from, and conversely contribute to, the familial paradigm posited earlier on the basis of selected stories. We will single out the Decalogue as a particularly important sample for this purpose.

Notes

1. This is in accord with Stanley Hauerwas's claim that "every ethic requires a qualifier" (*The Peaceable Kingdom: A Primer in Christian Ethics* [Notre Dame: University of Notre Dame Press, 1983], 17). In other words, my reference to "life" implies, in each instance, "that (particular understanding of) life." The same holds true for land and hospitality.
2. Of course, many Swiss were caught in a conflict between their national story and their sense of compassion for the sojourner rooted primarily in their biblical heritage.
3. Precisely this unavailability of a common understanding, not only with respect to individual concepts like "justice," but also with respect to an absolute common basis of religion as such, whether rooted in propositional truths or in universal experience, has been held against narrative theology generally. George Lindbeck has addressed this problem incisively in his monograph *The Nature of Doctrine: Religion and Theology in a Postliberal Age* (Philadelphia: Westminster Press, 1984), esp. 46–72.
4. The same is true of casuistic law in large measure, however, for even though it stipulates particular conditions for the validity of a certain law, the understanding can still be a universal one: *Whenever* these conditions prevail, such and such a law is valid. Further, Dale Patrick has shown how at least some casuistic laws (those called "primary" by him) developed in the direction of apodictic laws, thereby reducing Albrecht Alt's sharp distinction between these two categories; cf. Dale Patrick, *Old Testament Law* (Atlanta: John Knox Press, 1985), 23f.
5. This is evidenced clearly by the topical regrouping of Pentateuchal materials in the Mishnah. E. A. Speiser links the central importance of law in Judaism (and Islam), developed largely in Mesopotamian Talmudic (and in Islamic) schools, to the continued influence of "the overwhelming importance of law as the key to a cherished way of life" in ancient Mesopotamia; *Oriental and Biblical Studies: Collected Writings of E. A. Speiser,* ed. J. J. Finkelstein and M. Greenberg (Philadelphia: University of Pennsylvania Press, 1967), 322; cf. also 554. If Speiser is right, then the Old Testament's own subjection of law to story represents a noteworthy departure from a millennia-spanning religio-legal tradition.
6. Ultimately, the authority of laws was understood to be rooted in God's will, of course, but that will was often seen as mediated in the same direct manner, for example, through natural law accessible by reason, rather than through the biblical story in which the laws are embedded.

7. The law codes primarily referred to here are the Decalogue (Ex. 20:1–17; Deut. 5:6–21), the Book of the Covenant (or Covenant Code; Ex. 20:22–23:33), the Priestly Law (Leviticus 1–16), the Holiness Code (Leviticus 17–26), and the Deuteronomic Law (Deuteronomy 12–26). It should be noted, however, that some of these delimitations are debated. The tendency of form criticism to isolate these bodies of law (and smaller components within them) and to study them independently of their story context is now being balanced and corrected by canonical and literary methodologies. That the laws of the Pentateuch are not only inserted into the Pentateuchal story, but are intertwined with it in intricate interrelationships, has been argued especially forcefully by David Damrosch, "Law and Narrative in the Priestly Work," in his *The Narrative Covenant: Transformations of Genre in the Growth of Biblical Literature* (San Francisco: Harper & Row, 1987), 261–97.

8. Cf. T. W. Ogletree, *The Use of the Bible in Christian Ethics: A Constructive Essay* (Philadelphia: Fortress Press, 1983), 47–53.

9. For this characterization of Mesopotamian civilization, see Speiser, *Oriental and Biblical Studies,* 313–23: "Authority and Law in Mesopotamia"; and 534–55: "Early Law and Civilization."

10. The text is available in James B. Pritchard, ed., *Ancient Near Eastern Texts Relating to the Old Testament* (3d ed. with supp.; Princeton: Princeton University Press, 1969), 163–80. For the earlier law codes of Ur-Nammu, Lipit-Ishtar, and Eshnunna, see ibid., 523–25, 159–61, and 161–63, respectively. For a discussion, see Hans Jochen Boecker, *Law and the Administration of Justice in the Old Testament and Ancient East,* trans. J. Moiser (Minneapolis: Augsburg Publishing House, 1980), 53–65 (for the earlier codes), and 67–133 (for the Code of Hammurabi).

11. See Boecker, *Law and the Administration of Justice,* 55f.

12. See Rifat Sonsino, *Motive Clauses in Hebrew Law: Biblical Forms and Near Eastern Parallels,* SBL Dissertation Series 45 (Chico, Calif.: Scholars Press, 1980). Many scholars have followed B. Gemser ("The Importance of the Motive Clause in Old Testament Law," *Vetus Testamentum* Supplement 1 [1953], 50–66) in assuming that motive clauses are absolutely unique to the Old Testament. Sonsino (*Motive Clauses,* 153–55) reviews the question and sides with those who believe they find motive clauses in the Code of Hammurabi (e.g., laws 7, 9, 107, 136, 194, 232). It appears to me that such "motive clauses" are offering further legal clarification, rather than a motivation rooted elsewhere than in the particular law to which they are attached. They in no way parallel such motivations as the frequent reference, in Old Testament laws, to Israel's liberation from Egypt. But even if one would allow for a few genuine motive clauses in Near Eastern laws, this would not at all invalidate our argumentation.

13. This is especially true of Deuteronomic law; cf. Gerhard von Rad,

Studies in Deuteronomy, trans. D. M. G. Stalker, Studies in Biblical Theology 9 (London: SCM Press, 1953), 11–24.

14. Erhard Gerstenberger, *Wesen und Herkunft des "Apodiktischen Rechts,"* Wissenschaftliche Monographien zum Alten und Neuen Testament 20 (Neukirchen-Vluyn: Neukirchener Verlag, 1965), esp. 110–17. For a critique and alternative, see John Bright, "The Apodictic Prohibition: Some Observations," *Journal of Biblical Literature* 92, no. 2 (June 1973): 185–204. It is plausible to assume, with Bright, that apodictic prohibitions were at home in more than one life setting and that the clan instruction by the elders was only one setting (besides cultic recitation, priestly instruction, and prophetic preaching; cf. esp. p. 203).

15. The village circle (*sôd*) is well characterized in Ludwig Köhler, *Hebrew Man,* trans. P. R. Ackroyd (Nashville: Abingdon Press, 1957), 86ff.

16. Patrick, *Old Testament Law,* 4.

17. Ibid.

18. A preoccupation with law detached from story can again be found in the Mishnah and the Talmud, albeit in their own discursive style and without specification of punishment.

19. Speiser, *Oriental and Biblical Studies,* 542.

20. Cf. Walther Zimmerli, *The Law and the Prophets: A fStudy of the Meaning of the Old Testament,* trans. Ronald E. Clements, Harper Torchbooks (New York: Harper & Row, 1967).

21. For a fuller discussion of the Decalogue, see below, pp. 87–105.

22. Albrecht Alt, "The Origins of Israelite Law," in *Essays on Old Testament History and Religion,* trans. R. A. Wilson (Oxford: Basil Blackwell, 1966 [first German ed., 1934]), 79–132. Alt's designation of the Israelite cultus as the unique life setting of apodictic law has been questioned. Further, the bodies of law grouped together by him as "apodictic" show considerable formal variation. For a survey of these issues, see W. Malcolm Clark, "Law," in *Old Testament Form Criticism,* ed. John H. Hayes (San Antonio: Trinity University Press, 1974), 99–116; and Patrick, *Old Testament Law,* 21–24. However, the comprehensiveness of these lists of laws still makes them suitable samples of a trend in Old Testament law, namely, to characterize model behavior in a given realm of life, in contrast to an atomistic concern with individual laws.

23. In the canonical text, these laws are now separated by other materials, but their formulaic conclusion *môt-yûmāt* (RSV: "shall be put to death") identifies them as belonging to an earlier compact series. Alt ("The Origins of Israelite Law," 121) lists the following twelve laws: Ex. 22:19; Lev. 20:2; 24:16; Ex. 31:15; 21:17, 15, 12; Lev. 20:10, 11ff.; Ex. 22:18; 21:16; Lev. 20:27 (in an order approximately that of the Decalogue).

24. Boecker, *Law and the Administration of Justice,* 202.

25. Ibid., 202f.

26. Clark, "Law," 115.

27. Ibid., 102.
28. See above, p. 61, and n. 14.
29. Families even today do not have laws, although their internal dynamics are regulated by rather specific values.
30. Hans Walter Wolff has argued that the preaching of Amos was rooted in popular ethos as handed down in his hometown, Tekoa; cf. *Amos the Prophet: The Man and His Background,* trans. Foster R. McCurley (Philadelphia: Fortress Press, 1973).
31. Although in some such court proceedings earlier legal decisions may have been cited, this does not appear to be the case here. There is no allusion to a formal trial of Micah. Precedent is offered here in the form of a story recounting an event from the past.
32. J. J. M. Roberts, "Law," in *The Hebrew Bible and Its Modern Interpreters,* eds. D. A. Knight and G. M. Tucker (Philadelphia: Fortress Press, 1985), 92.
33. Speiser, *Oriental and Biblical Studies,* 539, citing J. C. Miles, in G. R. Driver and J. C. Miles, *The Babylonian Laws,* vol. 1, Legal Commentaries (London: Oxford University Press, 1952), 41.
34. The revision of certain aspects of the Covenant Code (Exodus 20–23) in the Deuteronomic Code (Deuteronomy 12–26) offers a good example of this dynamic. Within it, the adjustment of the older slave law as reflected in Ex. 21:2–11, in the later Deuteronomic Code (Deut. 15:12–18) illustrates the process of reform particularly well; cf. Boecker, *Law and the Administration of Justice,* 180–83.
35. A clear and often cited example of the roots of many of Israel's laws in the ancient Near Eastern context is the "law of the goring ox." We find it in the Covenant Code (Ex. 21:28–36) and, in similar versions, in the codes of Eshnunna and Hammurabi; cf. Pritchard, *Ancient Near Eastern Texts,* 163 and 176, respectively.
36. I say "also" because the old story context is not necessarily to be rejected. It can retain its own interpretive function, insofar as the latter can be conformed to the new and overarching story.
37. Emil Brunner, *The Divine Imperative: A Study in Christian Ethics,* trans. Olive Wyon (Philadelphia: Westminster Press, 1947), 132–39.
38. Ibid., 132. Is it accidental that Brunner, in quoting Ex. 20:2–3, omits the historical summary ("who brought you out of the land of Egypt, out of the house of bondage")?
39. Ibid., 133.
40. This is captured in the title of the English translation of Brunner's great work (*The Divine Imperative*). The original German title, *Das Gebot und die Ordnungen* (lit.: The Commandment and the Statutes/Orders) accentuates the contrast between the one and central (First) Commandment and the many and varied other laws that, according to the quoted passage, are nothing but technique or technology (*Technik*).

41. See above, p. 55f.
42. Brunner, *The Divine Imperative,* 135.
43. Patrick, *Old Testament Law,* passim, but esp. ch. 7: "The Written and Unwritten Law," 189–222.
44. Ibid., 198.
45. Ibid., e.g., 190. Similarly H. van Oyen, *Ethik des Alten Testaments, Geschichte der Ethik,* ed. H. van Oyen and H. Reiner, vol. 2 (Gütersloh: Gütersloher Verlagshaus Gerd Mohn, 1967), 50, 51, 59.
46. Ibid., 200–204.
47. Ibid., 203–5. Patrick notes, however, that the dialogical quality of legal discussion in Mishnah and Talmud prevented foreclosure in the form of a rigid, static system. In this it preserved a link to the unwritten law of preexilic Israel.
48. Ibid., 190.
49. This plea for a broader definition of the sources of Old Testament ethics is directed not only at Patrick, but also at van Oyen, Old Testament ethicists from whom the present study has profited greatly.
50. Christopher J. H. Wright, *An Eye for an Eye: The Place of Old Testament Ethics Today* (Downers Grove, Ill.: InterVarsity Press, 1983).
51. At one point, Wright (ibid., 158) speaks of law as expressing moral principles or "middle axioms"; but in spite of the similarity of language, these seem, for Wright, to be less comprehensive than my "middle level," or paradigmatic level, of values.
52. Ibid., 44. See above, p. 26f, for a discussion of Wright's understanding of paradigm.
53. This characterization is based on Wright's chapters 4–9.
54. Wright (ibid., 183–87) characterizes the family as Israel's extended kinship-structure related to the land; cf. our familial paradigm.
55. Ibid., 185.
56. Ibid., 201–12.
57. See chapters 5 and 6 for such treatment. Wright seems to grant some such need when he acknowledges the legitimacy and desirability of "comparing and contrasting the varying ethical emphases of different authors, editors and schools" (ibid., 64). My divergence from Wright at this point appears to be one of emphasis rather than substance.
58. Brief references to prior guiding principles (ibid., 25, 26) point in that direction.
59. Ibid., 186.
60. Bruce C. Birch, *Let Justice Roll Down: The Old Testament, Ethics, and the Christian Life* (Louisville, Ky.: Westminster/John Knox Press, 1991).
61. For the specialist in the field, it may be helpful to think of Birch's and my approaches in analogy to the Old Testament theologies of Gerhard von Rad and Walther Eichrodt, respectively. This analogy, however, is suggested in a most general way only; it should not be pressed.

62. Birch, *Let Justice Roll Down*, 158.
63. Ibid., 168.
64. Bruce C. Birch and Larry Rasmussen, *Bible and Ethics in the Christian Life* (Minneapolis: Augsburg Publishing House, 1976), 49–50 (with reference to James M. Gustafson), and 108–10. "Christian ethics needs to guard against every form of what might be called 'genre reductionism.' This is the effective selection, whether deliberate or not, of only certain kinds of biblical materials as the materials pertinent to ethics" (p. 109).
65. This problem in biblical ethics is parallel to the much-discussed question as to whether a systematized and focused theology of the Old/New Testament can be discerned or whether such an attempt is doomed to failure by the diversity of theologies contained in the various textual units. (For the Old Testament, these diverse positions are commonly associated with the names of Walther Eichrodt and Gerhard von Rad, respectively.)
66. In a programmatic essay, John Barton has outlined the fine historical-sociological grid that would have to be applied in a full analysis of the diverse ethical witness of the Old Testament; see "Understanding Old Testament Ethics," *Journal for the Study of the Old Testament* 9 (1978): 44–64. He suggests that the attempt to write *The Ethics of the Old Testament* be abandoned. Then, he believes, "the treatment of particular areas of Old Testament morality might actually be made easier by removing this ideal from the field of study" (p. 44).
67. This, of course, was the approach of the diachronically oriented earlier twentieth century. It dominates the classical study of Johannes Hempel, *Das Ethos des Alten Testaments,* Beihefte zur Zeitschrift für die Alttestamentliche Wissenschaft 67 (2d ed., Berlin: Verlag Alfred Töpelmann, 1964). Of course, as with all genuine historical study, Hempel's masterful work engages the contemporary mind in intense, if indirect, dialogue throughout. Barton, however, considers Hempel's attempt (and that of Walther Eichrodt, in his *Theology of the Old Testament,* vol. 2, trans. J. A. Baker [Philadelphia: Westminster Press, 1967], and other works) to capture the Old Testament's ethics in a historical-developmental scheme as still too unilinear and monolithic to do justice to the great variety of witnesses (Barton, "Understanding Old Testament Ethics," 44–50).
68. The favorite in this respect is, of course, the Decalogue; see chapter 4.
69. A parallel dynamic is evident in the effort to find a focused center (*Mitte*) for the Old Testament's theology.
70. I leave open the question whether these four supportive paradigms should be seen as forming a complete and closed paradigmatic substructure for the central paradigm, thus covering the Old Testament's ethics; or whether they constitute the major members in an open list of supportive paradigms, to which other, perhaps less important, paradigms

could be added. The former assumption is suggested by the presence of large literary segments and theological streams in the Old Testament that can be classified broadly as priestly, sapiential, royal, and prophetic. Open-endedness may be suggested by the fact that some materials, such as the apocalyptic texts, do not fit smoothly into these four fields.

CHAPTER 4

THE DECALOGUE

The Sampling Nature of Old Testament Law Codes

The laws of the Old Testament are extant in collections that astonish the modern reader by their apparent incompleteness and haphazardness. They vary considerably in extent and coverage, none of them apparently intending to regulate fully any larger area of life, or life as a whole. As to their content, they show a great mixture of what we would term religious and secular, cultic and ethical subjects. Smaller groupings are occasionally arranged topically, but on the whole the extant legislation has the appearance of an almost random sampling. What seems almost random to us was undoubtedly selected for the purpose of reforming or redirecting certain trends at specific times in Israel's history, in keeping with the functions of law codes in the ancient Near East generally. As these laws and law codes stand side by side now in their canonical form, however, those motives for selection have receded into the background. Although scholars can reconstruct, in part, Israel's developing legal history from them, they function now in their simultaneous total impact. All of them are gathered together under the name of Moses and work together in their totality to proclaim God's will in the covenant context of Mount Sinai.

They do this not by projecting a comprehensive legal system, but by sampling in a relatively unsystematized fashion the life God's people are called to live. They can function in this apparently haphazard way precisely because it is not on the level of concrete law that Israel's life of obedience to God achieved its focus and whole-ness. The positive laws in their smaller or larger collections offer samples pointing to an integrated value system, an ethos, that lies behind them and that generated them, as was discussed in chapter 3.

Now, the samples of that value system, extant in positive laws, do not all point equally to the same paradigms. For example, one particular law may promote the holy life as visualized by the priestly paradigm, whereas another addresses concerns of the good life in some other area. It is one of the claims of this study that all laws stand in some relation to the central "familial paradigm." Some express the value pattern of that paradigm immediately, whereas others offer samplings related to one of the subsidiary paradigms (e.g., the priestly paradigm), which in turn support the central paradigm.

An analogy may illustrate this. The display case of a salesman for the shoe industry may contain some samples of actual shoes, but also samples of laces, shoe polish, nails and tacks, felt soles, and so forth. Although several items may be products of the shoe company he represents, others may be made by subsidiary industries. Ultimately, however, the latter also serve the purpose of promoting the sale of shoes; they do this indirectly by demonstrating the quality of the products of the subsidiaries, which, in the end, affects the quality of the shoe company. Decoding the analogy, the shoe company stands for the familial paradigm, which captures the central thrust of the Old Testament's ethic. The sample shoes are laws that shape or safeguard that ethic directly. They may be laws that protect life, preserve the continuation of the family line, safeguard the family's claims to the inherited land, and ensure provision for the poor and hospitality to the stranger. The subsidiary companies in the analogy represent the subsidiary paradigms—priestly, wisdom, royal, and prophetic.[1] Their sample products, such as laces, tacks, or inlay soles, stand for laws that shape and safeguard these paradigms. For example, a law concerning the distinction between clean and unclean foods, or another defining access to the sanctuary, upholds priestly values, culminating in the concern that Israel be holy, as the Lord its God is holy. But this central priestly model of the good life is not an end in itself; it helps to ensure that God's people might live and multiply, retain their land, and have bounty enough to provide for the stranger. In other words, it serves the familial ideal.

To sort out from the present Old Testament collection all those laws that pertain to each paradigm, respectively, would be a task beyond the confines of this book. I will, instead, proceed to focus on one law collection, the Decalogue, to test its content in terms of our paradigms and to show, in particular, how the familial paradigm is the ideal that informs it.

The Decalogue's Comprehensiveness and Limitation

Comprehensive Function and Sampling Content

The Decalogue contains absolute, unconditional commands, without reference to specific circumstances or punishments.[2] In their comprehensive reference to large areas of life, these commands resemble maxims or principles. The Old Testament itself refers to them simply as the "Ten Words" (Ex. 34:28; Deut. 4:13; 10:4). Together they embrace so much of life that various attempts have been made to interpret them as covering all of life. I have already pointed out, however, that they cannot be seen as self-contained and self-interpreting principles or moral axioms.[3] In this respect, an exceptional place is occupied by the First Commandment, supported by the Second (Ex. 20:2–4; Deut. 5:6–8). Together they proclaim and protect the exclusive claim of Yahweh, defined as Israel's savior. In this confession the whole faith of Israel is summarized, and through it the other commandments are tied into the story of God's self-manifestation that has gone before.[4] Beyond this, I will argue that the Ten Commandments, just like the other law collections, are sampling rather than covering in scope.

The grandeur and centrality of the Decalogue within the canonical story, however, remains uncontested.[5] This code stands at the head of all subsequent legislation gathered under the name of Moses and, in a sense, comprehends the purpose of that legislation. It is God's call to Israel to respond to salvation with a new way of life. This new life can be summarized elsewhere as a total commitment of love (Deut. 6:4–5). The Decalogue explicates such love through a selection of commands regulating large and important areas of communal life. It is very important to remember this centrality of the Decalogue as we proceed now to dispute the frequent claim that its content embraces the totality of God's will for Israel and perhaps for humankind. In other words, we must distinguish between the Decalogue's centrality of function and its selectivity of content.

The Search for Comprehensive Coverage

The understanding that the Ten Commandments cover the major areas of life and thus embrace the whole scope of Old Testament (and even general) ethics within themselves has led to various attempts at grouping the ten in such a way as to suggest completeness. The earliest of these attempts is probably the traditional view of the two tablets, according to which the theological or God-directed commands are inscribed on the first tablet, and the ethical or neighbor-directed stand on the second. Together, the vertical and the horizontal dimensions of obedience suggest wholeness and completion.[6] Hartmut Gese, for example, states tersely: "The Ten Commandments are a summary of the Torah."[7] Structurally, this comprehensive coverage of Israel's existence is expressed, according to Gese, in five thematic commandment pairs. They are concerned with the exclusive nature of the relation to God (other gods, images), with holiness (name, Sabbath), with sexuality as basic to humanity (parents, adultery), with humanity in general (murder, slavery [stealing persons]), and with one's neighbor (testimony, household).[8] Walter Harrelson compares the Ten Commandments to the United States Bill of Rights and pleads for their adoption as the basic set of norms for contemporary society.[9] In keeping with this view, he engages in a thorough search for their original, supposedly brief and parallel, formulation.[10]

My last, and perhaps most striking example of the tendency to see comprehensive ethical coverage in the content of the Decalogue comes from the work of Walter C. Kaiser.[11] Having virtually equated Old Testament ethics with law,[12] he accords first place to the Ten Commandments. But he goes further. Following especially Stephen Kaufman, he considers the Deuteronomic Code (Deuteronomy 12–26) to have been structured in sections according to the Ten Commandments.[13] Further yet, he organizes his own treatment of the "Content of Old Testament Ethics" according to the content of the last six of the Ten Commandments (from the parents commandment on).[14] It is not surprising, then, that the Commandments, for Kaiser, also stand at the heart of Christian ethics.[15] No consensus has emerged, however, either with respect to the division of commandments among the two tablets, nor with respect to a different grouping of them along the lines of designating comprehensive areas of life supposedly covered.

Given the attempts of biblical scholars to interpret the Decalogue

as a comprehensive and programmatic summary of ethical requirements, it is no wonder that theologians and ethicists have followed
suit. This trend is represented radically by Klaus Bockmühl, for
example, when he states: "The Ten Commandments are the basic
contribution of the Christian Church to public life."[16] He goes on to
say that Christian proclamation has two foci, law and gospel. "The
law in the form of the Ten Commandments is comprehensible and
authoritative for every person."[17] This claim is made in the context of
the public debate in Germany concerning basic values. It is difficult to
imagine an equation of the Decalogue with ethics more complete than
this.[18]

Somewhat different, yet not altogether unrelated, is the search of
form critics for an original, uniformly structured Decalogue. Numerous attempts have been made to arrive at a set of parallel and brief
prohibitions.[19] This involves primarily the reformulation of the Sabbath commandment and the parents commandment into negative
statements and the deletion of the motive clauses in the first half of
the Decalogue. Such a search for a uniform and brief original
Decalogue would seem to enhance its stature. It is motivated by the
Romantic notion of earlier form criticism that literary forms are pure
and simple in origin and are only gradually distorted by transformations and accretions. In spite of many efforts, however, no consensus
on the original form of the Decalogue has emerged. It is difficult to
avoid the impression that assumptions concerning the completeness
and coverage of the Decalogue are also at work in this search for
formal symmetry. A terse and uniform structure is perceived to be
appropriate to a code approached with the prior assumption that it is
the central embodiment of all Old Testament (if not universal) ethics.

It is my contention that the Decalogue, in spite of its unassailed
centrality of position and function, neither qualifies as a comprehensive summary of the content of ethics, nor was intended and interpreted as such in the Old Testament. I will argue this on the basis of its
form as well as its content. As to its form, it is possible, though not
fashionable, to regard the canonical shape of the Decalogue as
reflecting an originally uneven collection of laws, some positive and
some negative, some with motive clauses and others without them.[20]
Alternatively, it can be regarded as an originally terse series of brief
commands (whether all negative, or mixed), which was subsequently
expanded. I prefer the former option. The complete inability of
scholarship to reach consensus with respect to a terse and symmetric
original form suggests the alternative route. The Romantic notion of

short and pure original forms distended by later insensitive or tendentious editors should finally be laid to rest. Like the other legal codes of the Old Testament, the Decalogue exhibits a selection of laws of varied formal structure.[21] Once this is recognized, it immediately also militates against the view that a comprehensive and unified summary of the totality of human obligations to God and neighbor is intended. The Decalogue, like other codes, should be considered as sampling several important aspects of the new life of obedience within the covenant, rather than as covering all of them.

If one accepts, on the other hand, the majority opinion with respect to a terse and symmetric original form of the Decalogue, one faces the problem of accounting for the additions (or subtractions). Why should the original formulator(s) have been so careful to achieve terse symmetry, whereas the later tradents, belonging to the same culture, showed such flagrant unconcern for it? Once again, the Romantic notion of ancient pure forms is not enough to explain this, especially because we know that symmetric sequences of sayings were known at all times (e.g., the Beatitudes, Matt. 5:1–10, for a "late" example). The Decalogue's present shape must be an embarrassment to all who make a comprehensive claim for its content, but it becomes appropriate as soon as one understands that content as being sampling rather than covering.

The Content of the Decalogue

Comparison with Leviticus 19

We turn now to the content of the Decalogue. The various attempts to group the Ten Commandments in such a way as to suggest coverage diverge considerably from one another, as we have seen. No one schema commands total allegiance. No matter how one stretches the blanket of the Decalogue to cover the large bed of ethics, it is too small. This becomes particularly evident when we compare the Decalogue with two other series of laws often considered somewhat parallel as to their apodictic form and as to their content: Lev. 19:1–18 (19–37) and Deut. 27:15–26.[22]

The first of these, Lev. 19:1–18 (19–37),[23] is presently embedded in the Holiness Code and introduced by the motivation to imitate God's holiness: "You shall be holy; for I the LORD your God am holy" (v. 2). As such, it falls within the ken of priestly ethics and will appear again in our discussion of the priestly paradigm.[24] It is evident immediately, on the basis of verse 2, that nothing less than a characterization of a life of holiness in its entirety can be expected to follow. How much of the subsequent text is to be included in this unit is not altogether clear. A completely new beginning is not made until 20:1, where a new instruction of God to Moses, parallel to 19:1, is introduced. On the other hand, the striking parallelism with the Decalogue ends with verse 17, and verse 18 appears to be a summarizing conclusion. Even if one considers the shorter option (vs. 1–18), a certain amount of distinctly ritual concern, beyond the Decalogue's Sabbath commandment, is present in the sacrificial instructions of verses 5–8. If the longer unit (vs. 1–37) is preferred, the combination of "social" content resembling the Decalogue with ritual instruction is more striking. But in either case, the material overlap with the Decalogue is impressive, Leviticus 19 offering close parallels to approximately eight of the ten Decalogue commands.[25] This extensive similarity in content is paralleled by the numerous apodictic precepts introduced by *lô* ([*thou shalt*] *not*), the formal hallmark of the Decalogue.

In other words, Leviticus 19, whether in its briefer or longer delimitation, parallels the Decalogue in its clear intention to characterize comprehensively the life lived in response to God's self-revelation. Leviticus 19's extensive overlap of content, as well as its wide representation of the Decalogue's most characteristic formal feature, suggests that the two series of laws have a similar aim. In addition, however, Leviticus 19 (shorter or longer option) contains a variety of laws not present in the Decalogue. We can summarize with Patrick: "The profound and the trivial were included to give a comprehensive picture of the life of holiness, and the result is a somewhat uneven and disorderly text."[26]

But are we to see the "profound" and the "trivial" as what parallels the Decalogue and what does not, respectively? I do not think so. We cannot equate the following commands with any provisions of the Decalogue; neither can we argue that they are less comprehensive principles than those found in it.

You shall not reap your field to its very border [and parallel provisions for harvesting other fruits]; . . . you shall leave them for the poor and for the sojourner. (vs. 9–10)

You shall not curse the deaf or put a stumbling block before the blind. (v. 14)[27]

You shall do no injustice in judgment; you shall not be partial to the poor or defer to the great. (v. 15)

You shall not hate your brother in your heart, but you shall reason with your neighbor[28] . . . but you shall love your neighbor as yourself. (vs. 17, 18)

When a stranger sojourns with you in your land, you shall not do him wrong. (v. 33)

This is not an exhaustive listing of all commands in Leviticus 19 that could possibly be considered to treat in a comprehensive fashion areas not covered by the Decalogue. These examples may suffice, however, to demonstrate my claim that certain weighty commands deeply rooted in the ethos of the Old Testament are present in this text, but absent from the otherwise largely parallel Decalogue.

Comparison with Deuteronomy 27:15–26

Space limitation forbids a similarly extensive analysis of the curse series of Deut. 27:15–26; a few comments must suffice to point out the similarity of the case. Once again, this series of twelve members is shown by its introduction and its covenant renewal setting (vs. 9–14) to aim at a characterization of the total life of obedience that Israel owed to God.[29] Like Leviticus 19, it shows an extensive overlap of content with the Decalogue.[30] It is also formulated apodictically, that is, as absolute principles, although the introductory word is *'ārûr (cursed be)* instead of the Decalogue's prevailing *lô'* ([*thou shalt*] *not*). And again we discover commands that treat large areas of life by way of broad principle, but cannot be equated with words of the Decalogue:

Cursed be he who misleads a blind man on the road. (v. 18)

Cursed be he who perverts the justice due to the sojourner, the fatherless, and the widow. (v. 19)

Cursed be he who lies with any kind of beast. (v. 21)

To confirm our argument, we can test it by moving in the opposite direction. Deuteronomy 27 lacks several commandments found in the Decalogue. Most prominent by their absence are the commandments concerning the Sabbath and stealing. And yet Deut. 27:26 states categorically:

> Cursed be he who does not confirm the words of this law by doing them.

The "words of this law" obviously refer to the preceding injunctions in curse form, but they also stand for the totality of the new life to which Israel is (re)committing itself here in a covenant renewal ceremony. How can they function in such a central and comprehensive manner if they lack certain of the commands of the Decalogue? Only if we interpret the Decalogue, together with other series like this, as sampling the quality of a life of obedience rather than covering it. Only then do we gain a true understanding, not only of the Decalogue, but of all Old Testament law.

I now digress into the New Testament for a moment to support this point. It is generally accepted that the Sermon on the Mount (Matthew 5–7) characterizes the new life of citizenship in God's kingdom. In that sense it is both central and comprehensive. However, the Sermon is notoriously haphazard, both in its coverage and in its formal structure. Further, Jesus interprets several commandments from the Decalogue in the Sermon, but apparently feels under no compulsion to comment on all ten. This creates a tension between the Sermon's central and comprehensive function and its almost random subject selection. We can understand it only if we see Jesus, as presented by Matthew, reverting to the Old Testament's understanding of law as sampling, rather than covering.

Conclusion

We conclude, then, that the Decalogue should not be equated with a comprehensive coverage of the whole of Old Testament (or Christian, or universal human) ethics. That is not to say that it was formulated carelessly. An analogy offers itself in the classical Christian creeds, such as the Apostles' Creed. It is certainly a careful formulation of the Christian faith and has served a central function throughout the church's history. At the same time, it is clear that it leaves out large segments of Christian confession. It responded to a particular need at a given point in God's economy. Similarly, the Decalogue was a careful and comprehensive characterization, by way of selective sampling, of the new life within the covenant.

The insufficiency of the Decalogue alone to capture fully what Israel owed to its covenant or overlord is underscored also by the canonical shape of the Sinai story. Although the Decalogue stands at the head of all Mosaic legislation and bears other marks of priority, it does not appear alone. Surely the other codes (the Covenant Code, the Priestly Code, and the Holiness Code) have not been placed at the foot of Mount Sinai merely out of reverence for them. Their cumulative presentation contains a message in itself. Israel is not expected to deduce its understanding of life in God's service from the Decalogue alone. Further instruction is needed. Such instruction is given a second-level status, to be sure, being mediated by Moses (Ex. 20:18–21; Deut. 5:22–23), yet it deserves its place in the Sinai context. Furthermore, it is not given in the form of an exposition of the Decalogue, but in formulations that range widely beyond it and have their own integrity of form and content.

The Decalogue and the Familial Paradigm

If the Decalogue can nevertheless claim to stand in for Israel's total life response to God, yet not by way of covering the content of the Old Testament's ethos, we must ask how that can be. How can the Decalogue, in spite of its selectivity of content, represent Israel's total life-response to God? It can do so only because its individual commands, mostly negative in formulation, evoked for Israel a positive ideal that was well known in its fuller shape. This ideal was rooted, in part, in Israel's unreflecting participation in general ancient perceptions of the good life. Several commandments of the Decalogue, as well as many of Israel's other laws, in many aspects resemble the content of other ancient Near Eastern law codes.[31] That broader heritage, however, was subjected to the correcting and rechanneling impact of Israel's very own story of faith. This duality in Israel's ideal of life is expressed centrally by the placement of selected life concerns shared with many peoples into the context of the Sinai covenant to represent Israel's life-response to God's salvation. It is the claim of this study, however, that the shape of this life stood before Israel's eyes in the form of a vivid, lifelike inner image, and not as a set of laws. In Patrick's words: "It is rather paradoxical to exemplify the positive by refraining from the negative, but such a paradox is typical of law and morality."[32]

What, then, is the positive paradigm or shape of life evoked by the

Ten Commandments? A first clue is given in the form of the address, the You/Thou of each commandment. The Sabbath commandment (Ex. 20:10 and Deut. 5:14) identifies this You as the head of the household, who has sons and daughters, servants and cattle, and sojourners dwelling under his protection.[33] Furthermore, he is expected to be able to direct their lives and to enforce the Sabbath rest. There can be no doubt that this You addresses the *paterfamilias,* the functioning head of the extended family or "father's house."[34] We must note immediately that this address, though personal, is not individualistic. The head of the household is appealed to precisely in that capacity, and through him the whole household is involved as well.[35]

This address is not self-evident; we could think of significant alternatives. Our modern expectation would be an individual address, directed at each person. Generally this is the way we hear the Decalogue today, whether in church or society. A second alternative would have been an address in the plural, aimed at all the people, as indeed we find it in many Old Testament laws.[36] Again, the Commandments might have been spoken to the king as the head of the nation or to the leadership of the people.[37] It is, therefore, a deliberate and significant move on the part of the Decalogue to single out the head of the extended family as the one on whose shoulders the responsibility for covenant obedience is preeminently placed. We must expect, therefore, that it will be life structured along kinship lines that will mark the positive ideal upheld by the Decalogue.

This expectation is immediately supported by the two most extensive motive clauses, attached to the Second and Fourth Commandments (concerning images and Sabbath), respectively. In the Second Commandment, the abstention from image making and idol worship is related to the welfare of the extended family that lived together, in three or four generations, under one tent-roof or in adjacent buildings. This living community was directly affected by any idolatry practiced by its head (Ex. 20:5–6). In the Fourth Commandment (concerning the Sabbath), the unit addressed through its head is defined as the extended family or father's house, as we already observed (Ex. 20:10)[38]

As to content, the first three commandments have general application, for they deal with Israel's exclusive relationship to the one God who has revealed himself under the name Yahweh (Ex. 3:13–16; 6:2–7) and has filled that name with meaning as he redeemed Israel (20:2). The allegiance to this God, and this God only, is of course incumbent on all Israelites alike. But as soon as we proceed, with the Fourth Commandment (Sabbath), to an explicit act of homage, it is an act of family-observance through which Israel is called to identify with her God as Creator (Ex. 20:11) and Redeemer (Deut. 5:14b–15). Obvious alternatives abound: Israel's response might well have been a pilgrim feast at the central sanctuary or a ritual performed by the king (or the priests or the tribal leaders). As it is, the only act of homage to God directly commanded in the Decalogue is a family-observance in the context of the father's house—the smallest, more or less self-contained and self-sufficient living unit of Israel.

In the next commandment (parents), the focus is on the flow of the generations. Will the generation that bears the weight of the family's existence now, through the *paterfamilias* addressed as You, preserve its identity by acknowledging its origins through due honor to its parental generation? On this continuity of identity depends the continuity of land tenure. Although the latter can be understood broadly as the existence of Israel in the promised land of Canaan, it undoubtedly means also the tenure of ancestral fields, title to which was held by the father's house as its "inheritance."[39] Although the order of the Ten Commandments is not identical in all references, it does not appear to be altogether haphazard. In Leviticus 19, revering of mother and father (in that order!) is first in the list, after the general exhortation to be holy. Similarly, in Deuteronomy 27 the curse against him who dishonors father or mother follows the curse against image making; that is, it comes immediately after the concern for loyalty to God. Therefore we will not go wrong if we deduce from the position of the parents-commandment as the first of the commands with reference to fellow humans a certain preeminence of the concern for the continuity of the extended family and of land tenure. Commandments six to nine (concerning killing, adultery, stealing, and giving witness) are briefest in formulation, least stable as to their order, and least specific in their reference to the kinship structure. Commandments six to eight (concerning killing, adultery, stealing) could be seen as protecting both members of one's own extended family and those of other families. The explicit protection of the institution of marriage underscores the priority of this institution over other social structures; thus there is no similar commandment to protect either the various class levels of community or the state as a whole.

In the Ninth Commandment (concerning false witness), the scope is explicitly widened to the "neighbor," that is, any member of the legal community. That community was the clan (*mišpāḥâ*), consisting of several extended families or fathers' houses. The commandment may well have particular reference to the crimes treated in the preceding three commandments, protecting a person against being falsely accused of these. We are still concerned primarily with the dynamics of life in the context of the kinship structure, however.

Finally, the Tenth Commandment (concerning the neighbor's property) turns explicitly from the preservation of one's own extended family to the protection of other families. It addresses life within the legal community, the clan, made up of extended families living adjacent to each other in neighboring tents or, in settled times, within a village. Much has been written about the meaning of this commandment in relation to the Eighth Commandment (stealing). It is most inviting to see the first clause (concerning the neighbor's house) to be the summarizing command, to which the remainder (wife, other possessions) forms a kind of motive clause expanding on "house."[40] Further, it is widely accepted that to "covet" (*ḥāmad*) has both a psychological and an external dimension, referring to inward desire for something, together with active steps to procure it.[41] Combining these two observations, this final commandment would then be concerned with the preservation of Israel's communal structure made up of extended families or fathers' houses. Members of one father's house were not to have designs upon other extended family units that might jeopardize the existence of the latter in any way. This underlines powerfully the familial thrust of the Decalogue.[42]

The Decalogue's Centrality of Place and Function

As we look back, we observe how the Decalogue contains a series of commands and prohibitions promoting and protecting the sphere of Israel's kinship existence in crucial areas. It does so over against other possible foci, such as the state or the cult. In themselves, the areas touched on are insufficient to embrace all, or even all of the most important segments of the familial realm. We must assume, however, that the concerns touched on, mostly in negative commands, evoked in Israel that vivid positive imagination that we have characterized earlier as the familial paradigm. It is for this reason that the Decalogue can stand in the canonical covenant story as representative of the central form of Israel's response of obedience to God, in spite of its own selective sampling of it.

To point out the restricted and selective coverage of the Decalogue as I have done in no way touches the centrality of the place and function it now occupies within the covenant story. Nor does it militate against the more universal interpretation of the Decalogue that may have begun in Old Testament times, is evident in the New Testament, and has marked the approach of the church. It does, however, remind us of the Decalogue's rootedness in the central values of Israel's familial ideal. This should warn us not to detach it from the stories and other texts that have shaped this ideal. Above all, we should be warned against isolating the Ten Commandments from the coherent positive level of value that shaped them and which they in turn protect. We should resist the trend to isolate them, understand them as self-authenticating principles, make them into comprehensive schemes of embracing the total realm of ethics, or even equate them with universal moral law that can equally well be discerned in classical Greece, in Buddhism, and in many other places. The Decalogue remains part of the story that shaped the ideal underlying it, and it loses its character and authority when detached from that story.

Notes

1. Laws are not equally common and useful in maintaining these paradigms. The largest volume of laws supports the familial and the priestly paradigms, although there are laws pertaining to the royal (e.g., Deut. 17:14–20) and the prophetic (e.g., Deut. 13:1–5; 18:9–22). The wisdom paradigm is upheld more frequently by proverbs and other forms of "counsel" than by laws, yet the content of such counsel resembles that of the laws so closely that Gerstenberger could argue for the derivation of apodictic law from wisdom; see above, p. 61 and n. 14.
2. See chapter 3, n. 22.
3. See chapter 3.
4. Norbert Lohfink, *Das Hauptgebot: Eine Untersuchung literarischer Einleitungsfragen zu Dtn 5–11,* Analecta Biblica 20 (Rome: Pontifical Biblical Institute, 1963). Dale Patrick (*Old Testament Law* [Atlanta: John Knox Press, 1985], 43) says: "More than any other word of Scripture, the first commandment articulates the religious revolution that brought Israel into being" (cf. also pp. 42–44). Cf. Emil Brunner, *The Divine Imperative: A Study in Christian Ethics,* trans. Olive Wyon (Philadelphia: Westminster Press, 1947), 132–39.
5. For a fine summary of the unique position and function of the Decalogue,

see Brevard S. Childs, *The Book of Exodus: A Critical, Theological Commentary*, The Old Testament Library (Philadelphia: Westminster Press, 1974), 397f. At the same time, Childs remarks about its content: "In what respect exactly the ten commandments differed from the Book of the Covenant in terms of content is nowhere explicitly stated" (ibid.). And further, "no single commandment [of the Decalogue] can claim a unique status, either in form or content. Each finds its parallel within the rest of the Old Testament law" (ibid., 399).

6. Walter Harrelson still finds such a division appealing; *The Ten Commandments and Human Rights* (Philadelphia: Fortress Press, 1980), 48, 92. He admits, however, that the two tables may refer to two copies of the entire list (p. 48), an option that I consider much to be preferred; see Meredith G. Kline, "The Two Tables of the Covenant," in his *The Structure of Biblical Authority* (Grand Rapids: Wm. B. Eerdmans Publishing Co., 1972), 113–30.

7. Hartmut Gese, "The Law," in his *Essays on Biblical Theology*, trans. Keith Crim (Minneapolis: Augsburg Publishing House, 1981), 65.

8. Ibid., 66f. To achieve this order, Gese has to interchange the commandments regarding killing and adultery.

9. Harrelson, *The Ten Commandments and Human Rights*, 13 and passim, esp. 186–93. It is not quite clear to me whether Harrelson holds the Decalogue to be that basic set of norms by virtue of its divine origin and/or its ontological rootedness in human existence, or whether he considers it a historically felicitous option for the United States, because every society needs some such set of norms.

10. Ibid., 40–43.

11. Walter C. Kaiser, Jr., *Toward Old Testament Ethics* (Grand Rapids: Zondervan Publishing House, 1983). The virtual subjection of the whole Bible by Rousas John Rushdoony, not only to the category of law, but also to the ordering principle of the Ten Commandments, moves even further in this direction; see *The Institutes of Biblical Law*, A Chalcedon Study with three appendices by G. North (n.p.: Presbyterian and Reformed Publishing Co., 1973).

12. With a passing nod to wisdom and prophecy, Kaiser says, "The heart of Old Testament ethics is to be placed squarely on the explicit commands found mainly in the Pentateuch, but also to a lesser degree in the Prophets and Wisdom books" (ibid., 42). None of the Prophets and wisdom books are, however, accorded separate treatment (if any at all) in Kaiser's 300-page work.

13. Ibid., 127ff.

14. Ibid., 139ff.

15. Ibid., 307–14.

16. Klaus Bockmühl, *Theologie und Lebensführung*, Gesammelte Aufsätze II (Giessen & Basel: Brunnen-Verlag, 1982), 102 (my translation).

17. Ibid. (my translation).
18. Harrelson's position, though less assertive in tone, moves in the same direction, however; see *The Ten Commandments and Human Rights*, esp. 186–93, and above, p. 101.
19. Eduard Nielsen's erudite study demonstrates the will of form-critical and traditio-historical scholarship to achieve this end, and the extent of hypothesizing to which it is ready to go; see *The Ten Commandments in New Perspective: A Traditio-Historical Approach*, trans. D. J. Bourke, Studies in Biblical Theology, Second Series 7 (London: SCM Press, 1968), 56–131. See also the more restrained approach of John J. Stamm and Maurice E. Andrew, *The Ten Commandments in Recent Research*, Studies in Biblical Theology, Second Series 2 (London: SCM Press, 1967), 18–22; and Harrelson, *The Ten Commandments and Human Rights*, 40–43.
20. Such an absence of concern for symmetry would also include the divergences between the Decalogue texts of Exodus 20 and Deuteronomy 5. For a strong case against the necessity of assuming a negative original for the two positively formulated commandments (Sabbath, parents), see Erhard Gerstenberger, *Wesen und Herkunft des "Spodiktischen Rechts,"* Wissenschaftliche Monographien zum Alten und Neuen Testament 20 (Neukirchen-Vluyn: Neukirchener Verlag, 1965), 43–50. He also argues convincingly that the shortest form of the prohibitive consisting of the negation *lō',* ("[you shall]" not) plus verb in the imperfect, as exemplified in the short Decalogue commandments, cannot have been the classical form; the latter requires at least the addition of an object to be meaningful, but often more, so that no uniform length can be the norm. Uniformity must not be expected of the individual members of prohibitive chains (ibid., 73–76).
21. It should be clear that I am not denying the existence of terse and symmetrically structured series of laws in the Old Testament. It is quite likely that the short commandments (on killing, adultery, stealing, and false witness) derive from such a series. Such series fragments are clearly present in the related list of laws in Leviticus 19; see Martin Noth, *Leviticus, A Commentary*, trans. J. E. Anderson, The Old Testament Library (Philadelphia: Westminster Press, 1965), 139–41. I am merely rejecting the notion that the Decalogue as a whole must be explained as such a series that was distorted later. Further, I am not denying the shaping impact of tradition or claiming that the extant form of the Decalogue is original. Once again, I am only rejecting the view that the impact of tradition had as its object a "pure" original.
22. See Patrick, *Old Testament Law*, 37–39; and Harrelson, *The Ten Commandments and Human Rights*, 26–33 (for Deuteronomy 27).
23. The comparison of Leviticus 19 with the Decalogue is most fruitful when limited to verses 1–18, the so-called ethical part of Leviticus 19; see Patrick, *Old Testament Law*, 37–39, 162; and Karl Elliger, *Leviticus,*

Handbuch zum Alten Testament, 1st series 4 (Tübingen: J. C. B. Mohr [Paul Siebeck], 1966), 245, 252, 254. On the other hand, commentators tend to agree that Leviticus 19, in its present form, constitutes a unity, albeit composed of many and diverse elements that have come together in a long and complex history of tradition; see Noth, *Leviticus,* 138f., and especially the exhaustive literary-critical and traditio-historical analysis of Elliger, *Leviticus,* 242–55. Even the generally recognizable thematic division into an ethical and a cultic part (vs. 1–18 and 19–37, respectively) is not consistent; Elliger (p. 255) posits an accentuation of this division by a later editor through the insertion of the first clause of verse 19. Therefore, even though I am basing my discussion mainly on verses 1–18, there is ample justification for keeping the full chapter in view.

24. See chapter 5.
25. Patrick, *Old Testament Law,* 39, 162. G. J. Wenham even claims that all Ten Commandments of the Decalogue are quoted or alluded to in Leviticus 19; *The Book of Leviticus,* New International Commentary on the Old Testament (Grand Rapids: Wm. B. Eerdmans Publishing Co. 1979), 264. It is generally acknowledged that Leviticus 19 has been shaped in conscious awareness of the Decalogue. Nielsen (*The Ten Commandments in New Perspective,* 142f.) holds that "in Lev. 19 we find the decalogue plainly used as a basis for the Levitical preaching." Elliger (*Leviticus,* 255) says, "The chapter [Leviticus 19] is the 'Decalogue' of the Priestly Codex" (my translation).
26. Patrick, *Old Testament Law,* 162.
27. Should it be objected that this precept does not cover all aspects of treating the handicapped, it could equally be pointed out that the adultery-commandment of the Decalogue does not cover all sexual aberrations, neither does the prohibition of images in the Decalogue cover all forms of idolatry. However, this precept samples a realm of ethical behavior not sampled in the Decalogue.
28. Jesus uses this command to interpret the Decalogue commandment on killing (see Matt. 5:21f.). However, that does not subsume the former under the latter, for one could surely hate one's brother without killing him and express such hate in other ways.
29. See Harrelson, *The Ten Commandments and Human Rights,* 26–33, for a helpful discussion of the function of these curses within the covenant framework, together with a tabulated comparison with the Decalogue.
30. Ibid., 32f., and Patrick, *Old Testament Law,* 39.
31. The emphasis here is on content, not form. With respect to casuistic laws, there is considerable formal resemblance, too; see above, p. 67 and n. 35. Whether true parallels to Old Testament apodictic law can be found in other ancient Near Eastern texts has been much debated, but need not concern us here. It is enough to note that all peoples had some legal restrictions on killing, adultery, false testimony, stealing, and so forth.

32. Patrick, *Old Testament Law,* 162. We experience the truth of this statement in other areas as well. It is so much easier for a physician to diagnose illness than to give an adequate description of health, or for a teacher to mark grammatical and orthographic errors than to characterize good style. See also Gerstenberger, *Wesen und Herkunft,* 110.

33. Childs (*The Book of Exodus,* 400) sees the commandments as addressed, not to any specific segment of the population, "but to every man." That is certainly true if it means that they apply to the actions of everyone. The last slave is obligated to keep the Sabbath, not to kill, and so forth. But this does not automatically imply that the "you" (singular) refers to everyone. Stamm and Andrew (*The Ten Commandments in Recent Research,* 104) suggest that the last five commandments ensure "a fundamental right of the free Israelite citizen," to whom the "you" then seems to apply. In this understanding, too, one has to distinguish between the free citizen, who is responsible in some sense not only for the observance of the commandments, but also for ensuring their observance in society, and those subordinate who are bound to observance, but do not carry responsibility for society.

34. It is not easy to define the scope of authority of the addressed "you"; it may have varied greatly from time to time and from situation to situation. It is important for our purpose, however, that the clues given in some of the commandments (as discussed below) invariably suggest a kinship context (marriage, extended family [father's house, *bêt'āb*], or judicial community [clan, *mišpāḥâ*]), rather than, for example, a priestly or royal administrative context.

35. The omission of the wife in the list of those commanded to observe the Sabbath has been interpreted to mean that she was included in the "you" of address; cf. Patrick, *Old Testament Law,* 59. On the other hand, she is listed among the possessions in the last commandment. Full clarity as to the relation of the wife to the addressed "you" seems beyond reach.

36. A mixture of singular and plural address is frequent in Old Testament law (e.g., Leviticus 19), whereas the consistent use of the singular, which marks the Decalogue, is rare and therefore especially significant; cf. Childs, *The Book of Exodus,* 394f.

37. Thus the Priestly law in Leviticus is characteristically addressed to Moses, who is to convey it to the people of Israel (e.g., 1:1–2) or to Aaron and his sons (e.g., 6:8); or it is addressed to Moses and Aaron jointly (e.g., 11:1).

38. This does not imply that these motive clauses were originally a part of the respective commandments, although that possibility should not be totally rejected. Whether original or not, they represent our earliest commentaries on the identity of the addressed "you."

39. "Inheritance" (*nahălâ*) is also used frequently with reference to the land holdings of a tribe (*šēbet*) and for God's gift to Israel of the land (of Canaan) promised to Abraham. Thus a certain fluidity of reference needs

to be preserved in our understanding of the motive clause of the parents-commandment; see Waldemar Janzen, "Land," *Anchor Bible Dictionary,* ed. David Noel Freedman (New York: Doubleday & Co., 1992), 4:143–54, esp. 144f.

40. Based on Exodus (20:17); cf. John J. Durham, *Exodus,* Word Biblical Commentary 3 (Waco, Tex.: Word Books, 1987), 299. The reversal of the order "house . . . wife" to "wife . . . house" in Deut. 5:21 must be a later rearrangement according to priority of value, the house now being regarded as a specific object (ibid.).

41. With Childs (*The Book of Exodus,* 427), who surveys extensively the evidence for and against this understanding of *ḥāmad* in Ex. 20:17 and Deut. 5:21, as well as the import of the parallel verb "desire" (*'āwāh,* hithpael) in Deut. 5:21 (pp. 425–28).

42. On the whole, I believe, the familial orientation of the Decalogue offered in this chapter is compatible with, and strengthened by, Gerstenberger's central thesis, namely, the derivation of prohibitives from clan ethos (*Wesen und Herkunft,* passim, esp. 110–17). Of course, Gerstenberger treats the prohibitive commands broadly, rather than the Decalogue specifically; but if he is right in his thesis, the exclusive use of such prohibitives in the Decalogue moves the latter into close proximity to Israel's familial or clan ethos (*Sippenethos*). It retains the stamp of this proximity even when employed within the covenant setting. I concur especially also with Gerstenberger's statement that "the head of the family (*das Familienoberhaupt*) must therefore be regarded as the protector and preserver of clan ethos" (*Sippenethos;* p. 116, my translation). He appears to weaken this claim somewhat, however, when he proceeds to say that the "you" (second person singular) characteristic of the prohibitives "probably directs itself exclusively to [all?] the male members of the family" (ibid.).

CHAPTER 5

THE PRIESTLY AND
WISDOM PARADIGMS

The Priestly Paradigm

Introduction

A remarkable observation in our study of the Decalogue was the total absence of reference to Israel's cult. Even the sole command- ment concerned with a religious observance, the Sabbath- commandment, focuses on an observance carried out within the family and clan. At the same time, the Old Testament contains extensive legislation and other materials devoted to the regulation of Israel's relationship to God through cultic practice. Israel was to be a holy people, set apart for God. Its ethic, seen from one perspective, can be described as its effort to become holy, in imitation of God's own holiness (Lev. 19:2, etc.).[1] We must ask, then, how the quest for holiness is integrated into an ethos that, as expressed in the Deca- logue, makes no mention of it.

One of the inner images or paradigms of the good life saw that life as a quest for holiness. According to Israel's central story, God had manifested his presence with his people to save them. Further, God continued to be present in their midst. This was experienced in the sanctuary, eventually identified with the Temple. God's presence there created a center of holy space, just as the Sabbath and the great festivals constituted holy time.[2] To live as God's people is consequently seen, at least from the priestly perspective, as living in constant awareness and recognition of God's hallowing presence. To be gathered around God makes Israel not only a people, but a "congregation" (Lev. 19:2). It also sets Israel apart from other peoples, making it holy (Lev. 20:26).

To live rightly, in this perspective, means first and foremost to orient all life, and not only cultic activity, toward the presence of God. The observance of pilgrim feasts accomplishes this by focusing life on the Temple. The provisions for distinguishing between "the holy and the common, and between the unclean and the clean" (Lev. 10:10) carry this awareness into every aspect of daily life. To live life in constant and zealous attention to Yahweh's holy presence constitutes the first great ethical imperative within the priestly paradigm of the good life.

The second great imperative is the natural consequence of Israel's calling to be a holy people. It is the imperative to be God's servants doing God's will. This imperative is not second in importance, for how can Israel live in constant orientation toward God and not seek zealously to do the will of that God? It is second only in the sense that it flows logically from the first. To be holy as God is holy means to be God's servant, as the opening and closing of Leviticus 19—a key chapter—show with exemplary clarity (compare v. 2 with v. 37). Between them they embrace a sampling of the specific content of the holy life.

When we reflect on that content, however, we gain a further insight that will be developed below. The aim of the holy life, when examined in some of its specifics, is remarkably close to the specifics of the familial paradigm. It revolves around issues related to life, land, and hospitality. We suggest for now, therefore, that the priestly paradigm is not a freestanding and complete vision of the good life,[3] but a vision subservient to a greater vision, the vision of the familial paradigm. But before we pursue these matters further, we must support this summary of the priestly paradigm by analyzing a sampling of specific texts.

Familial Ethos and the Zeal of Phinehas

We began our examination of the priestly paradigm in chapter 1 with a study of the story of Phinehas. We noted the explicit claim of that story that Phinehas had acted in exemplary fashion when he killed the offending Israelite and the Midianite woman. The exemplary dimension of his act was not its violence, however, but Phinehas's zeal for the Lord and his atoning for the people. These were hallmarks of true priesthood, and the Lord rewarded him and his descendants with "my [God's] covenant of peace [shalom]" (Num. 25:12), also called "the covenant of a perpetual priesthood" (v. 13).

Having studied the familial paradigm (chapter 2) and noted how the Decalogue addresses the head of the father's house (*bêt'āb*) as the primary ethical agent (chapter 4), we can now make several further observations. First, the offending act of one of the people of Israel (vs. 6, 8, 14), later identified as Zimri, is introduced as consisting of the fact that he "brought a Midianite woman to his family [lit. "to his brothers"]." Second, Zimri is deliberately and elaborately identified as "head of a father's house belonging to the Simeonites," and Cozbi, the woman, as daughter of the head of a father's house in Midian (vs. 14–15). In other words, the introduction of foreign sexual rituals is characterized here as a disturbance of the integrity of the kinship structure, aggravated by the fact that it is perpetrated by the head of a father's house, that is, by a primarily responsible ethical agent. Presumably the mention of the status of Cozbi's father implies that he, also head of a father's house, had consented to his daughter's move, or that he and his family were at least considered to be implicated in the events in some way.[4]

Phinehas's priestly action to stop the violation of the sanctuary and to preserve Israel's holiness, when seen in this light, is carried out with the ultimate aim of averting a disruption of life in the kinship structure. Or put differently, the priestly ideal is subservient to the familial ideal. We will pursue this theme below, but first we must turn to some further texts in order to develop a fuller understanding of that priestly ideal.

Gideon's Response to the Holy

It might seem logical to turn immediately to the relatively systematized instruction of the Priestly Code, the Holiness Code, and the Deuteronomic Code. However, because the goal of our investigation is not to portray the formulation of any given party or historical period within Israel, but rather to discover the broader, unwritten paradigms that informed such specific expressions, a different approach seems indicated. How did an Israelite act rightly in cultic matters? That is our question. The story of Gideon's call (Judges 6, esp. vs. 11–24), though outside the realm of priestly functions, strictly speaking, presents with apparent approval a man confronted with a theophany who responds rightly.[5] Very different from Phinehas, Gideon nevertheless exemplifies what an encounter with the holy God required.

It is an ethical story from the very start. In the typical pattern of the book of Judges, "the people of Israel did what was evil in the sight of the LORD" (Judg. 6:1), causing God to bring upon them the Midianites and other enemies. The threat to Israel's life and land is described vividly (vs. 1–5). As a result, "the people of Israel cried for help to the LORD" (v. 6). In the present text, a prophetic speech castigates Israel for forgetting her deliverance from Egypt and worshiping other gods (vs. 7–10). Surely as a further response to Israel's outcry, though this remains unsaid, Gideon experiences a theophany in which "the angel of the LORD came and sat under the oak at Ophrah" (v. 11). Gideon at first shows neither fear nor reverence. With the openness of the lament psalms, he pours his despondency into a respectful but outright challenge of God:

> Pray, sir, if the LORD is with us, why then has all this befallen us? And where are all his wonderful deeds which our fathers recounted to us, saying, 'Did not the LORD bring us up from Egypt?' But now the LORD has cast us off, and given us into the hand of Midian. (v. 13)

In a dialogue reminiscent of the call of Moses (Exodus 3), God commissions Gideon to deliver Israel in spite of Gideon's protestations of unworthiness and, upon his request, promises him a sign (vs. 14–18). Almost as if to catch up with a neglected duty, Gideon now brings a quickly prepared sacrifice on an improvised altar. The angel ignites it, a sure sign of acceptance (cf. 1 Kings 18:36–38). Though the angel of the LORD has been mentioned (in anticipation of what will follow) from verse 11 on, it is only now that "Gideon perceived that he was the angel of the LORD" (v. 22).[6] He reacts with an outcry of awe and fear, but is immediately reassured with the promise that he will not die (v. 23). He builds an altar and calls it "the LORD is peace (šālôm)" (v. 24). The story concludes with an etiological comment about Ophrah. In the extended Gideon account we learn how he executes his commission and delivers Israel from the Midianites.

With delicate art our story portrays a man engaged in survival measures and despondent concerning the access of the present generation to God's saving acts reported from the past. He is gradually overshadowed by a sense of holy presence and drawn into a proper response with the means that seem appropriate to him.[7] He receives an assurance expressed comprehensively in the name of the altar, "The Lord is shalom."[8]

What Phinehas took for granted and was zealous to defend, the Lord's holiness, must first emerge from mystery here and become reality. Traces of Israel's religio-historical roots in widespread ancient lore, such as the sacred tree of Ophrah, the primitive sacrifice, and the improvised stone altar, appear in the story. Just as Israel's familial paradigm shared much with the ancient world, its priestly paradigm does not conceal its pre-Israelite roots. But the general conception of the holy is transformed as it signifies a new experience of Yahweh, who appears again to confirm the meaning of his name as that of the one who redeemed Israel out of Egypt and continues to save. God becomes available to Israel in theophany and cultic response as the deliverer from threats to life and land. God is the source of shalom. For Israel as a people, the dynamics of this story were projected eventually onto a larger screen: not the oak tree of Ophrah, but Jerusalem/Zion; not the simple offering of a kid and unleavened cakes with a broth, but an elaborate sacrificial system; not a stone or even a constructed and named altar, but the grandeur of the Temple; not the localized attack of a neighboring nomad people, but the threat of world empires. But the central features of Israel's cultic response portrayed in this story remain paradigmatic throughout the Old Testament. Gideon's response to theophany paints the picture of a worshiper that informs the Old Testament's priestly paradigm.[9] But I hasten to add that theophany and cultic response serve the purpose of preserving life and land. Israel did not live in order to worship, but worshiped in order to live.

It might be objected that the acts of Gideon belong in the realm of worship, not ethics, and if ethics is defined as behavior directed toward humans and environment, the objection would be correct. Such a distinction between "horizontal" and "vertical" behavior, however, is foreign to the Old Testament. Both are called "service" (*'ăbōdâ*) in Hebrew and are intertwined in the law codes as well as in other texts. Therefore we do better to consider ethics as the quest for right behavior, without specifying the target of such behavior. It is only from practical and contemporary considerations that our small sampling of texts has been weighted somewhat toward those dealing with behavior on the "horizontal" plane, paying little attention to the many instructions pertaining to festivals, sacrifices, and other rites.

Leviticus 19: Israel as Holy Congregation

A text particularly informative concerning the priestly vision of right living is the collection of laws in Leviticus 19. We observed some of its features earlier and noted its proximity in form and content to the Decalogue (chapter 4). Like the latter, it has all of life in view. Its programmatic opening statement identifies right living with a quest for holiness, in imitation of God himself: "You [pl.] shall be holy; for I the LORD your God am holy" (v. 2). Israel is addressed as "congregation" (v. 1), and subsequent commands are generally (but not always) formulated in the plural.

Like the Decalogue, this series lacks uniformity of form and comprehensiveness of content. It displays, instead, that sampling quality of all Old Testament law codes discussed earlier (chapter 4). Within the body of the series can be found subcollections of laws clustering around certain topics, such as the concern to leave some of the harvest for the poor (vs. 9–10). As to content, approximately half of the injunctions of this chapter pertain to what we would call specifically religious or cultic matters. Even these, however, are frequently concerned with religious observances in the course of daily life, rather than with sacrifices, special rituals, or events at the central sanctuaries.[10] Thus there are regulations against interbreeding of cattle and other mixing of kinds, against eating fruit from newly planted trees during the first three years, or against consulting mediums or wizards. It is very doubtful, however, whether ancient Israelites perceived such laws to be different from those concerned with respect for parents, provision for the poor, avoidance of adultery, and the other "ethical" commandments that make up a good half of the chapter.

Instead, one gains the impression that Leviticus 19 addresses Israel as it lived its agricultural life with its daily routines and encounters, the same Israel that is in view in the Decalogue. And yet there is a difference. The Israel of the familial paradigm, living in fathers' houses on inherited lands, relating to other fathers' houses and clans, and harboring sojourners in its midst, is now viewed as a tightly knit congregation (*'ēdâ*, v. 1)[11] with eyes fixed on her holy God (v. 2).

Daily life is to be lived in constant awareness of God, and all its activities are related to God's presence and character, as the ever-repeated formula "I am the LORD (your God)" reminds the reader.[12] In this, Israel is a unified congregation, a fact emphasized throughout by the use of "his/your (own) people," "your neighbor," "your brother," "one another."

This people/congregation of God is reminded in various ways that its standing with God is of utmost importance. A properly brought peace offering to the Lord will be accepted, but an improper one will not qualify; instead, the bringer "shall be cut off from his people" (vs. 5–8). Oppression of neighbor, servant, or handicapped shall be avoided for "fear [of] your God" (vs. 13–14). One should not hate one's brother, "lest you bear sin because of him" (v. 17). Sexual relations with a slave woman under certain conditions may call for expiation by guilt offering (vs. 20–23). Certain fruits are holy (v. 24). Making one's daughter a harlot endangers the land, "lest the land fall into harlotry and the land become full of wickedness" (v. 29). Visiting mediums or wizards makes one "defiled" (v. 31). Thus the affairs of daily life are to be conducted with an eye to the Lord at all times, remembering that Israel is to be God's holy people and that it is dangerous to disregard the boundaries of holy living.

As God's holy people, however, Israel is reminded also of access to grace. Sacrifices brought properly will be accepted (v. 5). The tent of meeting, the priest, and the rituals of atonement are available in cases of sin (vs. 20–22). Under proper treatment according to God's instruction, the land will yield fruit richly (vs. 23–25). The congregation of Israel, in its quest for holiness, will embrace all its members as brothers, including the poor and the handicapped. Each will love the other as himself (v. 18), with explicit inclusion of the stranger sojourning in Israel, "for you were strangers in the land of Egypt" (v. 34).

In the conclusion, the phrase repeated throughout the chapter, "I am the LORD your God," is expanded to its full significance by the addition "who brought you out of the land of Egypt" (v. 36).[13] As in the Decalogue (Ex. 20:2; Deut. 5:6), it is a summary of the story of salvation, so that "you shall observe all my statutes and all my ordinances, and do them: I am the LORD" (v. 37). It is significant, however, that this motivation linking the family-oriented Decalogue to this priestly collection of laws stands at the end here, rather than at the beginning. There we find, as observed already, the programmatic call to holiness in imitation of a holy Lord (v. 2). The familial ideal of life is given here a cultic focus and placed in a cultic framework.

The Instruments of Holiness

Israel's call to live in constant awareness of God's holiness and to respond to it by allowing it to penetrate all aspects of daily life is expressed powerfully in the institutions and requirements of her unified cult. It is centrally represented by the Holy of Holies, filled intermittently with the glory (*kābôd*) of Yahweh according to Priestly theology, and constituting the dwelling place of Yahweh's Name according to Deuteronomic theology.[14] Surrounding it in concentric circles, there follow the Holy Precinct, the Temple Courts, the holy city Jerusalem/Zion, the Holy Land promised to Abraham and given to Israel, and eventually the realms of the nations extending to the farthest isles. Holy space is paralleled by holy time. It is regularly marked by the Sabbath and eventually centered in the Day of Atonement (Leviticus 16), surrounded by the three great festivals. Holy time extends in concentric circles to Sabbath years, jubilee years, and eventually the eschatological day of Yahweh.

Israel's response to the Lord's holiness is modeled by the high priest, the priests, the Levites, and eventually all members of the people, "a kingdom of priests and a holy nation" (Ex. 19:6). Commoners can temporarily attain a special status of holiness by becoming Nazirites (Numbers 6). All of these approach God's holiness according to duly prescribed ordination, purification, and examination at the Temple gates, to bring their sacrifices and praises in a continual and magnificently orchestrated devotion. But this life before a holy God, this constant observance of the line between the holy and the common, finds its minutest expression in the daily observation of the laws of clean and unclean pertaining to body, food, house, everything.

The Subordination of Priestly to Familial Values

Nevertheless, the quest for holiness, expressed in the symbolic structure just sketched and the texts that support it, is not the ultimate expression and aim of Israel's life of obedience. Life from a priestly perspective, imaged before Israel's eyes in the priestly paradigm or the ideal of the holy life, is subordinate to and supportive of the familial paradigm. As was said already, Israel did not live in order to worship, but worshiped in order to live. In a little-known ancient story, a man from the hill country of Ephraim hired a Levite to be his

113

house priest, and in that connection uttered a word that continues to characterize the purpose of the cult: "Now I know that the LORD will prosper me, because I have a Levite as a priest" (Judg. 17:13). Cult aims at life.[15] Deuteronomy expresses this theme throughout, not least in the cultic setting of 26:1–11. In this ritual of bringing the first fruits of the land "to the priest who is in office," the Israelite is, first, to rehearse the story of Israel's salvation from Egypt and reception of the land (vs. 5–7). Second, he is to engage in the presentation of the first fruits "and worship before the LORD your God" (v. 10). But these are only the penultimate acts required in the text. The third "you shall" takes him back into his daily life and his family context:

> And you shall rejoice in all the good which the LORD your God has given to you and to your house, you, and the Levite, and the sojourner who is among you. (v. 11)

Life and family, the gifts of the land, and the practice of hospitality represent the good toward which the cult is to lead, and that good is what we characterized as the familial paradigm. Nowhere is the priority of these familial values, as the aim of all obedience—both ethical and ritual—stated more clearly than toward the end of the Holiness Code, in Lev. 26:3–9:

> If you walk in my statutes and observe my commandments and do them, then I will give you your rains in their season, and the land shall yield its increase, and the trees of the field shall yield their fruit. And your threshing shall last to the time of vintage, and the vintage shall last to the time for sowing; and you shall eat your bread to the full, and dwell in your land securely. And I will give peace in the land, and you shall lie down, and none shall make you afraid; and I will remove evil beasts from the land, and the sword shall not go through your land. And you shall chase your enemies, and they shall fall before you by the sword. Five of you shall chase a hundred, and a hundred of you shall chase ten thousand; and your enemies shall fall before you by the sword. And I will have regard for you and make you fruitful and multiply you, and will confirm my covenant with you.

We must remember again that the canonical process placed the family-oriented Decalogue, and not a cultically oriented collection like Leviticus 19, into the primary position of representing Israel's life-response of obedience. Further, the symbolic system of Israel's cult, which we just considered in its monolithic unity and coverage, enjoyed only a limited historical reality in Israel. This is true not only according to modern critical reconstructions of Israel's history of religion, but also according to the Old Testament's own story. The Temple appeared late on the scene in the time of Solomon and was destroyed less than four centuries later by Nebuchadnezzar. Yet the continuing meaningfulness of obedience under new circumstances was strongly affirmed by the prophets Jeremiah and Ezekiel.

For such reasons I cannot agree with Walter Kaiser when he makes holiness "the central organizing feature of Old Testament ethics," citing Lev. 11:45.[16] And further: "Briefly stated, the mainspring of Old Testament ethics is: 'Be holy because I, the LORD your God, am holy.' It is an *imitatio Dei*." Now, when Kaiser sees "holiness as being a term practically equivalent for the 'Godhead' itself,"[17] one can hardly deny its centrality, for God is surely central to everything pertaining to Old Testament faith and life. But serious questions arise when Kaiser considers it "[e]specially significant for ethical modeling . . . that God's holiness means that he is free from the frailties and moral imperfections common to mankind,"[18] suggesting that the human ethical task is to strive for that same perfection. Is not God's holiness precisely his "otherness," which is never lost sight of throughout the Old Testament? Can we really see God and humans aligned and measured by a common yardstick of perfection applicable to both?[19] One could at best understand that in a strictly formal sense: God does perfectly whatever he expects of himself, and humans should also do perfectly whatever God requires them to do. But as soon as we ask concerning the substance of this perfection, the parallelism cannot be maintained. Humans cannot be and do, and are not meant to be and do, what God is and does.

Many motive clauses call on Israel to be gracious to the oppressed and the sojourners, for "You shall remember that you were a slave in the land of Egypt" (e.g., Deut. 24:22). Thus Israel was to imitate, in this instance, the "behavior" of God who redeemed it. However, an ethic of imitation cannot be extended to all areas. God creates and takes life according to divine decision; are humans to act with the same sovereignty? Or how can God be the model for honoring father and mother, not stealing, or not committing adultery? How can these and many other imperatives for humans be deduced from God's character and attributes? Walter Harrelson has shown that a significant difference between God and the Mesopotamian gods lies in the fact that in the Old Testament, behavior on the human plane does not mirror behavior on the heavenly plane.[20] In fact, we know nothing about God's attributes as such, only about certain of God's actions on the earthly plane. What Israel knew, however, was God's will *for Israel*.

God's holiness was to be effective as motivation, reminding Israel that it was a people accountable to God; God's holiness was not the model demonstrating the content of that will.[21] Rituals and practices symbolizing God's holiness and Israel's election to be God's holy people were to motivate Israel to fulfill its own special calling, but the content of that calling had to be embodied in models and instructions on the human plane.

Leviticus 25

Nowhere does the identity, in substance, between the priestly ethic and the familial ethic become more apparent than in Leviticus 25, with its provisions for the Sabbath year (vs. 1–7) and the jubilee year (vs. 8–55).[22] Presently this chapter is embedded in the Holiness Code and introduced as legislation given by God to Moses "on Mount Sinai" (v. 1). The latter phrase is uncommon among such introductions and is probably intended to underscore the foundational nature of the instructions that follow.[23] The land itself is to be allowed to keep the Sabbath every seventh year, undisturbed by the intrusion of Israel's agricultural activity. The immediacy of the relationship of the land to Yahweh is striking. Israel is simply not to interfere. Just as the people are to belong to the Lord, so is the land (cf. v. 23).

Verses 8–12 give a summarizing preview of the jubilee year legislation which then follows. The concern that the jubilee "shall be holy to you" (v. 12; cf. v. 10) is a summary of the central concern. We are clearly in the realm of priestly ethics here. As in Leviticus 19, the introductory address is directed to "the people of Israel" (v. 2), with subsequent addresses frequently (but not always) formulated in the plural. Israel is a large familial grouping, a fact recalled repeatedly by the terminology of "brother" and "neighbor." It is a people reminded again in central places (though less frequently than in ch. 19), that whatever is commanded ought to be motivated through constant awareness that "I am the LORD your God" (vs. 17, 55). And again this Lord, whose holiness shall be acknowledged, is the one who redeemed Israel from Egypt and gave her the land (vs. 2, 42, 55).

When we inquire, however, concerning the content of this observance of holiness, we find ourselves squarely in the realm of the familial ideal. Central to the priestly legislation of this chapter is the concern for the ongoing life of Israel, structured along kinship lines, on the ancestral lands given by God, with provision for inclusion of the poor and the sojourner. Periodic restitution of such life is the goal. Life, land, and hospitality, as the shorthand terms for the familial paradigm worked out earlier, summarize the ethical content of this chapter. Of particular interest is the function of the theme of hospitality. Central to it is God's sole ownership of the land, summarized in verse 23. This makes Israel's own status that of strangers and sojourners, or, in our language, landed immigrants or long-term guests: "The land shall not be sold in perpetuity, for the land is mine; for you are strangers and sojourners with me."[24]

This has several consequences. It means, first, that God has expectations of the land that are totally independent of its human inhabitants. The land is to observe the Sabbath "to the Lord," and Israel shall not interfere (vs. 1–8). A second consequence pertains to human acquisition of land. No one can acquire it "in perpetuity," that is, become its owner in an absolute sense. Humans can use God's land only as his guests, that means, in keeping with his will. And that will is to allot it equitably to Israel according to fathers' houses and clans, and to restore that order from time to time. A third development of the theme of sojourning or hospitality in the chapter is its application to the provision for the poor:

> And if your brother becomes poor beside you, . . . he shall be with you as a hired servant and as a sojourner. He shall serve with you until the year of the jubilee; then he shall . . . go back to his own family, and return to the possession of his fathers. For they are my servants, whom I brought forth out of the land of Egypt; they shall not be sold as slaves. (vs. 39–42)

Thus what we call social services or social security is handled by means of a sophisticated concept of hospitality operative on several levels.

Conclusion

In concluding our analysis of the priestly paradigm, we must ask what it contributes to the familial paradigm that it so powerfully promotes. Is priestly ethics simply the formulation of familial ethics by a certain group of people and institutions, using distinctive terminology and symbolism to express and promote what other groups in Israel said differently? Or does it bring to that ethic dimensions that would otherwise be lacking? The answer depends on our definition of ethics. If that definition is kept narrow, as right neighbor-related behavior, we must conclude that its promotion in priestly texts and contexts adds nothing we could not find in Israel's familial paradigm as spelled out elsewhere. In this case, priestly language and ritual become means to a social end. What remains as the main contribution of the priestly involvement in ethics is the zeal for the Lord that it generates by its powerful material and psychological means. Phinehas's model dimension would indeed form its core.

If on the other hand ethics is concern for right behavior not limited to a human target, then the priestly symbolism of acknowledging God's holiness constitutes ethical behavior in its own right, not limited to its intended impact on the "horizontal" plane. Then Gideon's simple sacrifice on his primitive altar had its own inherent ethical integrity; "right" had been done regardless of its further intended impacts and consequences. I have used the qualifier "intended" twice, and that deliberately. For ethics is more than action; it is also, and perhaps primarily, character formation. Will a person who "hallows" or "sanctifies" the name of Yahweh in total devotion not also become one who will do on the horizontal plane whatever he or she knows of Yahweh's will? Such a person will do that even where no explicit teaching or command connects a "vertically" directed act or ritual to a "horizontally" directed consequence. Klaus Koch has described this intangible effectiveness of the cult toward "justice" and "righteousness" as an "aura" that flows from genuine cultic practice, from the sanctuary, into the network of interhuman activity.[25] Only a perverted, self-serving cult becomes sterile in social effectiveness and sets itself in opposition to social ethics.

In summary, stories and other texts work together to shape before Israel's (and our) inner eye a vivid image of a holy people that worships God in constant awareness of his holiness, is motivated by this awareness to live out his will (expressed noncultically elsewhere) with zeal, and acquires in the course of this a character attuned to that will.

The Wisdom Paradigm

Introduction

Before the inner eye of Israel stood another comprehensive paradigm of life lived in constant awareness of the centrality of God. This awareness, like the knowledge of God's holiness, called every Israelite to total and dedicated obedience in all matters, down to the smallest capillaries of daily existence. It was kept aglow in a language and in institutions of its own and is preserved for us both in Israel's central story and in a distinctive literature. We must turn now to a study of the wisdom paradigm.

Wisdom was an intellectual-ethical pursuit resulting in a certain quality of life and in a literature with its own distinctive characteristics. Ancient Israel shared in this international pursuit, as is well known. Nevertheless, this broader quest received its distinctive stamp in Israel and was firmly tied into Israel's story of faith. We mention only three prominent features expressing this: (1) Wisdom elements appear throughout the Old Testament, and not only in the wisdom books (Proverbs, Job, Ecclesiastes).[26] (2) Two of the three wisdom books (Proverbs, Ecclesiastes) are placed under the name of Solomon, as the legal codes are placed under that of Moses. Thus they are incorporated into the historical framework of Israel's story.[27] (3) Wisdom is linked to Yahweh, the God who had chosen and redeemed Israel, with all the faith content associated with that name. Proverbs 1:7 expresses programmatically what marks Old Testament wisdom generally:

> The fear of the LORD is the beginning of knowledge;
>   fools despise wisdom and instruction.

Underlying the Old Testament's understanding of wisdom is the assumption that God has created and maintains an orderly universe. God's orders are embedded in its fabric and, if observed, are one avenue of revealing God's will. Such observation of divine design, both in the natural and in the human sphere, through generations accumulates experience. To acquire such experience from one's elders and to draw on it at the proper time leads to life, understood first of all concretely as survival, health, descendants, success, prosperity on the land, peace, honor, and so forth. To ignore it leads to death, that is, to failure, calamity, impoverishment, strife, dishonor, and literal death.

Wisdom, however, is by no means only a pragmatic striving for gain and avoidance of loss. It is a comprehensive ethical character ideal, namely, to do what is right,[28] thereby becoming a righteous person. Negatively, it means to avoid wickedness and the company and fate of the wicked (Psalm 1). On the whole, the wisdom mentality of the Old Testament is optimistic, trusting that God's design of the world is inclined in favor of life. It is possible to live rightly and become righteous. That God's design can also be mysterious and disturbing is expressed powerfully in Job and Ecclesiastes. The Old Testament knows well that the wisdom that one can trust in everyday life has its limited sphere; it is not sufficient to answer life's ultimate questions, nor is it given by God for that purpose.

As we study selected texts that point to the wisdom paradigm, we will again discover its subordinate role. It presents a vision of the right way that leads to life. This way becomes known through observation of God's design embedded in creation and through living harmoniously with that design. When we ask, however, concerning the content of that life to which the way of wisdom leads, our texts will take us into the realm of the familial paradigm again. It is life in a kinship structure, on land given as trust by God, with responsibility to care for others in a hospitality imitating God.

Holiness and Wisdom

We began our sampling of the wisdom paradigm with the story of Nabal, Abigail, and David (1 Samuel 25). In that story, the wisdom of Abigail consisted simply of the good sense that can evaluate a situation and choose the course of action that is life sustaining rather than destructive. Because such good sense is less a matter of outstanding intellectual giftedness than of the good use of ordinary intelligence and the profitable application of communal and personal experience, it is in principle available to all. Consequently, the short proverbs of Proverbs 10–31 are generally not addressed to anyone specifically, and the longer speeches of Proverbs 1–9 are styled as addresses from the older generation to the younger, from the wise teacher to "my son." This stands in some contrast to the priestly instructions. They, too, apply at times to Israelites in general, as for example, when they distinguish between clean and unclean foods. More frequently, however, they instruct a certain group or individual: high priest, priests and Levites, lepers, women who have given birth, bringers of certain sacrifices. The wider appeal of wisdom to all hearers is related to the general openness of the status of wise man or woman, as compared with the strictly defined hereditary lines of priests and Levites. Of course, certain well-defined ranks among those wise who stood in the king's service must also be assumed, although the particulars are no longer clear to us.

A more striking difference can be seen between the priestly focus on the act and the wisdom focus on character. Abigail is characterized as "a woman of good understanding" (v. 3), whereas Nabal is shown up by his name (nickname?) as one known for some time to be a fool. Wisdom and foolishness are seen as dimensions of character more than labels of individual actions. Hans Heinrich Schmid has pointed out a contrast, in this respect, between Israelite and general ancient Near Eastern wisdom. In the latter, individual acts, wise or foolish, contribute to the balance or imbalance of the universe. In Israel, the universe is in God's keeping, whereas individual wise or foolish actions gain their significance as they shape human character.[29] In keeping with this, the teachers of Proverbs 1–9 make a fervent appeal for "conversion" to wisdom and rejection of folly, for making a life choice when confronted by these two ways. It appears that an individual misjudgment on the part of a person considered wise would not immediately undo that status. On the other hand, a person's holiness/cleanness always pertained to a given moment. It could be undone by a contaminating act and restored by appropriate measures. Israel had persons reputed as wise men and women, but none known as holy men and women in the sense of Hinduism. In spite of these differences, the priestly and the wisdom paradigm share one important feature. Both appeal to every Israelite, inviting him or her to the quest for holiness and for wisdom, respectively. In this, they stand in contrast to the royal and prophetic paradigms, to be discussed in the next chapter. First, however, we must expand our understanding of the wisdom paradigm.

Popular, or Folk, Wisdom

Its Village Setting

Abigail's wisdom bears no marks of any institutional imprint. She is not associated with any wisdom group or setting, and she does not speak in any formally distinctive way. There were simply people with good sense in Israel, and she was one of them. Ludwig Köhler has characterized perceptively the social setting in which such popular wisdom could be nurtured, the "village circle."[30] After the day's work was done, the men of the village gathered in some central place, while the women and girls were still busy with the household chores. No one was forced to come, but everyone wanted to be there, to enjoy the fellowship, to exchange the day's news, to discuss the crops and the weather. If someone had returned from a trip or pilgrimage or if a traveler had asked for hospitality, there were stories to be told and heard. There must have been songs, too. Last, but not least, this was the place for the mental activity that we call popular wisdom, in contrast to the more sophisticated court wisdom that we shall refer to later. Experiences of the past were told, riddles proposed and solved, old proverbs repeated and new ones created. This could go on and on far into the night. The old men in the inner circle took the lead, while the younger folk on the fringes, and the women, who now had joined also, ventured an occasional word.

The village circle was the birthplace of Israel's popular ethos (or folk wisdom) and the primary channel for its transmission. Its literary stylization and fixation in collections like those of Proverbs 10ff. must be attributed to a further phase—probably to more formally trained scribes at the royal court and in the Temple.[31] In this process, the scribes added insights from their own courtly tradition with its strong international flavor. If Erhard Gerstenberger[32] and Hans Walter Wolff[33] are right, this popular ethos was also the soil from which sprang many of Israel's laws, cultic instructions, and prophetic impulses. The village circle was certainly the school of the common person.

Its Theological and Historical Nature

For its content, this ethos drew much from common ancient Near Eastern lore, but the imprint of Yahwist faith is also unmistakable. It was the widespread assumption of earlier critical scholarship that an older, international, and nontheological wisdom (represented in Proverbs 10ff.) was succeeded by a later, theological phase (evidenced in Proverbs 1–9). Against this, Gerhard von Rad has argued convincingly that the older proverbial wisdom, far from being a separate nontheological stream distinct from Israel's historical faith, rested securely in a context where the main lines of historical faith could still be taken for granted. Hence the wisdom teachers could devote themselves to the uncharted areas of daily life that lay between the highways of historical faith.[34] More than that, von Rad has drawn attention to three kinds of explicit theological statements in the older sections of Proverbs: (1) Proverbs with the central theme that God tests the heart (e.g., Prov. 16:2; 17:3; 21:2; 24:12). (2) Proverbs dealing with God's approval or disapproval of specific behavior or attributes (e.g., Prov. 11:1, 20; 15:8, 9, 26; 16:5, 7; 17:15; 20:10, 23; 21:3; 22:12), some corresponding closely to laws of Yahweh. (3) Most telling theologically is a group of proverbs speaking of limitations of human possibilities through God's autonomous reign (e.g., Prov. 16:1, 2, 9; 19:14, 21; 20:24; 21:2, 30f.; cf. also 16:33; 21:1; 25:2; 29:26). This must not be misunderstood as fatalism; the wise move confidently, as we have noted, but within the limits of God's sovereignty.[35]

Hans Heinrich Schmid also affirms the theological nature of proverbial wisdom, making the further point that ancient Near Eastern wisdom generally was also theological, rather than pragmatic only.[36] Furthermore, he counters the frequent claim that wisdom is nonhistorical. It is certainly not mythical, in the ancient Near Eastern sense, nor a collection of ever-valid truths in a Greek philosophical sense. In fact, wisdom is intensely concerned with the right time and context. Schmid summarizes the relationships of proverbs to history as a three-step process: (1) Very concrete (historical) experiences are observed and sifted. (2) These are handed down from father to son, teacher to student, in poetic and generalized formulations (proverbs) that in themselves seem timeless and universal. (3) They are, however, meant to be received in a particular historical situation and applied judiciously to it, to see whether they can become new historical reality at this new time and in this new place. Schmid observes that the temptation is to "freeze" wisdom on the second level and allow individual formulations to become contextless absolutes.[37]

Wisdom and Character

Wisdom Models

Very important for our purpose is Schmid's observation, referred to earlier, that a distinctive feature of Old Testament wisdom, as compared with general ancient Near Eastern wisdom, is the emphasis that the former places on the person, rather than on the individual deed.[38] The first question is not whether someone does right in a given situation, but whether someone is *ṣaddîq* (righteous, pious), rather than *rāša'* (wicked, evil). The contrast between the ethically approved and the ethically condemned person can be expressed in many word pairs. In keeping with its emphasis on character, the wisdom literature presents a nuanced typology of character.[39]

It is not surprising, in light of this concern for character, that the Old Testament holds up several prominent figures as models of a wise walk. Ever since von Rad's famous essay,[40] it has been recognized that Joseph (Genesis 37–50) mirrors a wisdom ideal. In the various crises that mark his adventurous journey, he makes those decisions that not only preserve his life, but lead to honor and renown. Eventually he becomes chief adviser to Pharaoh, because "there is none so discreet and wise as you" (Gen. 41:39; cf. 41:33). At the same time, and in true Israelite fashion, wisdom is more than autonomous human insight; it is gift and direction from God, as Joseph freely acknowledges (Gen. 45:4–8). And the end toward which God has endowed Joseph with wisdom is "to preserve life" (Gen. 45:5) in the context of the family.

Solomon, of course, is the patron of wisdom in the Old Testament. Royal wisdom expressed itself most prominently in good government and in the maintenance of justice, as we will discuss further below.[41] His wisdom, however, was not confined to the administrative and judicial areas, but was encyclopedic in scope, resulting in numerous proverbs and spreading his fame to far countries (1 Kings 4:29–34).[42] His renown was such that the Old Testament books of Proverbs, Ecclesiastes, and Song of Solomon are attributed to him.

Daniel, Esther, and the extracanonical book of Judith also have a wisdom-modeling dimension. Joseph Blenkinsopp comments that "we would probably have to say the same of almost all the religious narrative literature which has survived from the Graeco-Roman period."[43]

With these character models we have, of course, moved away from the popular ethos promoted in the village circle and have entered the realm of the more sophisticated court wisdom that eventually became the guardian and transmitter of all wisdom writings. The content of village wisdom, or popular ethos, is available to us only through these writings, of course, where it has already received an admixture of courtly and scribal concerns. Therefore, as we proceed now to lift out the ingredients that make up the wisdom paradigm, we must remain conscious of the fact that our extant canonical documents portray a two-sided figure. The image of the wise person is, on the one hand, that of an ordinary Israelite coping with the daily problems of agricultural and domestic life in the light of communal experience. On the other hand, it is that of a courtier in the service of the king, and ultimately, the wise king himself. Both images, however, portray persons who cope well with life through their recourse to experience, largely formulated into proverbs that capture in terse poetic form the empirical observations of many generations. That such coping well is, in the last analysis, a gift of grace from God, deeply roots the wisdom paradigm in the faith of Israel.

Joseph: A Familial-Royal Model

The courtly wisdom paradigm is most palpable in the model figures referred to above, especially prominently in Joseph.[44] He is able to direct the affairs of his people in such a way as to preserve life and enhance its quality through justice, prosperity, and peace. Although this may appear, from a human perspective, as personal dexterity in decision making, it cannot succeed unless it is, at the same time, the gracious leading of God. Joseph, looking back on his career marked by wise moves, acknowledges freely to his brothers:

> I am your brother, Joseph, whom you sold into Egypt. And now do not be distressed, or angry with yourselves, because you sold me here; for God sent me before you to preserve life. . . . And God sent me before you to preserve for you a remnant on earth [or: in the land], and to keep alive for you many survivors. (Gen. 45:4–7; cf. 50:20)[45]

Several points deserve attention. First, Joseph reminds his brothers that they, too, had had a plan (cf. their deliberations, Gen. 37:18–20), but that God's plan had overruled it. In Israel, true wisdom never meant merely to be clever, but rather to be in tune with God. Second, Joseph characterizes God's leading, expressed on the human level by Joseph's wise moves, as aiming at the preservation of life. In view is, first, the life of the brothers and their descendants, "on earth/in the land." Geography is important in the Joseph story itself, as well as in its functioning within the wider Pentateuchal story. In the land where Joseph's brothers belong, they would die of famine. In the land where food is available, their access to it depends on a potentially vengeful brother. Now the third theme of our familial paradigm, beside life and land, enters in: This brother, who himself has received hospitality in Egypt, now becomes the instrument of extending Egyptian hospitality to his brothers. But whereas the aim of God's leading has been the preservation of Jacob's family, those instrumental in making this possible through their hospitality, the Egyptians, are themselves preserved by means of Joseph's wise provisions for the years of famine. Though it is not said in these words, one gains the impression that all are God's strangers and sojourners, in the sense of Lev. 25:23.

Standing between seminomadic clan and imperial court, small-scale tribal concerns and international diplomacy, Joseph as a model of wisdom points in both directions. He is wise in the simple meaning of having good sense, like Abigail, to do what will preserve life and land by sharing it. He is wise also in the sense of Solomon, who asked and received wisdom for the complex decisions of a ruler, "for who is able [without God's gift of wisdom] to govern this thy great people?" (1 Kings 3:9).[46]

Job 31: A Familial-Wisdom Model

To explain the meaning of plain good sense cultivated by popular ethos is not altogether easy. Proverbs 10ff. abounds in individual proverbs depicting right actions and attitudes in the context of the extended family and the village. Frequently they contrast the right and wrong way of relating between husband and wife, parents and children, neighbors with each other, humans and animals. They extol diligence over laziness, truth over deceit, liberality over stinginess, care and compassion over selfishness. These and other themes pertaining to everyday life in family and community stand intermixed, however, with others that have the royal court and the life of the scribal class in view, and with a multitude of proverbs that could be applied anywhere. It would be an exercise in circular reasoning to select a certain group of proverbs as those depicting for us the paradigm of popular wisdom, for that paradigm would already have provided us with the selecting principles. Only if we could discover longer coherent presentations of model traits clearly pertaining to the kinship-village setting could we use them to analyze the content of the paradigm to which they point. Such a presentation, however, could not be expected to have its literary origin in the actual folk setting; no minutes were taken in the village circle. It would have to be the work of the literary wisdom circles, but one that has as its subject the highest ethical aspirations of those living in a kinship context.

Such a text has been preserved for us in Job 31. Job is clearly described as the head of a father's house in the Prologue (Job 1–2) and the Epilogue (42:7–17). Whatever tensions may exist between the prose framework of the book and the embedded Dialogue between Job and his friends, this setting and characterization is not affected by them. Georg Fohrer has subjected this chapter to an extensive analysis from which we will draw several observations.[47] The chapter ends the Dialogue of the book of Job with his three friends, not only by being the conclusion of Job's final speech (chs. 29–31), but also by making further replies from his friends impossible.[48] This happens when Job concludes his twelve- (originally ten?) member[49] series of protestations of purity (vs. 1–34, 38–40) with a final challenge (vs. 35–37). Such an "oath of purity" effectively ended debate and committed the case to divine decision.

Although Fohrer compares the form of the series of ten/twelve protestations to various such series in the Old Testament, including the Decalogue, and traces the function of the oath of purity to the legal and cultic realms, he finds the ethical content of the chapter to be solidly rooted in wisdom. "Wisdom teaching was the place of origin for the ethics found in Job 31."[50] At the same time, he details how the ethic of this chapter transcends wisdom ethic by far in its stress on attitude and intention. "It cannot be disputed that the Job who utters the oath of purity in chapter 31 stands almost alone upon an ethical summit."[51] Fohrer makes repeated cross-references to the Sermon on the Mount. At the same time, he maintains the solid wisdom orientation of this chapter. In spite of its lofty ideals, to which we will return below, the chapter offers us a useful portrait of the ideal *paterfamilias,* or household head, seen from a wisdom perspective. What were his marks?

First, we note with Fohrer that "the perceptible sinful deeds, which ordinarily came to an Israelite's mind, are absent in Job's oath of purity from the very beginning."[52] Such misdeeds as rape, adultery, stealing, or murder need not even be discussed, for they are warded off in the temptation stage already (vs. 1, 9, 7, 29, respectively). Instead, if we transpose the negative protestations of purity into their positive opposites, we see a man who relates to the people and things of his familial-communal surroundings with gentle care, preserving their integrity and ensuring their welfare. He preserves the integrity of the opposite sex, and therewith that of the family and its structures (vs. 1–4, 9–12). He gives fullest rights to his servants, including the right of legal action, and that on the basis of seeing them as fellow creatures of the same God (vs. 13–15). He makes no move to acquire the property of others (vs. 7–8), nor does he allow his own possessions to tempt him to idolize them (vs. 24–25); instead, he uses them to sustain the poor and the fatherless (vs. 16–23). Even his land has no reason to complain of his exploitation (vs. 38–40).[53] His relationship to the community is marked by truthfulness (vs. 5–6); his image and reputation have no need to be based on deceit, nor are they subject to popular pressure (vs. 33–34). His magnanimity is not limited to the poor of his household and community (vs. 16–23, the largest section in the chapter), but extends in hospitality to the sojourner and wayfarer (vs. 31–32); more than that, it forbids him to rejoice in the ruin of even his enemies (vs. 29–30).

This is the familial paradigm seen in wisdom perspective. As portrayed in Job 31, it transcends the familial paradigm discussed earlier by its emphasis on inwardness and intention. As to content, however, it covers the same areas. The overlap with the Decalogue is extensive; we need only think of the concern of both texts with idolatry, family and servants, adultery, enmity, truthfulness, and covetousness. The concern for the Sabbath is missing here, but the care of the poor and the sojourner occupies considerable space. Certain nuances and emphases are different, to be sure. In keeping with Proverbs 1–9, sexual temptation ranks high, as does a conciliatory attitude to enemies (cf. Prov. 25:21f.). But there is nothing in the Decalogue or in Job 31 that is incompatible with the other, or with the familial paradigm as characterized earlier. Just as legal lists like the Decalogue or Leviticus 19 are sampling, rather than covering, in nature, we must assume the same of a "wisdom decalogue" like Job 31.

Conspicuously absent from the list of Job's positive characterizations are references to ritual observance. It would be quite wrong, however, to consider his a secular ethic. First of all, Job's oath of purity is itself a "religious observance" addressed to God. Further, there are numerous reminders in the chapter that Job's ethical conscientiousness is motivated by a constant awareness of life lived before God. Though the names for God in this chapter are the older *'ĕlôah, 'ēl,* and *šadday,* as in the Dialogue generally, we must assume that, at least for the final canonical author, they were identical with the Yahweh of the Prologue, the Epilogue, and the theophanies (38:1; 40:1, and 42:1); and with the God (*'Ĕlōhîm*) to whom Job brought burnt offerings on behalf of the potential sin of his children (1:5). As von Rad pointed out concerning wisdom's supposed secularity,[54] the familial ideal of Job 31 must now be seen as lived out within the horizon of the Old Testament's great historico-theological themes, supplementing rather than ignoring them. Surely Job's special concern for the poor, the sojourner, the servant, and the land must now be read within the interpretive story context of the tradition of the exodus from Egypt and the gift of the land.[55] What a "righteous" person like Job expected from Yahweh, in the context of a firm belief in Yahweh as the guarantor of justice in times of trouble, is spelled out in Psalm 37, generally considered a wisdom psalm. The righteous can expect to "be still before the LORD" (v. 7), who will vindicate him. We note especially the repeated emphasis in that psalm on the gift of life, posterity, and land to the righteous, who is marked especially by waiting and liberality. Here the wisdom ideal has been linked solidly to Yahweh, the God of salvation. Of course, it is Job's special problem that his suffering seems to annul the validity of such assumptions. Although the book of Job in its totality grapples with that difficulty, it certainly does nothing to detract from the ethical ideal of Job as such.

Royal, or Court, Wisdom

We must briefly consider the ethical paradigm of court wisdom at its points of variance from popular wisdom. As was mentioned earlier, Joseph shows some of the hallmarks of court wisdom, but its major model is Solomon. Royal wisdom, of course, has its place in the realms of government and of justice. In his famous dream at Gibeah, Solomon asks God to give him "an understanding mind [lit. "a listening heart"] to govern thy people, that I may discern between good and evil" (1 Kings 3:9). To govern well is intimately bound up with the maintenance of justice. Consequently, the fulfillment of Solomon's request is immediately demonstrated in his wise decision in the case of the two women, of whom each claimed to be the mother of the surviving child (1 Kings 3:16–28). That story concludes with the statement that all Israel "stood in awe of the king, because they perceived that the wisdom of God was in him, to render justice" (v. 28). The specific content of this royal calling takes us into the royal paradigm and will therefore be discussed in the next chapter.

The close association of wisdom with royal virtue is also demonstrated by the use of common terminology to express the ideals of both. As Ahuva Ho has shown in a detailed study, *sedeq* ("right, rightness") is a key term expressing the highest ethical quality and goal of a king's rule, but also of the wise life generally.[56] In both spheres, it has a tendency toward the right observance and exercise of legal justice. Its related noun *sĕdāqâ* ("righteousness") is in narrative texts a term for "the proper behavior and acts of man,"[57] and for wisdom, it is "a way of life. It is a philosophy."[58] Such examples of overlap in key ethical terms confirm that there was close contact between wisdom instruction and the royal court.

A detailed analysis of wisdom admonitions has led Wolfgang Richter to the conclusion that there was a school in Jerusalem to train upper-class young men in wisdom to prepare them for government service.[59] That is entirely possible, but for lack of direct evidence it must remain a hypothesis. It is widely accepted, on the other hand, that there was a learned scribal class in Jerusalem that gathered and preserved in writing not only the wisdom writings (cf. Prov. 25:1), but much of our Old Testament.

The Limits of Wisdom

A discussion of the wisdom paradigm would not be complete without special attention to the concern for the limits of wisdom. One of the chief marks of the wise, if not the chief mark, is their awareness that their competency has definite boundaries; it is, so to speak, surrounded and defined by God's autonomous reign. According to von Rad, the theologically most telling group of older proverbs is the group that draws attention to this fact.[60] The tree of the knowledge of good and evil and the tree of life (Genesis 2–3) may belong to the same theme. Job's confrontation with God, when finally granted to him, is at the same time a confrontation with the limits of his own capacity to understand (Job 38–42). Fohrer makes the interesting point that Job, in his confident (and apparently justified) assertion of an unsurpassable righteousness in his oath of purity (ch. 31), paradoxically becomes guilty by transcending the human limitation as he claims an ethical victory over God. He turns his case into the issue as to whether man or God is right, and "[h]is ethically perfect behavior would lead him into the worst kind of sin," namely, the sin of wanting to be like God.[61] In a beautiful poem now embedded in the book of

Job (ch. 28), the poet searches in vain for access to wisdom. Its hiddenness with God leads the poet to the almost resigned but trusting conclusion:

> Behold, the fear of the Lord, that is wisdom;
> and to depart from evil is understanding. (v. 28)[62]

In the context of royal wisdom, the limitations of the wise are nowhere spelled out more strikingly than in the contest between Hushai and Ahithophel, two renowned wise men at the court of David, and then of Absalom (2 Sam. 15:31–37; 16:15–23; 17:1–14, 23). Both are renowned, with Ahithophel perhaps holding an edge, for "in those days the counsel which Ahithophel gave was as if one consulted the oracle of God" (16:23). Hushai remains David's loyal friend, but "Ahithophel is among the conspirators" (15:31). This moral aberration, together with David's prayer that God should "turn the counsel of Ahithophel into foolishness" (15:31), work together toward his undoing. Absalom and his followers side with the (deliberately misleading) counsel of Hushai against Ahithophel, "for the LORD had ordained to defeat the good counsel of Ahithophel, so that the LORD might bring evil upon Absalom" (17:14). It is not quite clear from the story whether Ahithophel's fall is to be attributed to his exercise of his wisdom in an unrighteous cause, or to the fact that even the highest human competence must yield to the inexorable plans of God.[63] The fact that Ahithophel could not accept defeat but went and hanged himself (17:23) highlights the implied critique of the reputation that equated his counsel with the oracle of God.

The uniqueness of the concern for human limitation in the wisdom paradigm becomes clear when we take note that there is nothing comparable in any of the other ethical paradigms. The call to family shalom is not accompanied by a warning that it might go too far, nor does the priestly paradigm contain an inbuilt warning against too great a holiness. A king, to anticipate our investigation, cannot be too just, nor a prophet too zealous a proclaimer of the word of God given him. Of course, all of these can pervert their calling, but the consciousness of the limits of wisdom pertains to true wisdom, not to the aberrations into folly, against which there is also plenty of warning. As it is, to be wise means to be wise within limits; but these limits can be accepted joyfully, for they constitute the surrounding presence of a God well disposed to his trusting creatures.

Notes

1. Walter C. Kaiser (*Toward Old Testament Ethics,* [Grand Rapids: Zondervan Publishing House, 1983], throughout; see esp. 139–51) considers striving for holiness the "central organizing feature" of Old Testament ethics (p. 139). Without denying the importance of the quest for holiness, the present study holds it to be only one of several organizing principles of the Old Testament's ethical thrust.

2. It is noteworthy that the Old Testament, unlike the mythologies of the ancient Near East, does not attribute primeval origin to the Tabernacle and Temple. It reports their construction by Israel at particular times in history. Nevertheless, such physical and historical realities are gifts of divine grace that mediate God's holy presence in a sort of sacramental fashion. The Sabbath, though associated with creation (Gen. 2:1–3), functions in a similar way. Its historical development within Israel, however, is beyond clear reconstruction.

3. This is Kaiser's position. See above, n. 1.

4. It is quite possible that the linking of the actors in the story to their respective fathers' houses (vs. 14–15) is a secondary addition (Philip J. Budd, *Numbers,* Word Biblical Commentary 5 [Waco, Tex.: Word Books, 1984], 280). This in no way weakens the suggestion that ethical behavior is here seen, in typical Old Testament fashion, to play itself out primarily in the family context.

5. Precise delimitation is difficult here. The larger Gideon pericope consists of chapters 6–8, framed by a Deuteronomistic opening (6:1–10) and closing (8:33–35). This framework embraces a number of older elements. Judges 6:11–24 is widely recognized as a unit (e.g., J. Alberto Soggin, *Judges: A Commentary,* trans. J. S. Bowden, Old Testament Library [Philadelphia: Westminster Press, 1981], 113–22), although the close thematic connection with 6:25–32 cannot be denied (cf. Robert G. Boling, [*Judges: Introduction, Translation and Commentary,* Anchor Bible 6A (Garden City, N.Y.: Doubleday & Co., 1975), 130], who regards the two pericopes as a unity). For our purpose, verses 11–24 are of chief interest, although their present function within the Deuteronomistic framework forms the horizon of our interpretation. Within these verses, certain tensions are evident also, especially between the call of Gideon (vs. 11–17) and the etiology of the altar of Ophrah (vs. 19–24), verse 18 functioning as a redactional bridge; cf. John Gray, ed., *Joshua, Judges and Ruth,* Century Bible (new ed.; London: Nelson, 1967), 296. In spite of these tensions, however, verses 11–24 are held together in a final editorial unity.

6. Although some interpreters have wanted to make the alternation between the angel's (or messenger's) speech and that of the Lord a criterion for distinguishing sources, it is better to see the messenger and the Lord

as essentially indistinguishable; thus Soggin, *Judges,* 114, and Gray, *Joshua, Judges and Ruth,* 296. This identity is not at all evident to Gideon at first, however, but emerges only gradually. When it breaks through (probably by v. 17), it elicits both the desire for greater certainty in form of a sign, and action appropriate as response to the holiness of God. Gray (ibid., 298) notes correctly that a certain tension remains between Gideon's earlier recognition of the true speaker addressing him and the recognition expressed in verse 22.

7. Gray (ibid., 296) captures well the personal dynamics underlying such a process when he writes: "Doubtless human associates who raised scruples and were instrumental in nerving a man's holy resolve were so understood [i.e., as divine messengers], and the encounter with the angel of the Lord might even be the personification of a man's spiritual conflict when faced by what he recognized as a divine challenge."

8. This name now functions as a promise of normal life and well-being restored by Yahweh, even if the pericope may once have served as an etiology.

9. How Gideon's "primitive" concern for the holy, together with his fear lest he die, is expressed in formal priestly instruction can be seen in Lev. 10:1–11.

10. In addition to the opening (vs. 1–2) and closing (vs. 36b–37), religious/cultic concerns are found in verses 4–8, 19, 23–25, 26–28, 30, and 31, that is, mostly in the latter half of the chapter. Verses 20–22 deal with a nonritual offense (sexual relations with a slave woman), which nevertheless requires ritual expiation.

11. By contrast, the Decalogue (both in Exodus 20 and Deuteronomy 5) simply addresses "you" (sg.). In its present Deuteronomic framework, however, Moses speaks to "all Israel" (Deut. 5:1), which is later characterized as "all your assembly" (*qāhāl;* v. 22), a term often used in association with "congregation" (*'ēdâ*). Here the original focus on the Israelite household has already been replaced by a focus on the people understood as a religious gathering.

12. In addition to the opening and closing (vs. 2 and 37), some version of this formula occurs fourteen times in this chapter.

13. See the classical treatment of this "formula of self-introduction" in Walther Zimmerli, "I Am Yahweh," in his *I Am Yahweh,* trans. Douglas W. Stott (Atlanta: John Knox Press, 1982; original German, 1953), 1–28.

14. For a comparative characterization of these two different theologies, both expressing the accessibility of the transcendent God at Israel's central sanctuary, see Gerhard von Rad, "Deuteronomy's 'Name' Theology and the Priestly Document's 'Kabod' Theology," in *Studies in Deuteronomy,* trans. D. M. G. Stalker, Studies in Biblical Theology 9 (London: SCM Press, 1953), 37–44.

15. One could easily see here no more than a summary of ancient under-

standing of magic, in which the cult represented a sacred technology for the achievement of human desires. In its early historical setting, Judg. 17:13 may indeed have meant little more than that. In the canonical context of the Old Testament, however, it becomes a comprehensive statement of Israel's distinctive faith. It expresses that life flows from God and that Israel's enjoyment of life is dependent on ensuring that God remain central; in other words, on Israel's receptivity for God's holiness in its midst. That alone would lead to life.

16. See above, n. 1.

17. Kaiser, *Toward Old Testament Ethics,* 143.

18. Ibid., 140. Jesus' call to be "perfect" after the model of God (Matt. 5:48) must be interpreted as "merciful," with its Lukan parallel (6:36).

19. Kaiser acknowledges this otherness too, as *one* of the two sides of God's holiness, the other being God's "righteousness and goodness" (*Toward Old Testament Ethics,* 143). The latter, of course, will in no way be denied here; it is only the assumption that it can provide "ethical modeling" (ibid., 140) that seems problematic in the Old Testament context. That God's incarnate presence in Jesus Christ includes ethical modeling, on the other hand, will be a strong assertion in chapter 7.

20. Walter Harrelson, "The Significance of Cosmology in the Ancient Near East," in *Translating and Understanding the Old Testament: Essays in Honor of Herbert Gordon May,* ed. Harry Thomas Frank and William L. Reed (Nashville: Abingdon Press, 1970), 237–52. "More fundamental [than the relocation of Mesopotamian mythological motifs onto the historical plane] for an understanding of the contrast between Meso-potamian and Israelite cosmology, however, is the fact that the Israelite people so persistently resisted the temptation to explain their lives on the basis of analogy with the life of Yahweh" (p. 249).

21. We note that Lev. 11:45 and 19:2 read "*for [kî;* also "because"] I (the LORD your God) am holy," not "*as [kĕ]. . . .*" By contrast, Matt. 5:48 says, "You, therefore, must be perfect, *as [hōs;* not *hoti,* "because"] your heavenly Father is perfect."

22. This chapter is marked by great complexity of structure and style. Its division into two very unequal parts, verses 1–7 and 8–55, is at least partially explained by the inclusion, in the second part, of the theme of "redemption" (vs. 24ff.). Though related to the jubilee theme of restitu-tion, the various redemption laws are not necessarily tied to the year of jubilee (Martin Noth, *Leviticus, A Commentary,* trans. J. E. Anderson, Old Testament Library [Philadelphia: Westminster Press, 1965], 189; Karl Elliger, *Leviticus,* Handbuch zum Alten Testament, Erste Reihe 4 [Tübingen: Verlag von J. C. B. Mohr (Paul Siebeck), 1966], 339–43). The style of the chapter, though "Priestly" throughout, is equally marked by variety, fluctuating between third person speech and personal address, the latter in the singular or in the plural. A long history lies behind the

present text; Noth (ibid., 85) believes it to extend from early monarchic to early exilic times. Nevertheless, this chapter, in all its diversity, is pervaded by the same concern, "the *restitutio in integrum* or restoration to an original state" (ibid., 183).

23. Thus Noth, *Leviticus*, 185.

24. For this understanding of land, see also Pss. 39:12; 119:19; cf. Josh. 22:19; Jer. 2:7; 16:18, and Waldemar Janzen, "Land," in *Anchor Bible Dictionary*, ed. David Noel Freedman (New York: Doubleday & Co., 1992), 4:144f.

25. Klaus Koch, *The Prophets*, vol. 1: The Assyrian Period (Philadelphia: Fortress Press, 1983), 50–62, esp. 58–59. In his sensitive, albeit cautious, interpretation of Amos's critique of the cultus, Koch rejects the widespread view that sees justice (*mišpāt*) and righteousness (*sĕdāqâ*) as ethical ideals affirmed by Amos (and other prophets) in a polemic against cultic practice. On the contrary, says Koch, the prophetic indictment of the cult is based on the failure of the latter in its proper function, namely, to generate justice and righteousness.

26. See Don F. Morgan, *Wisdom in the Old Testament Traditions* (Atlanta: John Knox Press, 1981).

27. For Job's place within this framework, see J. Gerald Janzen, *Job*, Interpretation (Atlanta: John Knox Press, 1985), 10–12, and throughout.

28. Ahuva Ho puts it well: "Wisdom is the means by which one acquires divine attributes. *Sdq* [rightness] has become the goal. Effective and dedicated learning will result in *sdq*." (*Sedeq and Sedaqah in the Hebrew Bible*, American University Studies, Series 7, Theology and Religion 78 [New York: Peter Lang, 1991], 51).

29. Hans Heinrich Schmid, *Wesen und Geschichte der Weisheit: Eine Untersuchung der altorientalischen und israelitischen Weisheitsliteratur*, Beihefte zur Zeitschrift für die alttestamentliche Wissenschaft 101 (Berlin: Verlag Alfred Töpelmann, 1966), 155–63. Although Schmid makes these observations especially with respect to Proverbs 10ff., our application of them to Old Testament wisdom generally seems warranted.

30. Hebrew: *sôd*; see Ludwig Köhler, *Hebrew Man*, trans. P. R. Ackroyd (Nashville: Abingdon Press, 1957), 86–91.

31. Because of the transmission of all wisdom, including any popular wisdom that has survived, by learned circles, some have questioned the existence, or at least the preservation in the Old Testament, of such a popular ethos. It is indeed impossible to sort out within the book of Proverbs materials that demonstrably originated in the village circle. On the other hand, Otto Plöger reminds us correctly that wisdom instruction understands itself as the continuation of parental instruction (*Sprüche Salomos [Proverbia]*, Biblischer Kommentar zum Alten Testament 17 [Neukirchen-Vluyn: Neukirchener Verlag, 1984], 22); cf. also Waldemar Janzen, "Education in the Old Testament and in Early Judaism," in

Janzen, *Still in the Image: Essays in Biblical Theology and Anthropology* (Newton, Kans.: Faith & Life Press, 1982), 92–108.

32. Erhard Gerstenberger, *Wesen und Herkunft des "apodiktischen Rechts,"* Wissenschaftliche Monographien zum Alten und Neuen Testament 20 (Neukirchen-Vluyn: Neukirchener Verlag, 1965).

33. Hans Walter Wolff, *Amos the Prophet: The Man and His Background,* trans. Foster R. McCurley (Philadelphia: Fortress Press, 1973).

34. Gerhard von Rad, *Old Testament Theology,* vol. 1: *The Theology of Israel's Historical Traditions,* trans. D. M. G. Stalker (London: SCM Press, 1975), 433–37.

35. Ibid., 437–41.

36. Schmid, *Wesen und Geschichte der Weisheit,* 144–55.

37. Ibid., 79–84. Although Schmid makes these observations in the context of discussing Egyptian wisdom, they are equally valid for Israelite proverbial wisdom.

38. This observation is shared by Roland E. Murphy, "Wisdom in the OT: B.3. Wisdom and Moral Action," *Anchor Bible Dictionary,* ed. David Noel Freedman (New York: Doubleday & Co., 1992), 6:925: "The approach of wisdom to morality is much broader than that of the Decalogue in that it aims at character formation."

39. For example, John Paterson suggests a threefold characterization of the person meeting disapproval in Proverbs, in ascending severity: the teachable fool (*petî,* "simple"; *hāsēr lēb,* "without sense"), the hardened fool (*kĕsîl, 'ĕwîl,* "thick of heart," i.e., despising instruction), and finally, the arrogant fool (*lēs,* "scoffer"; *nābāl* "fool" [par excellence]); see *The Wisdom of Israel,* Bible Guides II (New York: Abingdon Press, 1961), 63–68.

40. Von Rad's interpretation of the Joseph story in this light remains a classic in its sensitivity and penetration, even if we may not accept the hypothesis regarding a Solomonic enlightenment into which it is set. See Gerhard von Rad, "The Story of Joseph," in his *God at Work in Israel,* trans. John H. Marks (Nashville: Abingdon Press, 1980 [original German, 1954]), 19–35. Von Rad's sapiential interpretation has not gone unchallenged; see below, n. 44.

41. For a discussion of the persistent Old Testament association of wisdom, in particular the wisdom of rendering judgment, with kingship, see Norman W. Porteous, "Royal Wisdom," in *Wisdom in Israel and in the Ancient Near East,* Rowley Festscrift, Supplements to *Vetus Testamentum* III, ed. M. Noth and D. Winton Thomas (Leiden: E. J. Brill, 1960), 246–61. This association continues, according to Porteous, the judicial function of the "Judges" (*šōpĕtîm*) and extends beyond the monarchy into the messianic expectations. In the association of royal wisdom with the establishing of justice, we encounter also the proximity of the wisdom paradigm to the royal paradigm.

42. For a study of these two dimensions in the texts characterizing Solomon's wisdom, and an attempt to relate their origins to a time not much later than that of Solomon, see Martin Noth, "Die Bewährung von Salomos göttlicher Weisheit," in *Wisdom in Israel and in the Ancient Near East*, 225–37.

43. Joseph Blenkinsopp, *Wisdom and Law in the Old Testament: The Ordering of Life in Israel and in Early Judaism* (New York: Oxford University Press, 1983), 40; cf. also pp. 37–40 for a brief discussion of select wisdom models in the Old Testament and in the Apocrypha.

44. To claim Joseph as modeling a wisdom perspective does not make it necessary to adopt von Rad's interpretation (see above, n. 40) in its entirety. For a brief summary of critiques leveled against it, see Claus Westermann, *Genesis 37–50: A Commentary*, trans. John J. Scullion (Minneapolis: Augsburg Publishing House, 1986), 26f. Westermann himself sees the Joseph story in the wider sense as consisting of a Joseph story in a narrower sense (chs. 39–45) embedded in elements of the Jacob story (chs. 37; 46–50). The former again consists of a melding of an original family theme (strife and reconciliation) with a political-royal theme (How can a brother rule over his brothers?). (Ibid., 22–25). It cannot be our task here to resolve the complex issues involved in the analysis of the Joseph story. Suffice it to point out that the degree to which an interpreter rejects von Rad's claims regarding wisdom features in the story usually depends on the degree of strictness employed in the definition of wisdom. I for one am persuaded that the story's wisdom content is extensive, although it alone does not offer an adequate key to the story's structure and composition. As Blenkinsopp puts it, "The entire story breathes the atmosphere of the sages" (*Wisdom and Law*, 38).

45. Von Rad ("The Story of Joseph," 29–35) traces the theme of God's leading with particular sensitivity. It is grace, not fate, that moves the story forward. At the same time, God's grace, when overruling even evil human designs, eventually does confront Israel's confident trust in wisdom derived from experience with the opaque mystery of God's ways. We experience this powerfully in Ecclesiastes.

46. Westermann rightly recognizes the union of familial and royal themes in the Joseph story (see above, n. 44).

47. Georg Fohrer, "The Righteous Man in Job 31," in *Essays in Old Testament Ethics: J. Philip Hyatt, In Memoriam*, ed. James L. Crenshaw and John T. Willis (New York: KTAV Publishing House, 1974), 1–22.

48. With this chapter we reach the climax and end of Job's speeches in his own defense. Ludwig Köhler (*Hebrew Man*, 134–39) has suggested that the whole Dialogue in Job (chs. 3–31) reflects formally the proceedings of the legal assembly in the gate. Whether one accepts this analysis *in toto* or not, it seems clear that chapter 31 represents an oath of innocence in a

"forensic context" in which Job is the accused and God the accuser and judge; see Norman C. Habel, *The Book of Job, A Commentary,* Old Testament Library (Philadelphia: Westminster Press, 1985), 438–40. To what extent one should assume, with Habel (ibid.), a covenant context is less clear.

49. Ibid., 8. J. Gerald Janzen holds (with Robert Gordis) to a list of fourteen sins, a "double heptad"; see *Job,* 212f. Whether ten, twelve, or fourteen members constitute the list is less important for our purpose than the fact that these significant numbers underscore the programmatic way in which the righteous person is presented here; we are not dealing with a haphazard collection of characteristics.

50. Fohrer, "The Righteous Man in Job 31," 9.

51. Ibid., 19.

52. Ibid., 14.

53. The fact that Job's affirmation of blamelessness with respect to his land follows the concluding verses 35–37 (including his "signature," v. 35) has led some interpreters to see it as misplaced or appended. Habel (*The Book of Job,* 438–40), however, reading the passage in a covenantal context, points out that covenant unfaithfulness was ultimately evidenced by alienation from and of the land. He recalls in this connection the curse on the ground (Gen. 3:17) resulting from Adam and Eve's sin. J. Gerald Janzen (*Job,* 215f.) presents a masterful analysis of "Job's Evocation of the Garden Story," in verses 38–40. Rather than misplaced or appended, Job's land-related self-imprecation effectively clinches his protestations of innocence and at the same time heightens the significance of the relationship to the land within the total wisdom portrayal of the righteous human being.

54. See above, pp. 122f.

55. J. Gerald Janzen demonstrates the continuity between Job and Israel's theological tradition throughout his commentary. For an introductory listing of several themes evidencing such continuity, see his *Job,* 10–12.

56. Ho, *Sedeq and Sedaqah,* 57, 144, 147, 150, and passim.

57. Ibid., 143.

58. Ibid., 144.

59. Wolfgang Richter, *Recht und Ethos: Versuch einer Ortung des weisheitlichen Mahnspruches,* Studien zum Alten und Neuen Testament 15 (Munich: Kösel-Verlag, 1966), 182–89.

60. Von Rad, *Old Testament Theology* 1:438–41, and Gerhard von Rad, *Wisdom in Israel,* trans. James D. Martin (London: SCM Press, 1972), 97–110.

61. Fohrer, "The Righteous Man in Job 31," 20.

62. The limits of human access to wisdom, experienced painfully in Job and Ecclesiastes, need not—and generally did not—dishearten the search for wisdom through experience and its application to daily living. Thus a

statement very similar to verse 28 is offered as the positive reference point for the wisdom quest in Prov. 1:7. See also von Rad's perceptive treatment of "The Self-Revelation of Creation" (*Wisdom in Israel*, 144–76).

63. Blenkinsopp (*Wisdom and Law*, 5) sees at work here "inevitable tensions between this new [court] wisdom of international stamp and indigenous resources (e.g., appeal to an oracle or a seer for guidance)." Both in the court history of David (2 Sam. 9:20; 1 Kings 1–2) and in the story of the Fall (Genesis 3), the potential of wisdom is shown in its destructive capacity for overreaching itself, and is subordinated to the free agency of God.

CHAPTER 6

THE ROYAL AND PROPHETIC PARADIGMS

The Royal Paradigm

Introduction

The royal and prophetic paradigms belong together for at least two reasons. First, both of them stand in some contrast to the priestly and wisdom paradigms, for the royal and prophetic paradigms functioned as paradigms for the ordinary Israelite only in an indirect sense. King and prophet were representatives of the people and mediated between God and people, but the ordinary Israelite was not expected to imitate them; in fact, it would have been quite impossible to do so. By contrast, the ordinary Israelite could and should seek holiness and wisdom. It might be objected that the ordinary Israelite could also not be expected to aspire to the position of high priest or priest, yet the ideal of holiness was not absolutely dependent on these offices. The holiness of God could be acknowledged and thereby shared, in a sense, apart from the existence of these offices. By contrast, a royal ideal or a prophetic ideal could not have been aspired to apart from the actual exercise of the royal or prophetic offices.[1]

Second, the royal and prophetic paradigms belong together on the basis of their relationship to each other. Although the ideal prophet was one who kept in line all the other offices in Israel by means of the divine word given to him, none was as frequently and directly the target of a prophetic message as was the king. This was undoubtedly so because of the ever-present temptation for the kings to undo Israel's "prophetic counterculture" by leading it back into those ancient Near Eastern modes of thought, life, and worship from which God had redeemed it through the calling of Abraham and the prophetic ministry of Moses.[2]

Ideal and Ambiguity of Kingship

The Ideal

The royal paradigm, then, focused heavily on the one expected to embody it, the king. He, rather than the people generally, was expected to represent in Israel a way of right living. This way of the king, to be sure, affected the life of the people, and, as we will see, there was a sense in which they partook in living it out.

Because of its focus on the king, the royal paradigm is presented for us less in terms of characteristics than of characters. Good kings and bad kings are portrayed and compared, especially in the Deuteronomistic History and in the largely parallel books of Chronicles. David stands out as the primary model, not without faults, to be sure. He is preceded and followed by Saul and Solomon. Each of these two, though not without exemplary characteristics, functions more as an antimodel than a model. In the further story of kingship, David offers the yardstick by which other kings are evaluated. Others like Hezekiah and Josiah undergird his image. Antimodels are also not lacking, prominent among them Jeroboam I of Israel and Manasseh and Jehoiakim of Judah.

Although model kings make their impact through the composite and complex picture of their personalities, certain chief characteristics do stand out. First among these is the recognition of accountability to God, over against the inclination of all autocratic rulers ancient and modern to act in their own self-sufficient autonomy. A second characteristic of the royal ideal is the use of the power of office toward the end of justice rather than self-aggrandizement. Although the exercise of justice characterized the ideal king in neighboring cultures as well, its specific context was defined, for the king in Israel, by Israel's own story of faith. Here we observe again, as we did with respect to the priestly and wisdom paradigms, that the content of the royal paradigm issues in the familial paradigm.

We will sample texts that present the royal ideal through models or antimodels of kingship. We will also examine the nature of royal justice in Israel. First, however, we must pay some attention to the peculiar ambiguity that attaches to kingship in Israel due to the uneasy sense that the institution as such might rival the lordship of God.

The Ambiguity

We were introduced to the royal paradigm by the story of David's sparing of Saul's life (1 Samuel 24). Because the story revealed the inherent temptation of kingship, we encountered the royal paradigm in the form of an antimodel. Saul, Israel's first king, meets us as one who fails at the heart of Israel's royal ideal, the execution of justice. Instead of being the guarantor of justice, he is seen pursuing one of his subjects, fearing for his own throne, and attempting to consolidate and protect his power. At the same time, that story holds out the possibility and the promise that one "more righteous than I" (i.e., David; v. 17) shall become king (v. 20). This is the tension that accompanied kingship throughout its duration in Israel. On the one hand, kingship inclined inherently toward the monarchies of the surrounding nations from which it had been borrowed, "that we also may be like all the nations" (1 Sam. 8:20). On the other hand, there was the continued hope, borne up by limited signs of fulfillment, that a new and different form of monarchy under Yahweh could emerge in Israel (e.g., Deut. 17:14–20).

This continued tension was preceded, of course, by the prior tensions surrounding the introduction of kingship in the first place. Historically, this must have been an extended struggle between Israel's seminomadic tribal structure and the predominant form of government of the sedentary population. We see evidence of it in Gideon's refusal to establish a dynasty (Judg. 8:22f), Abimelech's short-lived reign (Judges 9), and Samuel's failed dynastic thoughts (1 Sam. 8:1–3). The main struggle came, of course, in the events that surrounded the eventual establishment of kingship under Saul, David, and Solomon. Various interpreters have judged the introduction of kingship to have been the tragic turn in Israel's history. In analogy to a "Constantinian fall" of the church, they claim, it undid the distinctive calling of the Mosaic alternative community and led the people back into a pattern marked, according to Walter Brueggemann, by an economics of affluence, a politics of oppression, and a religion of immanence.[3] Millard C. Lind,[4] has argued forcefully that the turning point is to be seen in David, but Frank Moore Cross[5] and

Brueggemann[6] prefer to see the turning point in Solomon. Viewing Solomon from the perspective of the Mosaic vision of an alternative community, Brueggemann arrives at the devastating judgment: "Solomon managed a remarkable continuity with the very Egyptian reality that Moses had sought to counter."[7]

Models and Antimodels

Canonical Considerations Concerning Kingship

If Brueggemann's judgment is true—and, noting his careful qualifications, I think it is—one might well ask whether an inquiry into Old Testament ethics should be looking for a royal paradigm of the good, God-pleasing life at all. Must not such a "paradigm" inevitably lead away from the will of Yahweh into some form of compromise, if not outright idolatry? Before we accept such a negative conclusion, however, we ought to consider certain further facts. First, the biblical narrative treats the historical struggles for kingship rather tersely. It allows for a moment of ambiguity in the beginning, when Samuel resists the popular request for a king (1 Samuel 8).[8] Almost immediately, however, the narrative reports his compliance, politically an act of acculturation (v. 20) and theologically a concession from God (vs. 7 and 22). After that, monarchy as Israel's form of government is no longer challenged, not even in the context of the rebellion that split the nation into North and South (1 Kings 12).[9] The fringe phenomenon of the Rechabites, with their retention of the desert lifestyle, is admired by Jeremiah (Jeremiah 35) but not held up as a model for restructuring the state. Neither do the other prophets call Israel back to a premonarchical tribal structure, in spite of their repeated recalling of an ideal time in the wilderness (e.g., Hos. 2:15; 11:1ff.; 13:4ff.; Jer. 2:1ff.). Once introduced, kingship was there to stay until it was ended by foreign conquerors in the events of 721 B.C. and 587 B.C. What remained was the question concerning the proper nature of kingship under Yahweh.

A second consideration is imperative on the basis of the canonical process. The believing communities of Israel and the church have retained as canonical scripture not only the premonarchical story, but also the story of monarchy. They have, furthermore, not selected the critical strands in that story, but two versions (the Deuteronomistic History and the Chronicler's History) that place even the critical accounts into frameworks of basically positive disposition toward kingship.[10] In addition, they have included large segments of psalmody and wisdom literature in the canon and testified to their close connection with the monarchy by associating them with the names of David and Solomon, respectively. Consequently, a canonical approach to Old Testament ethics must also come to terms with kingship, not only as a historical reality in Israel, but as a possibility of modeling obedient living under God. It must, therefore, inquire concerning the biblical paradigm of obedient kingship, marred and embattled as it may have been.

David

In the encounter of David and Saul (1 Samuel 24) treated earlier (chapter 1), we were introduced, among other things, to the promise that David would be a more adequate king than Saul and "that the kingdom of Israel shall be established in your [David's] hand" (v. 20). Space does not allow us to develop the manifold ways in which David is lifted up as the model king in such varied Old Testament documents as the Deuteronomistic History, the Chronicler's History, Isaiah, and the Psalter, to name only the major ones. By comparison, neither Saul, Israel's first king, nor Solomon, at the peak of the monarchy's splendor, inform the Old Testament's image of the good king as powerfully as does the image of David. To be sure, it is a composite image. In the Deuteronomistic History, divergent earlier strata are integrated to present a divinely empowered, God-chosen figure, called to succeed to and transform the office of the Judges. He shows one persistent quality in all the ups and downs of his turbulent life. It is encapsuled in the expression that "his heart was wholly with the Lord," applied by the Deuteronomistic Historian as a yardstick to other kings of Judah and Israel (cf. 1 Kings 11:4; 15:3). In other words, this narrative presents him as a king who rules in dependence on Yahweh, in contrast to Saul, who veers into policies of expediency (1 Samuel 13 and 15), and Solomon, whose "wives turned away his heart after other gods" (1 Kings 11:4) and who made the yoke of the people heavy (1 Kings 12:10).

In 1 Chronicles, David emerges as the real founder of the Temple cult, even if the Temple was built after his time. In the royal psalms, we see him as the adopted son of God (Ps. 2:7; 89:26f.) who establishes God's reign over his enemies, whereas the psalm headings prefer to characterize him as the sufferer crying to God. He is the recipient of a promise and a commission that are to accompany his successors (2 Samuel 7; cf. 23:1–7). These having failed, God himself will ensure the establishment of his worldwide reign of justice and peace through a new and greater David, according to a long prophetic-messianic tradition.

Brueggemann, despite his critique, acknowledges the need to recognize the theological contributions of the monarchic period. He summarizes them as (1) the full and formal articulation of creation faith, in which "the king-temple-royal-city complex is the guarantor of both social and cosmic order"[11] and (2) messianism, in which "the Davidic king is understood as an advocate for the marginal ones and so potentially figures as an agent of the Mosaic vision."[12]

Beyond David

Even though the royal ideal of the Old Testament is closely tied to David, it would not be totally appropriate to identify his (composite) image fully with the royal paradigm. The wisdom of Solomon and the peaceful international relations that marked his era also contribute positive elements to the total paradigm. (e.g., 1 Kings 3; 4:29–34; 8; 10:1–10). Other kings of the Davidic line, most prominently Josiah (2 Kings 22–23), though approved of in the Deuteronomistic History by means of the yardstick of David, have a certain independence of stature.[13] Thus Josiah, especially when seen against the foil of Manasseh, models the king as reformer and as bulwark against idolatry in a way not seen in the accounts of David himself (cf. 2 Kings 22:1–23:27).

Somewhat parenthetically, we also take note that even the image of foreign rulers is not totally negative. The Pharaoh of the exodus, the quintessence of the God-resisting autonomous world ruler, is held in balance with the Pharaoh of Joseph's time who preceded him in the biblical account. Not even an imperial ruler is destined by his sociological position alone to play the role of the grand antagonist of God and oppressor of people. The odds may be stacked against the office, but there was that earlier Pharaoh—so the story reminds us—who did not consider it beneath his dignity to employ the God-given wisdom of a foreign prisoner in order to make provisions to feed his people and preserve their life (Genesis 41). In later times there would be further world rulers who would perform God's plans unwittingly, like the Nebuchadnezzar of the Deuteronomistic History and the books of Jeremiah and Ezekiel. Others would be receptive to a measure of insight and repentance, like the Cyrus of the book of Ezra (1:2–4) and the Nebuchadnezzar of the book of Daniel (4:34–37). The point to be made is that the Old Testament in its canonical balance does not attribute inherent ethical value, whether positive or negative, to any one social structure. It is not biblical to say that kingship as such is condemned in the Old Testament, or that premonarchical tribal existence is approved of as such. Israel, in her long history, moved through many forms of sociopolitical existence. Every one of these was marked by human imperfection and was open to abuse, but each was also a medium capable of being transformed and drawn into God's service. This is true also of kingship.

The Centrality of Justice/Righteousness

Psalm 72: Justice with Messianic Horizons

From the broad parameters of the royal paradigm sketched so far, it is necessary to move back toward its center. In our story of David and Saul (1 Samuel 24), we observed already that the issue between them was one of righteousness, reaching a climax in Saul's confession, "You are more righteous than I" (v. 17). Righteousness means here the preservation of the life of the other, even the enemy (vs. 17–19). No other feature of the royal paradigm is as central as this. Psalm 72 gives paradigmatic expression to the centrality of justice/righteousness (*mišpāṭ/ṣĕdāqâ*) among the duties of the king:[14]

> Give the king thy justice (*mišpāṭ*), O God,
>   and thy righteousness (*ṣĕdāqâ*) to the royal son!
> May he judge thy people with righteousness,
>   and thy poor with justice!
> Let the mountains bear prosperity for the people,
>   and the hills in righteousness!
> May he defend the cause of the poor of the people,
>   give deliverance to the needy,
>   and crush the oppressor!
> . . . .
> In his days may righteousness flourish,
>   and peace (*šālôm*) abound, till the moon be no more!

May he have dominion from sea to sea,
  and from the River to the ends of the earth!

. . . .

For he delivers the needy when he calls,
  the poor and him who has no helper.
He has pity on the weak and the needy,
  and saves the lives of the needy.
From oppression and violence he redeems their life;
  and precious is their blood in his sight.

. . . .

May there be abundance of grain in the land;
  . . . may men blossom forth from the cities
  like the grass of the field!
May his name endure for ever,
  his fame continue as long as the sun!
May men bless themselves by him,
  all nations call him blessed!

(vs. 1–4, 7–8, 12–14, 16–17)

In this psalm, attributed to Solomon by its heading, the administration of justice/righteousness is characterized as a gift from God. We are reminded of Solomon's prayer for wisdom in his dream at Gibeah (1 Kings 3:9), as a result of which "the wisdom of God was in him, to render justice (*mišpāṭ*)" (v. 28). This endowment is available to the king in special abundance, no doubt, because of his special relationship to God as God's adopted son (Ps. 2:7). Nevertheless, it is a gift of grace conferred on him at least in part as the result of prayer, both his own (cf. Solomon's prayer; and Ps. 2:8) and that of his people (v. 15); in fact, Psalm 72 must have functioned in some liturgical context related to the maintenance of the flow of royal justice.[15] The object of the king's administration of justice is designated in three concentric circles: the outer circle includes all nations and their rulers (vs. 8–11); the second embraces the people of God (v. 2); and the third and central circle singles out the poor, needy, oppressed, and weak for special attention (vs. 2, 4, 12–14). The creation of justice is operative on two levels. First, it is achieved through the king's active support of the poor and oppressed; he judges them (understood positively; v. 2), defends their cause (v. 4), delivers them (vs. 4, 12), has pity (v. 13), saves their lives (v. 13), and redeems them from oppression and violence (v. 14). Conversely, he crushes the oppressor (v. 4) and subjects all kings and nations (vs. 8–11), with the implication that the latter oppose God's justice/righteousness in some sense.

Second, the active pronouncement of God's justice among the inhabitants of the earth has an integrative and beneficial effect on nature itself, causing it to yield abundantly (vs. 3, 16), including human fertility (v. 16). The king's role on this level must undoubtedly be seen against an earlier background of an autonomous interplay between human and nonhuman forces. Human, and especially royal, action would directly unleash consequences in nature. In the context of Yahwistic faith, however, such consequences can be understood only as God's blessing upon an obedient king. The effect of a good king is comprehensively captured in the image of verses 6–7:

> May he be like rain that falls on the mown grass,
>   like showers that water the earth!
> In his days may righteousness (*sĕdāqâ*) flourish,
>   and peace (*šālôm*) abound, till the moon be no more!

Righteousness (*sĕdāqâ*) and peace (*šālôm*), equated here in poetic parallelism, are the summarizing catchwords for the reign of a good king. More precisely, their relationship should probably be understood here as it is elsewhere, namely, that *sĕdāqâ* is the activity that results in the state of *šālôm*, that is, wholeness, integration, prosperity (Isa. 32:16–17).[16] Such a state represents the fulfillment of the Abrahamic promise:

> May men bless themselves by him,
>   all nations call him blessed!
>   (v. 17b; cf. Gen. 12:3)

It is clear that such a vision transcends by far the possibilities and limits of the Davidic royal line in Jerusalem. Brevard S. Childs states the case succinctly:

> Because David's rule had become a type of God's reign, an adumbration of the eschatological rule of God, mythopoetic [*sic*] language could be applied to the reigning monarch as the emissary of God's righteous rule. When the Hebrew psalmist spoke in such an ideal fashion, he was confessing his hope in God's rule which would be ushered in one day by God's anointed.[17]

Nevertheless, this ideal with cosmic horizons speaks a clear language also concerning those more limited goals that a Jerusalemite king ought to strive to achieve. In brief, it is the creation of *šālôm* through redemption achieved by means of *ṣĕdāqâ*, the latter to be executed through both judicial and military activity.

The King and the Law

On a formal level, this ideal approximates that of some ancient Near Eastern concepts of kingship outside of Israel, especially in Mesopotamia.[18] Thus Hammurabi opens the Prologue to his code with the claim that the gods Anu and Enlil named "me, Hammurabi, the devout, god-fearing prince, to cause justice to prevail in the land" and closes it on the same note: "I established law and justice."[19] Similarly, he begins the Epilogue—a text replete with references to his justice—with the words "The laws of justice, which Hammurabi, the efficient king, set up . . ."[20]

Perry B. Yoder points out three ways in which ancient Near Eastern kings promoted justice: (1) by publishing law collections, (2) by deciding individual cases, and (3) by instituting economic and social reforms.[21] In the Old Testament the case is clearly different insofar as the king is not the source of law. All law has its source in God and is understood as God's covenant will. As such, its ideal custodians are the priests (Deut. 17:18). When the written scripture gained prominence with the discovery of the Book of the Law (Deuteronomy) in the time of Josiah (2 Kings 22; 621 B.C.), the sage or scribe assumed increasing importance, though in many cases that office must have been held by priests as well.[22] Less clear is the king's involvement in the execution of the law. Many interpreters consider him to have held high profile in the administration of legal justice in Israel.[23] On the other side, Hans Jochen Boecker, largely following Georg Christian Macholz, presents a weighty case for a much more restricted role of the king. He argues that the king's judicial authority extended to three groups: (1) the military personnel, (2) the royal court, and (3) the royal city of Jerusalem. It left the local jurisdiction of the village elders essentially untouched.[24] In view of the widespread ancient Near Eastern pattern of royal jurisdiction, the allusions to the execution of justice by the king in certain psalms (e.g., Psalm 72, above) and other texts, and the inclusion of the king and his officials in the prophetic indictments for injustice, Boecker's characterization does seem too restrictive, but it cannot be ignored or readily refuted.

Even if one assumes a somewhat limited functioning of the king in the administration of legal justice, there remains much additional scope for his effectiveness toward its establishment and preservation. First, there is his leadership in the matter of faithfulness to Yahweh, including the nation's subjection to Yahweh's law. Conversely, his influence may sway the nation toward apostasy. In other words, the king is ideally the obedient First Worshiper and Citizen and, on the other hand, potentially the First Apostate. The Deuteronomistic History traces a veritable zigzag pattern of royal modeling in this respect. Second, the king can maintain justice, in a broader sense than that of legal verdicts, through the curbing of violence in the land, that is, through appropriate police action. Third, and by no means unimportant, the king can refrain from exploiting his own position of power toward injustice and oppression. Ahab, in his legal murder of Naboth, offers a counterexample (1 Kings 21). Fourth, the king can develop positive policies, for example, in the area of trade, to further shalom-justice. And fifth, the king's military ventures to subdue his and the people's enemies are largely interpreted as righting the wrongs done to Israel, even if they fell short, historically, of subjecting the earth. Thus, in spite of considerable diversity of function, the Old Testament shares with other ancient Near Eastern cultures, such as Babylon, the centrality of justice in the royal ideal.

Distinctive Israelite Kingship

Justice and Story

We must remind ourselves, however, of the dangers of a reductionist usage of concepts. The recognition of justice as the aim of kingship in both Israel and the ancient Near East establishes a merely formal parallelism. Justice becomes meaningful only as it is filled with content by a story, and that story is not identical for Israel and other ancient nations. The justice of Hammurabi, for example, has been achieved when, among other things, each wrongdoer and each person wronged has received punishment or redress in accordance with his or her social status in the Babylonian class structure. But that very class structure appears as injustice, or absence of shalom, in the egalitarian faith of the people redeemed from Egyptian slavery. This is not to argue that Israelite justice is unique as to its content; on the contrary, it shares much with the Code of Hammurabi, with other ancient legal codes, and with universal human perception of justice. Nevertheless, the partial overlap with other stories does not undo the need to fill the term "justice," when read in the Old Testament, and the ideal of kingship generally, with the content that they receive in the context of Israel's own story.

To safeguard the integrity of the meaning provided by that story, it is particularly helpful to observe where that story defines itself consciously over against alternatives. To do so, we will now turn to certain passages where the nature and the limits of kingship are discussed explicitly.

The Law of the King

Most prominent among these passages is the Deuteronomic law of the king (Deut. 17:14–20). Kingship is introduced here within the tension that marked its whole history. It is the result of popular demand, in imitation of the nations round about (v. 14; cf. 1 Samuel 8). Nevertheless, the king will be one "whom the LORD your God will choose" (v. 15), a statement reflecting the possibility that this holder of an essentially non-Israelite office could also be drawn into God's service. This possibility is endangered, however, by several features characteristic of foreign kingship and also experienced repeatedly in Israel's monarchies. First among these is the undue elevation of the king above his people, issuing inevitably in a class structure. To prevent this, the Deuteronomic law requires the king to be chosen "from among your brethren" (v. 15; cf. v. 20). The danger of developing a chariotry with foreign (Egyptian) help may well lead in the wrong direction, as the model of Solomon demonstrates (1 Kings 10:26–29), and is therefore forbidden (v. 16). An extensive harem and undue royal splendor ("greatly multiply for himself silver and gold," v. 17) are further forbidden dimensions. They remind one of Solomon whose "wives turned away his heart after other gods" (1 Kings 11:4) and whose taxation system contributed greatly to the demise of his kingdom. In a general way, the royal ideal promoted here is the opposite of the picture of the king drawn in Samuel's warning (1 Sam. 8:11–18) and in the indictments brought against Solomon in the Deuteronomistic History (e.g., 1 Kings 11:1–10, 33; 12:4).

The positive features of a distinctive Israelite monarchy are gathered into one criterion, namely, the king's subjection to God. Toward this end he is to make himself "a copy of this law," to meditate on it and to carry out its requirements (vs. 18–19). Von Rad (leaning on Alt) goes too far, however, when he sees in this prescription only the negative aim of restraining the king from any interference with the goals of the Deuteronomic legislation.[25] In modeling the fear of the Lord by subjecting himself to his will, the king as the "First Worshiper and Citizen" could exert a most powerful positive effect, a theme fully exploited in the Deuteronomistic History. At the same time, subjection to the law lends substance to the king's central duty, the ensuring of "justice." We saw that this duty in itself is formally parallel to the Babylonian ideal of kingly duty. But the Israelite king is not to equate it with his own will, either as the chief legislator for the gods, or as divine like a pharaoh. He is to allow Israel's covenant story with its covenant stipulations to inform the discharge of his duties. That will automatically ensure that "his heart may not be lifted up above his brethren" (v. 20); instead, it will assure him position and authority as *primus inter pares* (first among equals).[26]

Davidic Line and Messianic Hope

Although we have discussed the remarkable Israelite ideal of a kingship subordinated to law in its Deuteronomic formulation, this ideal is not limited to that formulation. The Deuteronomistic History adopts it throughout, but elsewhere in Jerusalemite theology it is also not absent. There is widespread belief that God's promise to establish the Davidic dynasty (2 Samuel 7) implied an "unconditional covenant," which was only gradually transformed into a "conditional covenant," mainly under the influence of the "conditional" Mosaic covenant. That seems quite unlikely, however, if for no other reason than the fact that even in the ancient Near East generally very definite responsibilities and expectations accompanied the royal office. If little is said about these in 2 Samuel 7 and certain other passages, it is more likely that the king's duties were taken for granted, rather than that his election was "unconditional." Already in the "last words of David" (2 Sam. 23:1–7), dated early by most interpreters, the accountability of the Davidic king to Yahweh is assumed to form an integral part of the "everlasting covenant" (v. 5):

> The Spirit of the LORD speaks by me,
>   his word is upon my tongue.

The God of Israel has spoken,
　the Rock of Israel has said to me:
When one rules justly over men,
　ruling in the fear of God,
he dawns on them like the morning light,

. . . .
But godless men are all like thorns that are thrown away.

(vs. 2–4a, 6a)[27]

In how far this just rule expected of David was equated with a distinctly Yahwistic understanding of justice, or was informed by more general ancient Near Eastern royal ideology, is a matter for debate. By the time of the composition of Psalm 89, possibly before the exile,[28] the exuberant picture of the Davidic king's everlasting election and universal rule (vs. 25–29) was solidly placed under the requirements of the Torah and its sanctions:

If his [David's/the king's] children forsake my law (*tôrâ*)
　and do not walk according to my ordinances,
if they violate my statutes
　and do not keep my commandments,
then I will punish their transgression with the rod
　and their iniquity with scourges;
but I will not remove from him my steadfast love,
　or be false to my faithfulness.

(vs. 30–33)

Isaiah of Jerusalem, against the background of a failing Davidic dynasty, already proclaimed an eschatological era in which the Torah of Yahweh goes out from Zion (Isa. 2:3) to establish worldwide and lasting justice and peace (2:4).[29] It would be ushered in by a new Davidic ruler who embodies the ideals of kingship under God:

Of the increase of his government and of peace
　there will be no end,
upon the throne of David, and over his kingdom,
　to establish it, and to uphold it
with justice and with righteousness
　from this time forth and for evermore.

(9:7)

153

There shall come forth a shoot from the stump of Jesse,

. . . .

He shall not judge by what his eyes see,
   or decide by what his ears hear;
but with righteousness he shall judge the poor,
   and decide with equity for the meek of the earth.

(11:1, 3b, 4a)

This panorama was taken up and developed by other prophets in the context of announcing the Day of the Lord (Jer. 23:5–6; Ezek. 34:17–31; 37:24–28; Zech. 9:9–10).

Thus the Old Testament's royal paradigm visualizes a king who subjects himself to God, upholds justice, and thereby creates shalom. The content of royal justice is provided by Torah, Israel's narrative and legal tradition whose ethic we have earlier characterized as the familial paradigm. The king upholds it not only by his executive power, but also through his own stature as the representative Israelite or First Worshiper and Citizen. He does not embody Israel, however, as the pharaoh embodied Egypt, but remains one among his brethren, *primus inter pares*. In other words, he helps Israel to live the good life, but he neither determines what that should be nor lives it out in their stead.

In the beginning of this chapter we noted that the royal paradigm focuses on the king and, in a sense, is not an ethical ideal to be lived out by the individual Israelite. Although that is true, we must qualify this limitation now. As representative First Worshiper and Citizen, the king was called to be *the* representative Israelite. Humans as such, however, are also shown to share in the main royal temptation, namely, the wish to be like God (Gen. 3:1–7). In this broad sense, every Israelite—yes, every human—shares in the royal role and faces the challenge to live it according to the royal paradigm.

The Prophetic Paradigm

Introduction

The prophetic paradigm is not fully parallel to the three subsidiary paradigms (priestly, wisdom, royal) discussed so far. Each of these three could be characterized as a distinctive inner image or ideal of the God-willed life. Its distinctiveness was associated in each case with the sphere of activities and values proper to its chief functionaries (priests, sages, king). The people generally were then invited to participate in each of these spheres through seeking holiness, wisdom, or justice, even though not all could become priests, sages (as formal status), or kings. They could live to some extent the holy life modeled and promoted by the priests, and so forth.

It is different in the case of the prophets. There was, at first glance, no sphere of life with characteristic activities and values that was modeled and promoted by the prophets in Israel. Although the representatives of the other subsidiary paradigms could and should invite the people to be holy, wise, or just like they, a prophet could in no way ask others to emulate his or her "prophetic life." It was peculiar to the prophetic calling that it was uniquely addressed to certain persons by God. One could not aspire to it as a way of life or imitate those thus called.

Instead, it was the function of the prophets to exhort the leaders in the other realms—priests, sages, king—to live in keeping with the paradigms they represented in a special way. Beyond that, and especially from Amos on, they included the people as a whole in their challenges to live in true holiness, wisdom, and justice. We will study selected texts again to see the prophets at work in extending these challenges. Because each of these paradigms ultimately served to promote the familial paradigm, however, we will come to see that as the ultimate goal of prophetic preaching also.

As the prophets recalled the various leaders and the people to faithfulness within the different realms or paradigms, the prophets met with growing rejection, opposition, and persecution. They were tempted to the easier way of preaching what was pleasant to the people's ears, rather than the challenging and judging words from God. To remain a true servant of God's word could no longer be taken for granted and thus became a virtue to be sought. Eventually, this striving to be God's true servant became identified with suffering.

In this way, and as a secondary development, a distinctive prophetic paradigm or ethical ideal emerged. At its center stood faithful service to the point of suffering. With time, such suffering came to be seen as the role not only of individually called prophets but also of all those who lived by God's word. Thus the prophetic paradigm became, like the other subsidiary paradigms, a comprehensive ideal of right living for all Israel. We will sample texts—foremost among them

Isaiah 40–55—that demonstrate this new inner image of the God-pleasing life. But, as in the case of the other subsidiary paradigms, we will note how the prophetic paradigm is also not its own end, but one way toward the overarching familial paradigm.

Prophet and King

The Naboth Story Again

The story of Naboth's vineyard (1 Kings 21), introduced in the first chapter, leads straight to the heart of prophetic activity. The shalom of an Israelite household has been undone. The king, instead of offering to Naboth recourse to justice, becomes the agent of oppression. At that point, the prophet Elijah enters the story and hurls God's verdict at Ahab. God sends a prophetic word when life has been violated, when inheritance/land has been alienated, and when hospitality has been replaced by egotistic concern for self.

That the first two conditions prevail in our story is starkly obvious. Naboth has lost his life, and his family its inherited land. Hospitality, a term defined in our study as the unquestioning sharing of life resources with others even at personal risk and for no other reason than need, is less obviously a factor in our story. And yet, is not the absolute claim to property regardless of the rights or needs of others, as displayed by Ahab and Jezebel, the precise antithesis of hospitality as just defined? A deadly calm settles over the scene. A certain peace (shalom) after conflict has been achieved, of which Jeremiah says that it is no peace (Jer. 6:14). Walter Brueggemann has described this state as a "numbness," an "apathy" marked by "the loss of passion, which is the inability to care or suffer."[30] It becomes the "task of prophetic imagination . . . to cut through the numbness."[31] Elijah is God's agent to do just this.

The Turn in the Eighth Century

In the earlier egalitarian society of Israel, the action of Ahab and Jezebel in the ninth century still appears to have been somewhat exceptional, yet a harbinger of things to come. Approximately a hundred years later, by the middle of the eighth century, the exception had become the rule. The inherited land of the fathers' houses had become stock-in-trade for the politically and economically powerful. That the impulse toward the development of a class structure had proceeded from the royal court seems most likely, but the ruthless encroachment on inherited land now proceeded from many angles. Of course, down to the end of the monarchies of Israel and Judah, the king himself remained a potential oppressor. At the same time, the hope stayed alive that a king subject to the word of the Lord would remain a recourse for the oppressed against the variety of exploiters besetting them. By the same token, the king could incur double guilt by engaging in oppressive exploitation himself and by neglecting his duties as guarantor of God's justice. Jeremiah 22:1–5 expresses both dimensions:

> Thus says the LORD [to Jeremiah]: "Go down to the house of the king of Judah, and speak there this word, and say, 'Hear the word of the LORD, O King of Judah, who sit [sic] on the throne of David, you, and your servants, and your people who enter these gates. Thus says the LORD: Do justice and righteousness, and deliver from the hand of the oppressor him who has been robbed. And do no wrong or violence to the alien, the fatherless, and the widow, nor shed innocent blood in this place. For if you will indeed obey this word, then there shall enter the gates of this house kings who sit on the throne of David, riding in chariots and on horses, they, and their servants, and their people. But if you will not heed these words, I swear by myself, says the LORD, that this house shall become a desolation.' "

This prophetic word from the LORD recalls the reigning king toward compliance with the royal paradigm, the hallmark of which is subordination under Yahweh and the establishing of justice and righteousness according to his word. There is still some hope even at this late time[32] that the king and his successors might indeed listen—that a royal line might legitimately continue a kingship compatible with the image of David, whose name is twice invoked. On the other hand, the double temptation of doing injustice and tolerating the injustice committed by various agents is near at hand.

The agents of injustice were many, and their oppressive acts cut to the very heart of existence as defined in Israel's exodus story. That story led from diminished existence in a foreign land to a redeemed life in a land signifying tangibly God's covenant grace. By the eighth century, a concerted commercial onslaught on that gift of grace threatened the reversal of salvation history. The uprooted masses of the people would increasingly lead a diminished existence as an exploited, servile class under the ruthless domination of a class of taskmasters, albeit from among their own people.

The New Class of Leaders

In this new situation, the older pattern of prophetic proclamation, in which the prophet addressed primarily the king, both in promise and judgment, underwent a significant transformation. Because the new oppressors were many, the prophetic addresses reached out beyond the king. Often the legitimate offices of Israel had become self-serving and perverted. Consequently, they became the target of prophetic invective:

> Hear this, you heads of the house of Jacob
>   and rulers of the house of Israel,
> who abhor justice
>   and pervert all equity,
> who build Zion with blood
>   and Jerusalem with wrong.
> Its heads give judgment for a bribe,
>   its priests teach for hire,
>   its prophets divine for money.
>   (Micah 3:9–11a)

The violation of the Israelite family's claim to its inheritance/land stands at the center and is vigorously condemned by Amos, Isaiah, and Micah. This violation of God's gift of grace must inevitably lead to the withdrawal of that very gift:

> Woe to those who are at ease in Zion,
>   and to those who feel secure on the mountain of Samaria,
> the notable men of the first of the nations,
>   to whom the house of Israel come!
> . . . .
> Therefore they shall now be the first of those to go into exile.
>   (Amos 6:1, 7a)

> Woe to those who devise wickedness
>   and work evil upon their beds!
> . . . .
> They covet fields, and seize them;

and houses, and take them away;
they oppress a man and his house,
    a man and his inheritance.
Therefore thus says the LORD:

. . . .

In that day they shall take up a taunt song against you,
    and wail with bitter lamentation,
and say, "We are utterly ruined;
    he changes the portion of my people;
how he removes it from me!
    Among our captors he divides our fields."

(Micah 2:1–4)

In the same century, however, Israel's royal paradigm was con-fronted with yet another challenge. The exodus story had awakened in Israel faith in a God whose desire and ability to deliver the oppressed from a mighty oppressor was borne out by historical experience. God had shown both the will and the power to crush Pharaoh. To such a God, Israel was to commit itself in covenant, and to such a God Israel's king was to subject himself. With the dramatic rise of the Neo-Assyrian Empire under Tiglath-pileser III (745–27 B.C.), the matter of royal subjection to Yahweh posed itself in a new form: Could the king afford to subject himself in total obedience to a God whose ability and/or willingness to deliver was not borne out by historical developments? Did not the Assyrian emperor's success demonstrate that Israel's God would not or could not save his people? Could the kings of Israel and Judah permit themselves to be governed in their policies by a God who allowed the advance of the Assyrian (and later, the Babylonian) avalanche of power unchecked?

The first dramatic encounter between king and prophet on this matter is recorded in Isa. 7:1–9. Assyria is advancing. A flurry of power politics to establish an effective alliance against it has em-broiled Ahaz of Judah in warfare with neighboring Syria and Israel. Isaiah addresses the king with a warning and a challenge: "Take heed, be quiet, do not fear, and do not let your heart be faint . . ." (v. 4). We must hear his call to be quiet, here as elsewhere (e.g., Isa. 30:15), as a call to abandon all attempts to manage history through autonomous exercise of military and diplomatic self-preservation. Von Rad has linked this prophetic approach to the holy wars of earlier times.[33] Just as Israel's original possession of the land was understood as a gift of God, independent of military realities, so the matter of her retention

159

of the land now had to be left totally to Yahweh's decision. Hans Wildberger prefers, instead, to understand Isaiah's message as a consistent application of Davidic theology, within which the continuance of Davidic rule was also granted as a gift.[34] God would uphold the line of David as promised through Nathan (2 Samuel 7). In either case, the king was faced with a decision between autonomous royal politics and subjection to dependence on Yahweh. The tension replicated the one that surrounded the origins of kingship in Israel, where God rejected Saul and approved of David. Ahaz now decided to go the way of autonomous power politics, as did most of the kings of Israel and Judah after him. This way led unavoidably to defeat and exile, for the North in 722 B.C., and for the South in 587 B.C.

Prophet and Priest

The preexilic prophets directed their charges largely at the kings of Israel and Judah and at the abuses related to a monarchy that had departed from Israel's royal paradigm. Kingship, however, was not the exclusive target of prophetic attack. Wherever a group became instrumental in deflecting the people from God's way, a prophet might pronounce divine judgment. Next to the failure of the royal ideal, it was the failure to realize the priestly ideal that became the object of prophetic censure. In the cultic expressions of religion, just as in the royal domain, inheres a hazard to become self-serving. Holiness wants to contain itself within the cultic sphere. It is this self-containment that the prophets targeted repeatedly in the name of the Lord:

> I hate, I despise your feasts,
>> and I take no delight in your solemn assemblies.
> Even though you offer me your burnt offerings and cereal offerings,
>> I will not accept them,
> and the peace offerings of your fatted beasts
>> I will not look upon.
> Take away from me the voice of your songs;
>> to the melody of your harps I will not listen.
> But let justice roll down like waters,
>> and righteousness like an ever-flowing stream.
>
> (Amos 5:21–24)

After a similar judgment on self-contained religious activity (Isa. 1:10–15), Isaiah expands on the content of justice:

> Wash yourselves; make yourselves clean;
>> remove the evil of your doings
>> from before my eyes;
> cease to do evil,
>> learn to do good;
> seek justice,
>> correct oppression;
> defend the fatherless,
>> plead for the widow.
>
> (Isa. 1:16–17)

Because the prophets did not promote an ethic of their own, but were instruments to recall the other offices and realms toward their proper paradigms, they often resorted to forms of speech characteristic of those realms, reshaping these forms for their own purposes. Thus Isaiah, in the verses just quoted, exhorts those practicing self-serving worship to seek true (cultic?) cleansing. Similarly, Isaiah tests, as it were, the would-be holiness-seekers in Zion by means of a gate liturgy such as must have been exchanged between worshipers and priests at the Temple gates[35] (cf. Pss. 15 and 24:3–4):

> The sinners in Zion are afraid;
>> trembling has seized the godless:
> "Who among us can dwell with the devouring fire?
>> Who among us can dwell with everlasting burnings?"
> He who walks righteously and speaks uprightly;
>> who despises the gain of oppressions,
> who shakes his hands, lest they hold a bribe,
>> who stops his ears from hearing of bloodshed,
>> and shuts his eyes from looking upon evil,
> he will dwell on the heights;
>> his place of defense will be the fortresses of rocks;
>> his bread will be given him, his water will be sure.
>
> (Isa. 33:14–16)[36]

Jeremiah's "Temple Sermon" belongs here as well:

The word that came to Jeremiah from the LORD: "Stand in the gate of the LORD's house, and proclaim there this word, and say, Hear the word of the LORD, all you men of Judah who enter these gates to worship the LORD. Thus says the LORD of hosts, the God of Israel, Amend your ways and your doings, and I will let you dwell in this place. Do not trust in these deceptive words: 'This is the temple of the LORD, the temple of the LORD, the temple of the LORD.'

"For if you truly amend your ways and your doings, if you truly execute justice one with another, if you do not oppress the alien, the fatherless or the widow, or shed innocent blood in this place, and if you do not go after other gods to your own hurt, then I will let you dwell in this place, in the land that I gave of old to your fathers for ever." (Jer. 7:1–7)

The prophetic judgments on self-contained cultic activity have often been used to portray prophets and priests as inherent antagonists. Prophets were said to be concerned with ethics and priests with ritual. It appears more appropriate, however, to regard the prophetic condemnation as directed against the intolerable simultaneous practice of cultic activity and social injustice, rather than against the existence of the cult as such. "I [Yahweh] cannot endure iniquity and solemn assembly," says Isaiah (1:13). It is the side-by-side existence of these two, without any apparent sense of incongruity, that evokes Yahweh's ire. In Isa. 33:14–16, the holiness of God, which the worshiper expects to meet in the cultic context, has become unendurable for those guilty of social injustice. In Amos 5:21–24, God has moved out of reach altogether.

Klaus Koch has argued forcefully and convincingly, in the context of interpreting Amos, that the prophets, rather than rejecting the cult as such, had the highest expectations of it. It is precisely the sanctuary—Bethel, in the case of Amos—that constitutes the "center" of the land; "what happens there unleashes fearful billows of disaster over the land."[37] Positively, righteousness and justice (*mišpāṭ* and *ṣĕdāqâ*) from God are mediated through the cult. They proceed as an aura, analogous to a fluid flowing forth, and make righteousness/justice possible throughout the land. They affect human relationships, but extend to the land itself, creating harmony between it and its human inhabitants. During monarchical times, the king becomes their mediator.[38] The effectiveness of this aura can be described as follows:

. In the enthusiasm of the feast, sharers in the ritual experienced the presence of God and recognized one another as brothers. This aroused a sense of the solidarity between all Israelites, a consciousness of community, not only between God and man but between man and nature. It was an awareness that probably cannot be achieved today by even the most careful teaching.[39]

Instead, Amos contends, the sanctuaries pour forth a negative aura, generated by rebellion (*pešaʿt*) against Yahweh as Israel's legitimate overlord. Such an aura of rebellion destroys Israel's chances of living a successful and satisfying life based on the "ontological trinity of god, country and people."[40]

Following Koch's perceptive analysis, I believe that the case of Amos illustrates paradigmatically the role of the preexilic prophets with respect to the priestly-cultic sphere. Instead of rejecting the latter in principle, they had highest expectations of it and attacked it so fiercely precisely for that reason. They envisioned a cultus that would transmit the holiness of God to the people as a life-giving, motivating, and restoring power. For Isaiah (2:2–4), this would eventually become reality and extend beyond Israel to embrace the nations. It would operate in a twofold movement between them and "the mountain of the house of the LORD, Zion. First, "all the nations shall flow to it," and then, conceivably in the sense of Koch's "aura," "out of Zion shall go forth the law (*tôrâ*), and the word (*dābār*) of the LORD from Jerusalem," to effect justice and peace to the ends of the earth.

But the hour was late. Only tentatively and with limited expectations could Amos say:

> Seek god, and not evil,
>> that you may live;
> and so the LORD, the God of hosts, will be with you,
>> as you have said.
> Hate evil, and love good,
>> and establish justice in the gate;
> it may be that the LORD, the God of hosts,
>> will be gracious to the remnant of Joseph.
>
> (Amos 5:14–15)

Thus the prophets maintain a residue of hope, now and then, for the realization of the royal and the priestly paradigms, up to the very end of the Davidic rule (cf. Jer. 22:1–5, quoted above) and of preexilic Temple worship (cf. Jer. 7:1–7, quoted above) in Jerusalem.[41]

Prophet and Sage

The prophetic indictments of departures from the royal and priestly paradigms could not but touch court wisdom. Wise men as an educated class with expertise in politics and law were characteristically attached to the royal court, and probably to the Temple, ever since the days of David and Solomon. Their service to the king covered a broad range of counsel and expertise. To the priestly realm they were indispensible primarily in their function as scribes and as experts in the interpretation of the law.[42]

William McKane has presented a strong case for an inherent antagonism between prophets and wise men, at least in the preexilic era.[43] He bases his thesis on the view that the sages who formed a distinct intellectual elite were inherently secular in their orientation, basing their counsel on pragmatic considerations in utter disregard of Yahwistic faith. He finds unacceptable von Rad's characterization of the wise as functioning within a broader framework of Yahwistic orientation and an awareness of the limits of human wisdom.[44]

In view of the basically theological nature of wisdom in Israel, as discussed earlier, and of the well-recognized incorporation of much wisdom speech and perspective into the prophets' own proclamation,[45] I am persuaded that the prophets did acknowledge a proper Israelite wisdom paradigm within the framework of Yahwistic faith. Their indictments of wisdom must be seen as directed against its deviation from its proper role in Israel, and not as outright rejection of a worldview incompatible with Yahwism. In this respect, their stance toward wisdom and its practitioners was therefore analogous to their stance toward kingship and priesthood as just characterized.

A case in point is the often-quoted verse Jer. 18:18 (cf. Ezek. 7:26):

> Then they said, "Come, let us make plots against Jeremiah, for the law shall not perish from the priest, nor counsel from the wise, nor the word from the prophet."

By inference, Jeremiah has accused each of the three professional groups of failing in its own specific and proper calling. It is clear that Jeremiah does not reject priests and prophets as such, but sees a proper role for them, which they have betrayed. By analogy, we must assume that he also reckons with the existence in Israel of a proper administration of "counsel" (*'ēṣâ*) by professional persons called "wise" (*ḥākān*). It is insufficient to argue, as McKane does, that the prophets, rejecting the secular wisdom movement, generated a reinterpretation of wisdom vocabulary to fit the proclamation of the historical faith of Israel.

McKane has, nevertheless, put the attacks of the prophets on aberrant wisdom into sharp profile. It may be sufficient here to sample one instance of prophetic indictment of wisdom related to government and king, and one of wisdom related to priesthood and law. The first instance comes from Hezekiah's reign, where Isaiah combats forcefully the attempts of the royal court to engineer an alliance with Egypt. In Isa. 19:11–15, the prophet points out how Yahweh can thwart the wisdom of the Egyptian royal counselors to lead the country toward its own judgment purposed by Yahweh. In Isa. 31:1–3 we find a complementary passage indicting the Israelite side of the political scheming with Egypt on the basis of pragmatic political considerations, refusing to consult Yahweh who alone is truly wise.[46] It should not be assumed, however, that Yahweh's use of their own wisdom to confound the Egyptians is an indication that wisdom as such—even Egyptian wisdom—is wrongheaded in principle. In the story of the contest between Ahithophel and Hushai we have an example of how Yahweh can draw even genuine wisdom into his service toward judgment (2 Sam. 16:15–17:14; esp. 17:14). Further, in Isa. 31:1–3 the pragmatism of those who do not "consult the LORD" (v. 1) is contrasted with a recognition of Yahweh as the source of wisdom (v. 2). Isaiah attempts to convert his hearers toward a true wisdom that subordinates itself to Yahweh's sovereignty; in other words, a wisdom that remains conscious of its limits.

An instance of prophetic indictment of wisdom in the service of religion and law, rather than politics, is found in Jer. 8:8–9:

> How can you say, "We are wise,
>   and the law of the LORD is with us"?
> But, behold, the false pen of the scribes
>   has made it into a lie.
> The wise men shall be put to shame,
>   they shall be dismayed and taken;
> lo, they have rejected the word of the LORD,
>   and what wisdom is in them?[47]

The attack on the wise is powerful; but again, as in Jer. 18:18, the wise are associated with priest and prophet (v. 10). We must assume that they, like priest and prophet, are measured by their own proper paradigm and found wanting, rather than that they are rejected here as inherently incompatible with Yahwistic faith.

The Good Life in Prophetic Perspective

In the introduction to this chapter, I indicated that the goal of prophetic preaching is sought in two stages. First, the prophet recalls toward a life in keeping with the other three subsidiary paradigms. But as each of these ultimately promotes the familial paradigm, prophetic preaching must also be seen as ultimately sustaining the familial paradigm. Two sample texts will illustrate this.

Jeremiah's Letter

If we want to hear the prophets' own positive formulations of an ethos for God's people, we can do no better than to listen to their words concerning the future beyond the judgment. This new future begins immediately with the people's life in exile, extends to a restored life in their re-given land, and is projected to its full dimensions in an eschatological future. In these prophecies addressing the future, the royal and the priestly paradigms become increasingly transformed into models transcending ordinary life. They become visions of the Messiah and the holy mountain or the New Jerusalem. As such they become guarantors of a life that is once again described in terms of what we have presented earlier as the center of Old Testament ethics, our "familial paradigm."

The opening verses of Jeremiah's letter to those recently exiled to Babylon illustrate this new beginning:

> Thus says the LORD of hosts, the God of Israel, to all the exiles whom I have sent into exile from Jerusalem to Babylon: Build houses and live in them; plant gardens and eat their produce. Take wives and have sons and daughters; take wives for your sons, and give your daughters in marriage, that they may bear sons and daughters; multiply there, and do not decrease. But seek the welfare of the city where I have sent you into exile, and pray to the LORD on its behalf, for in its welfare you will find your welfare (*šālôm*). (Jer. 29:4–7)

This is an interim ethic for the duration of the exile, but at the same time it recalls Israel in exile from despair or (internal, passive) resistance to a life under promise, moving the people toward fulfillment and blessing.[48] It calls for an understanding of place. Babylon is not the promised land. It might be a no-place for Israel, but it shall be understood by the remnant of the people as its place assigned by God. So designated, it holds the promise and potential of life, even though the exiles were dragged there as a consequence of God's judgment and human cruelty. Life, then, is the new task, and it is life structured in families and extending into the future in the flow of generations. But not even as exiles in a foreign land were the people to capsule themselves off in their struggle for existence. Even captivity has room for others, not only the other, but also the foreigner; in this case, the enemy: "Seek the welfare of the city where I have sent you into exile!" Life, land, and "hospitality," the familial paradigm of the good life, are made possible by God in unlikely circumstances, but this possibility is also to be sought in prayer, from God, for the foreign captors![49] The goal is summarized as shalom (RSV here: welfare), both for the enemy and for self.

The Interim Ethic of Ezekiel 18

Interim ethic, yet lasting in the sense that it is stripped down to basics, can also be found in Ezekiel 18. Just as in Jeremiah's letter, the concern here is the possibility of life in exile. The chapter begins with an apparently widespread popular complaint, expressed in a proverb. In a bitter or cynical tone, it states that earlier generations, through their sins, have effectively robbed the present generation of its land and its future (vs. 1–2; cf. Jer. 31:29). The present generation appears ethically emasculated by past history; it is incapable of ordering its life in ways that count. Not so, says the Lord through his prophet. It still matters ultimately whether one lives in righteousness (*sĕdāqâ*) or in wickedness (*riš'â*), as a righteous person (*saddîq*) or a wicked person (*rāšā'*) (v. 20). One way leads to life, including all that this term had meant for Israel in better times, whereas the other leads to death. But God's will is for life, and to this end God makes a special offer of life based on individual repentance.[50] The solidarity of the chain of generations was intended as a blessing ("Be fruitful and multiply . . ." Gen. 1:28), but had turned into the solidarity of rebellion. The solidarity of Israel as a people was intended as solidarity in blessing (Gen. 12:1–3), but had also turned into solidarity in rebellion. Now God announces the end of that solidarity of the generations, not as they function to continue life and symbolize hope (as in Jer. 29:4–7;

see above), but as they impose a determinism of history. The proverb "The fathers have eaten sour grapes, and the children's teeth are set on edge" (v. 2) shall no more be repeated. Each generation will be able to break out of a deterministic pattern (vs. 5–18). Furthermore, each individual will be able to break out of the sinful patterns of his or her own life (vs. 21–28).

Much has been written about a supposed turn in the Old Testament from corporate to individualistic thinking and ethics in Jeremiah and Ezekiel. It has also been realized that such is not the case.[51] Israel continues to exist. For our purposes it is important to note that it is God's grace that can turn the violent destruction of the structures and symbols of peoplehood into a new freedom for life. The discontinuity of traditions experienced by Judah in exile can become God's means of grace, just as God could turn the city of exile into a new God-given place of life (Jeremiah 29). In other words, apparently individualistic ethics is God's emergency possibility where corporate ethics has failed.

I say "apparently individualistic," for the thrust of this chapter must be interpreted within the vision of Ezekiel for the "house of Israel." This vision not only projects a future for God's purified people, but a future in its re-given holy land.[52] In a comprehensive and important study, Gordon H. Matties has characterized the content of the appeal for repentance in Ezekiel 18 as a "revisioning" of Israel as a people.[53]

The old institutions of control (kingship, priesthood, etc.) have fallen away, but the story, or *tôrâ*, remains. Israel is in a "liminal"[54] situation, on the threshold either of succumbing to meaninglessness or of following the call to form a new community. Such a community would have to be an "interpretive community" made up of individuals voluntarily committing themselves to it. Interpreting the potentially chaotic reality of exile, it would restructure its view of life around the will of God, thus becoming a "community of character" (Hauerwas's term). The laws in Ezekiel 18 function as "lines of demarcation" for this new community of the future. Though priestly in its language and orientation, Ezekiel's vision is deeply rooted in Israel's kinship structure, as even the frequent reference to the "house of Israel" (in the sense of "father's house") indicates. Consequently, the new Israel, in this vision, is a gathering of tribes around Yahweh's holiness.[55]

We proceed now to consider some specific matters of content in Ezekiel 18. In a methodical survey of three generations (cf. Ex. 20:5), the prophet announces the graciously preserved possibility of each person to choose the way of life through significant ethical behavior, in spite of the loss of the institutions intended earlier to safeguard the way of the people under God. The content of the righteous life still open to the Israelite in exile is sampled for us in verses 5–9:

> If a man is righteous and does what is lawful and right—if he does not eat upon the mountains or lift up his eyes to the idols of the house of Israel, does not defile his neighbor's wife or approach a woman in her time of impurity, does not oppress any one, but restores to the debtor his pledge, commits no robbery, gives his bread to the hungry and covers the naked with a garment, does not lend at interest or take any increase, withholds his hand from iniquity, executes true justice between man and man, walks in my statutes, and is careful to observe my ordinances—he is righteous, he shall surely live, says the LORD God.

In contrast to Jeremiah's letter, the formulations here are negative for the most part, showing some analogy to Job's protestations of innocence (Job 29 and 31) and to the gate liturgies (e.g., Pss. 15 and 24:3–4).[56] Like legal collections, such lists are selective, yet not randomly so. Basic is allegiance to the one God, to the exclusion of idol worship. Concern for ritual cleanliness is sampled briefly. But the major enumeration treats various aspects of concern for the oppressed and needy. Finally, there is the inclusive "walks in my statutes, and is careful to observe my ordinances," which makes clear, if that were needed, that the items specifically enumerated earlier are to be read in *pars pro toto* fashion; they merely sample a much greater ethical ideal.

In sum, the prophet presents no new ethic for a new time, nor does he promote a specifically prophetic paradigm; instead, he recalls his people to the familiar concerns of Old Testament ethics. The point to be made is that these concerns are still valid; they have neither been made ineffective by the people's past history of disobedience, nor become impossible to live out due to the collapse of their politico-social and religious supporting structures. It is still the prophet's task to recall his people to the life modeled in its ethical paradigms.

Second Isaiah: Prophet of Hope

The New Exodus

Walter Brueggemann has called this new prophetic thrust, following upon the era of "radical criticism," "prophetic energizing and the emergence of amazement."[57] He points out that prophetic hope has its focus in the "sovereign faithfulness of God. . . . It is that overriding focus which places Israel in a new situation and which reshapes exile, not as an eternal fate but as the place where hope can most amazingly appear."[58] This is precisely what we sampled in Jeremiah 29 and Ezekiel 18. However, with Brueggemann it is Second Isaiah who "serves as the peculiar paradigm for a prophet of hope."[59]

Second Isaiah announces salvation to his people in exile. He acknowledges fully the legitimate function of the exile as God's punishment (Isa. 40:1–2; 43:25–28). In doing so, he affirms retroactively the theology of the preexilic prophets. In his own proclamation, however, the announcement of salvation predominates. It is based both on the fact that Israel has served its term of punishment and on God's free decision to confirm the election of this people and to take the initiative in its salvation. This "new thing(s)" (Isa. 42:9; 43:19; 48:6) that God will bring about is a new exodus, modeled on the earlier exodus from Egypt.[60] The persistent exodus typology alone would lead one to expect a new Sinai as well, that is, a new covenant conclusion confirming the relationship of the saved to God and calling them to a new life, possibly by the proclamation of a new law. Nothing like this is made explicit. The momentum of God's saving acts carries the day. That the exiled and newly redeemed Jacob/Israel is called to be God's obedient people is taken for granted on the strength of the earlier promises and covenants.

The Servant of Yahweh

The response of Israel to her God, who through redeeming her lays claim to her whole life, receives highest profile in Second Isaiah through the prominent title of "servant." A servant is one who responds obediently to the master's will. Prominent men in the past had been designated by this title, like "Moses my servant" (Josh. 1:2) and "my servant David" (e.g., 2 Sam. 3:18). Now the whole people are repeatedly called "Jacob/Israel, my servant" (Isa. 41:8; 44:1; 45:4; 49:3).[61] In this title, the total life response expected by God from his people is comprehended.

A vast literature has treated every aspect of the servant theme in Second Isaiah. In the course of our ethical inquiry we must focus on the content of the service expected. In contrast to the detailed legal definitions of the new life that constitutes the canonical account of God's call to his people at Sinai, very little is said here to explicate this life as servant. There are no new commandments or their equivalent. Occasional references to familiar ethical key terms can be found throughout the book (e.g., justice 42:1–4; torah, 42:21; commandments, 48:18), giving the impression that nothing important has changed with respect to their content and significance.[62]

Instead, the new dimension of the service now required is to proclaim the (known) will and way of God to the nations; not only to proclaim it in words, but to model it:

> Behold my servant, whom I uphold,
>> my chosen, in whom my soul delights;
> I have put my Spirit upon him,
>> he will bring forth justice to the nations.
> . . . .
> I am the LORD, I have called you in righteousness,
>> I have taken you by the hand and kept you;
> I have given you as a covenant to the people,
>> a light to the nations,
>> to open the eyes that are blind,
> to bring out the prisoners from the dungeon,
>> from the prison those who sit in darkness.
>> > > (Isa. 42:1, 6–7; cf. 49:6)
> Listen to me, my people,
>> and give ear to me, my nation;
> for a law (tôrâ) will go forth from me,
>> and my justice (mišpāṭ) for a light to the peoples.
>> > > (Isa. 51:4)

Such a widening of outreach is the first new feature of Israel's service. Or is it really new? The original exodus story did contain the theme of the peoples that observed God's deliverance of Israel, and trembled (e.g., Ex. 15:12–18).[63] Perhaps the new element in Second Isaiah is the fact that the nations are now not only the incidental and terrified witnesses to God's acts; they are deliberately invited to recognize God's salvation of Israel as a light that invites and attracts them as well:

> Behold, you shall call nations that you know not,
>> and nations that knew you not shall run to you.
>> > > (Isa. 55:5a)

All Israel has now become "a prophet to the nations" (Jer. 1:5).[64]

A second new element in the nature of Israel's service emerges as a matter of timing. In the first Exodus narrative, the new life defined by the law took effect only after the rescue from Egypt. In fact, Deuteronomy sees it as being truly in force only after the crossing of the Jordan. The Israel of the new exodus in Second Isaiah, by contrast, begins its servant role while still in exile. This means, in effect, that the shouldering of the deprivations and sufferings of life in exile, in "Egypt," is itself a fulfilling of the servant role, just as the "Suffering Servant" of Isa. 52:13—53:12 begins his service by suffering. Although the good life is usually understood as the doing of justice, the accent has now shifted to the suffering of injustice, whereas the balancing of that injustice is left to God's own justice (e.g., Isa. 42:4; see above).

That leads us to the third and closely related distinction of the new call into service. Whereas the redeemed of the first exodus collaborated with God in establishing themselves in the land by force of arms, the new service does not call for arms. God, in his justice, will work Israel's salvation through the Persian emperor Cyrus (44:28; 45:1–6) and not through his servant Israel. Again we can ask whether this "passive" role is really new. In the exodus narrative we read, "The LORD will fight for you, and you have only to be still" (Ex. 14:14; cf. Isa. 7:4; 30:15f.).[65] And yet, just as in the case of Israel's witness to the nations, something new has come. In the exodus from Egypt, Israel's "stillness" indicated that her efforts were superfluous in view of God's might. Here in Second Isaiah, Israel's meek role, culminating again in the Suffering Servant, is an act of active service through (actively!) shouldering the role of the nonwarrior.[66]

In sum, Second Isaiah does not abrogate the earlier prophetic efforts to align the people with God's will for them, a will most basically comprehended in the familial paradigm. God himself will give his people, threatened as to their very existence, a new life in its own land. Beginning even before that, however, God will use his servant to extend the hospitality of God's salvation to the nations. We see the triad of life, land, and hospitality with a worldwide horizon.

Brevard Childs has shown how the stripping away of any historical introduction and the attachment of Second Isaiah to First Isaiah has effectively eschatologized Second Isaiah.[67] The limited fulfillment that his prophecy experienced in the partial return of the people and the rebuilding of Jerusalem in the late sixth century B.C. does not exhaust this prophecy; it remains a vision for God's further future. Consequently, its ethic of servanthood is also not taken up in its full pathos and grandeur by such postexilic prophets as Haggai, Zechariah, and Malachi. Suffice it to say that they take up, at least in their ethical concerns, the role of the earlier prophets. It would remain for the Suffering Servant of the New Covenant, Jesus Christ, to initiate a fuller realization of this prophecy.

The Prophet as Model Israelite

The Older Prophets

I have tried to characterize the ethical role of the prophets as agents of realigning Israel with the familial paradigm, and eventually of pronouncing God's judgment on the people's irreversible deviation from it. They fulfilled this agency primarily by attempting to realign the "helping agencies" of monarchy and cultus, together with their wise counselors and scribes, toward their own proper paradigms. I emphasized that the prophets did not promote an ethical paradigm of their own. There is no peculiarly right "prophetic life" comparable to a wise or a holy life. And yet, as prophecy became established in Israel, there emerged eventually the image of a true prophet, as compared with the anti-image of a false prophet. In the time of Elijah and Elisha already, we can observe a conscious preoccupation with the person of the prophet. What kind of a person is he, madman or saint? How does one treat him properly? (Cf. 2 Kings 1; 2:23–25). In Deuteronomic theology we have the most explicit theoretical characterization of a true prophet of Yahweh (Deut. 13:1–5; 18:15–22). Moses sets the standard for further prophecy (18:15, 18). Beyond that, the Deuteronomic concerns for the prophet are remarkably similar to those for the king (17:14–20). Like the king, he is to be "from among you, from your brethren" (18:15; cf. 18:18). This implies that Deuteronomy is well aware of prophetic phenomena outside of Israel and of the dangers for Israel from their model and activity. Their claim to authority lay in their special effects and powers (13:1–2), which they might use to lead Israel to worship other gods. The prophet like Moses, on the other hand, was to base his authority solely on Yahweh's word (18:18), which can be authenticated only by the test of history (18:21–22). Like his brethren, from among whom he is called, he is subject to God's command. This command will address him personally and specifically (18:18), and conceivably lead him, and the people through him, in new ways. But it will in no case take the people outside of God's will as revealed at Sinai (13:4); any such attempt would be "rebellion against the LORD your God, who brought you out of the land of Egypt" (13:5). In all this, we sense the strong identification of the prophet with his people.

Jeremiah

It is Jeremiah, as Sheldon Blank has pointed out,[68] in whom this identification of the prophet with his people becomes paradigmatic. It is for this reason that so much of his outer and inner biography has been preserved. The reflection of the people's life in Jeremiah's life is forcefully presented in Jer. 16:1–4, 8–9:

> The word of the LORD came to me: "You shall not take a wife, nor shall you have sons or daughters in this place. For thus says the LORD concerning the sons and daughters who are born in this place, and concerning the mothers who bore them and the fathers who begot them in this land: They shall die of deadly diseases. They shall not be lamented, nor shall they be buried. . . . You shall not go into the house of feasting to sit with them, to eat and drink. For thus says the LORD of hosts, the God of Israel: Behold, I will make to cease from this place, before your eyes and in your days, the voice of mirth and the voice of gladness, the voice of the bridegroom and the voice of the bride."

Blank,[69] as well as von Rad,[70] also draw attention to the total identification of Jeremiah with the destiny of his people in the words that he spoke to Baruch, when the latter was lamenting his miserable situation:

> Thus says the LORD, the God of Israel, to you, O Baruch: You said, "Woe is me! for the LORD has added sorrow to my pain; I am weary with my groaning, and I find no rest." Thus shall you say to him, Thus says the LORD: Behold, what I have built I am breaking down, and what I have planted I am plucking up—that is, the whole land. And do you seek great things for yourself? Seek them not; for, behold, I am bringing evil upon all flesh, says the LORD; but I will give you your life as a prize of war in all places to which you may go. (Jer 45:2–5)

In other words, Jeremiah and Baruch, who is drawn into Jeremiah's hardships, are not to seek exceptional treatment; they are to identify with the coming suffering of their people by shouldering their own burdens as signs of the way awaiting their people.

Jeremiah is neither the first nor the last to portray the destiny of his people in his own person. Hosea before him was called to live out the people's faithlessness and God's persistent love by marrying a harlot and remaining faithful to her in spite of her unfaithfulness (Hosea 1–3). Ezekiel "lived out" the fate of his people in bizarre symbolic actions, as when he lay on his side as a sign of punishment:

> For I assign to you a number of days, three hundred and ninety days, equal to the number of the years of their punishment; so long shall you bear the punishment of the house of Israel. (Ezek. 4:5)

Further examples are found in 4:4—5:12; 12:1–16; 24:15–24. According to Blank, Ezekiel provides the word that is equivalent to "paradigm" as used here, namely, *môpēt* ("sign," "token," "omen," "portent," Ezek. 12:11; 24:24).[71]

The Merging of Prophet and Israel

The focusing of the role and destiny of the people in the model of the true prophet, to the point of identification of the two, finds its fullest expression in the Servant of God in Second Isaiah. I have outlined above how Second Isaiah calls Israel in exile to an ethic marked by a distinctive form of servanthood. The more fully Israel would live as God's servant, the closer it would come to the model upheld in the Suffering Servant of Isa. 52:13—53:12. But who is that Servant? Theories abound, divided generally into "corporate" and "individual" interpretations.[72] The former see the Servant as Israel personified, whereas the latter look for an individual figure, whether historical (Moses, Jeremiah, Jehoiachin, Second Isaiah himself, an unknown sufferer, and others) or predicted for the future. "Fluid" theories have attempted to see continuity between the two.[73]

From the standpoint of our inquiry into paradigms, Blank's interpretation is suggestive and inviting:

> According to what is, in my opinion, the most satisfying interpretation of the "servant" figure, the Servant of God is a personification of the people of Israel, as a prophet after the manner of Jeremiah.[74]

The servant is not a person, but a personification, a figure of speech. Such a view shows a conflation of paradigms. If Israel lives out the ideal of "servant" as given in Second Isaiah, it will demonstrate, to the point of overlap, the features of the model prophet. And in turn, to the extent that a prophetic figure will live out the prophetic paradigm to its fullest, that prophet will at the same time represent the people at its best. To think of this doubly paradigmatic figure in such a way resolves the tension between community and individual. To understand the Servant/Prophet as a personification absolves us from the search for a historical referent. Whether this personification was as directly inspired by Jeremiah as Blank claims, or rather the result of the developing understanding of a prophetic paradigm along the lines suggested by Blank himself, may be left open.

Finally, the book of Jonah completely abandons the form of the prophetic oracle addressed to the people, in favor of portraying the prophetic paradigm.[75] It reports Jonah's attempt to escape his prophetic calling and his reluctance to carry God's word as a light to the nations and accept the fact of its saving power among the foreigners and enemies. Thus Jonah portrays the temptations both of the prophet and of the people to fail to conform to their respective paradigms. Just as in the case of the Servant in Second Isaiah, it is gratuitous to debate, at least from a canonical perspective, whether Jonah is an individual prophetic figure or a personification of the nation, for the two have inextricably become one.

Thus the work of the prophets, originally intended to help Israel and its leaders to remain aligned to their respective paradigms without promoting a paradigm of its own, was itself transformed into a paradigmatic way of life that eventually comprehended the other paradigms within itself. Obedience to God's word and suffering on account of the inevitable opposition to it became central to this prophetic paradigm. It became foundational for the suffering yet vindicated Servant Jesus Christ and the suffering yet redeemed servant community founded by him. Though Jesus Christ also embraced paradigmatically the offices of king, priest, and sage, these were qualitatively transformed by the attributes of the suffering and redeemed servant. He was the lowly king; the self-sacrificing priest; the bringer of a wisdom not of this world. Above all, he was the Son of God, as Israel had been God's son. In that role he was the embodiment of Israel. That these components of the paradigm of Jesus Christ were not abruptly innovative, but deeply rooted in the Old Testament's paradigmatic pattern, will be the topic of our next and final chapter.

Retrospect

In the preceding chapters I have presented a paradigm of human existence under God that highlighted three dimensions:

1. *Life.* Paradigmatic human existence was shown to be existence in community structured along familial lines. Fulfillment in life, to use a modern term, was not achieved individualistically, as for example, through personal adventure or professional achievement. Nor was it corporate in the context of some larger community overriding the familial structures, such as citizenship in a state. It meant, instead, to be embedded in the texture of the generations and to participate harmoniously as a member of a community (and ultimately a humanity) where relationships were understood on the model of genealogy. This was life with a promise of future.

2. *Land.* Life in familial community was seen as existence in a specific place on the map. Every familial unit was to posses land, the means of production and sustenance, living on its "inheritance" as God's guests. This was life with a promise of home and security.

3. *Hospitality.* With this term I described that openness to, and responsibility for, the welfare of others without which familial existence and possession of land would become little more than tribal selfishness. The characterization of interhuman responsibilities as hospitality preserves the integrity of closely knit groups and of private property. It is distinct from "brotherhood of man" or "equality and fraternity," where long-range and significant belonging is replaced by immediate and shallow association. It is also distinct from collective ownership, with its tendency to produce a subtle hierarchy of the advantaged and the disadvantaged. Life as hospitality is life with a promise of new brothers and sisters, parents and children, and of home away from home, beyond one's familial context.

I called the combination of these perspectives the Old Testament's "familial paradigm." I attempted to show how the ethical modeling dimensions of many Old Testament stories and other genres combine to allow this "definition" of the God-willed life to emerge. We saw the origins of many of its component features in general human or ancient Near Eastern experience and lore, but we observed further how this raw material was shaped increasingly by Israel's creation-salvation story. I took special pains to demonstrate that Israel's legal tradition is not a self-contained body of ethical norms, but stands in the service of promoting, ensuring, and safeguarding the life modeled in the familial paradigm. We reminded ourselves, and do so here again, that the terms life, land, and hospitality are to be understood as focal terms or shorthand for perspectives contained in stories and other texts, and should not be made into isolated and self-explanatory principles or concepts. Only a constant re-reading of the texts that inform these terms will safeguard them against acquiring independent meanings deviating from the Old Testament.

Having presented this familial paradigm as the center and goal of the Old Testament's ethos, I proceeded to show that four other Old Testament paradigms, each in its own way encompassing all of life, are nevertheless not competing but supporting models for the familial paradigm. The priestly, sapiential, royal, and prophetic paradigms are distinctive modes of seeking the same God-willed life, not new definitions of it. Stated differently, they are ways toward living ethically, not new contents of such living.

I believe that this paradigmatic structure embraces the canonical Old Testament's ethical message in a comprehensive way. In its several paradigms it gathers up ethical content expressed in a great variety of literary genres. It provides a focus in the familial paradigm that is more proper and adequate than a single principle, such as love, justice, or shalom, can offer. Instead of making individual texts, such as the Decalogue or the social justice oracles of the prophets, central through reductionist selection, it provides a framework within which these, too, can function more adequately as they are integrated into the Old Testament's total ethical thrust.

In briefest summary, we can say that the Old Testament's ethical directive points the way to true, God-intended humanity. To be truly human in this sense is to be holy, to be wise, to be just, and to serve, if necessary to the point of suffering. True humanity both embraces and transcends these distinctive ethical quests.

Notes

1. For the royal office, it may be objected that Adam, and with him every human being, has been granted royal authority over the rest of creation (Gen. 1:28; cf. Ps. 8:5–6). This, however, is metaphoric language to characterize the relationship of humanity to the created world; it cannot

be used to define the individual Israelite politically, socially, or as to ethical responsibility, in relation to the king.

2. For a clear and forthright characterization of the prophetic role, modeled by Moses, of keeping God's people from abandoning their distinctive community of justice to be reenculturated into the dominant "imperial religion," modeled by Pharaoh, see Walter Brueggemann, *The Prophetic Imagination* (Philadelphia: Fortress Press, 1978), 11–27.

3. Brueggemann, *The Prophetic Imagination, 36.*

4. Millard C. Lind, *Yahweh Is a Warrior: The Theology of Warfare in Ancient Israel* (Scottdale, Pa.: Herald Press, 1980), 114–44. Similarly, Norbert Lohfink, "Die davidische Versuchung," in *Kirchenträume: Reden gegen den Trend* (Freiburg: Herder, 1982), 91–111.

5. Frank Moore Cross, *Canaanite Myth and Hebrew Epic: Essays in the History of the Religion of Israel* (Cambridge, Mass.: Harvard University Press, 1973), 237–41.

6. Brueggemann, *The Prophetic Imagination, 31.*

7. Ibid., 37.

8. Whatever the literary prehistory of the text of 1 Samuel 8–12, the attempt of literary-critical scholarship to dissolve this ambiguity by separating two sources with clear perspectives, one pro-monarchical and the other anti-monarchical, has obscured the verdict of the canonical narrative on the origins and character of Israel's early monarchy and, in my opinion, the more likely historical reality. For an inviting alternative, see Baruch Halpern, "The Uneasy Compromise: Israel Between League and Monarchy," in *Traditions in Transformation: Turning Points in Biblical Faith* (Cross Festschrift), ed. Baruch Halpern and Jon D. Levenson (Winona Lake, Ind.: Eisenbrauns, 1981), 59–96.

9. The people gathered at Shechem request of Solomon's son a change from Solomon's style of governing, but they do not question the institution of monarchy as such. The seceding ten Northern tribes immediately enthrone Jeroboam I as their own king.

10. The positive disposition of the Chronicler's History toward kingship and the Davidic dynasty is generally recognized. That the Deuteronomistic History, in spite of its persistent critique of individual kings, is marked by a positive view of kingship has been argued convincingly by Gerald E. Gerbrandt, *Kingship According to the Deuteronomistic History,* SBL Dissertation Series 87 (Atlanta: Scholars Press, 1986). We also remember in this connection that the very prophets who challenged the kings most forcefully projected the new (messianic) age as a purified Davidic rule.

11. Brueggemann, *The Prophetic Imagination, 39.*

12. Ibid., 40. It is well known that the king's association with creation theology and his mandate to maintain justice for the underprivileged show considerable continuity with ancient Near Eastern royal ideologies; see Keith W. Whitelam, *The Just King: Monarchical Judicial Authority in*

Ancient Israel, JSOT Supplement 12 (Sheffield: JSOT Press, 1979), 17–37. At the same time, the subjection of these continuities to the shaping impact of Yahwistic faith, far from being a limited Deuteronomic dream (Deut. 17:14–20) as some think, extends throughout the history of monarchy in Israel and becomes most palpable in the interaction between prophet and king.

13. Besides David, the Deuteronomistic History treats two kings (Hezekiah and Josiah) with full approval and six with partial approval, according to Gerhard von Rad, *Old Testament Theology,* vol. 1: *The Theology of Israel's Historical Traditions,* trans. D. M. G. Stalker (London: SCM Press, 1975), 336.

14. For a discussion of the relationship of justice/righteousness to shalom, see Perry B. Yoder, *Shalom: The Bible's Word for Salvation, Justice and Peace* (Newton, Kans.: Faith & Life Press, 1987), esp. 13–15, 97. On the centrality of justice among the king's duties, see 96–99, and von Rad, *Old Testament Theology,* vol. 1, 322. For a characterization of justice (*mišpāṭ*) and righteousness (*ṣĕdāqâ*), see Klaus Koch, *The Prophets,* vol. 1: *The Assyrian Period,* trans. M. Kohl (Philadelphia: Fortress Press, 1967), 56–62, esp. 59. Although presented in the context of their use by Amos, Koch's profound analysis of these terms has a much wider validity. See also Ahuva Ho, *Sedeq and Sedaqah in the Hebrew Bible,* American University Studies, Series 7, Theology and Religion 78 (New York: Peter Lang, 1991).

15. For a summary of the expectations and hopes placed here in the king regarding the implementation of justice, see also Hans-Joachim Kraus, *Psalms 60–150: A Commentary,* trans. Hilton C. Oswald (Minneapolis: Augsburg Publishing House, 1989), 77.

16. Yoder, *Shalom,* 13–15. For an overview of the semantic range of shalom, see 10–13. For *ṣĕdāqâ,* see our characterization based on Ho, *Sedeq and Sedaqah,* above p. 130.

17. Brevard S. Childs, *Old Testament Theology in a Canonical Context* (Philadelphia: Fortress Press, 1986), 120.

18. Yoder, *Shalom,* 94–96; Whitelam, *The Just King,* 17–37.

19. James B. Pritchard, ed., *Ancient Near Eastern Texts Relating to the Old Testament* (3d ed. with supp.; Princeton: Princeton University Press, 1969), 164f.

20. Ibid., 177.

21. Yoder, *Shalom,* 95f.

22. For a discussion of the differences between Israel and Mesopotamia in this respect, see Roland de Vaux, *Ancient Israel,* vol. 1: *Social Institutions* (New York: McGraw-Hill, 1965), 150f.

23. Thus de Vaux, ibid., 151f. According to de Vaux, the story of Absalom's appeal to the people (2 Sam. 15:1–6) "shows that there was at Jerusalem a king's court, to which every man in Israel could appeal" (p. 152). But

the king was not only the final court of appeal; "recourse could also be made to him in the first instance" (ibid.). An impressive and nuanced picture of the king's judicial authority and practice, ideal and actual, is given in Whitelam, *The Just King*. Although presenting the case for far-reaching judicial authority on the part of the king, Whitelam also dispels the theory that the king acted as the highest court of appeal.

24. Hans Jochen Boecker, *Law and the Administration of Justice in the Old Testament and Ancient East,* trans. J Moiser (Minneapolis: Augsburg Publishing House, 1980), 40–49.

25. Gerhard von Rad, *Deuteronomy, A Commentary,* trans. Dorothea Barton (Philadelphia: Westminster Press, 1966), 119.

26. Dale Patrick, (*Old Testament Law* [Atlanta: John Knox Press, 1985], 120) summarizes: "Submission to the law is the great equalizer, and only by accepting his equality can he [the king] retain his position among his brothers."

27. The conditional nature of the promise accompanying the Davidic dynasty is consistently emphasized in the later parts of the Deuteronomistic History, beginning with David's admonition to Solomon in 1 Kings 2:1–4. For a survey of this theme, see also Gerhard von Rad, "The Deuteronomistic Theology of History in the Books of Kings," in *Studies in Deuteronomy,* trans. D. M. G. Stalker, Studies in Biblical Theology 9 (London: SCM Press, 1953), 74–91.

28. Kraus (*Psalms 60–150,* 203) argues for a preexilic setting of the psalm, possibly at a "royal festival of Zion," although he recognizes that some have placed it into or after the exile. Arnold A. Anderson reviews several positions, extending from pre- to postexilic dating, accepting as "reasonable" that "the Psalm may have been composed *c.* 520 B.C. against the background of the hope that the Davidic kingdom might soon be restored," but assumes that older cultic material was drawn on. See *Psalms 73–150,* New Century Bible Commentary (Grand Rapids: Wm. B. Eerdmans Publishing Co., 1972), 631.

29. For a discussion of the question of authenticity of these verses, see Hans Wildberger, *Isaiah 1–12: A Commentary,* trans. Thomas H. Trapp (Minneapolis: Fortress Press, 1991), 85–87. Similarly, Wildberger reviews the question of authenticity of 9:1–7 and 11:1–9 extensively (pp. 389–93 and 465–69, respectively) and decides in favor of Isaianic authorship in each case. With Wildberger, I accept the Isaianic authorship of these passages.

30. Brueggemann, *The Prophetic Imagination,* 46,

31. Ibid., 49.

32. This passage, a prose parallel to Jer. 21:11–12, has often been assigned to a Deuteronomic redactor, in which case its time and setting would depend on one's assumptions about such redaction. William L. Holladay, however, has argued persuasively for authentic Jeremianic authorship,

assigning the passage to the early reign of Jehoiakim, with the year 601 as the *terminus ad quem;* see *Jeremiah 1: A Commentary on the Book of the Prophet Jeremiah Chapters 1–25,* ed. Paul D. Hanson, Hermeneia (Minneapolis: Fortress Press, 1986), 580–82. He points to a certain amount of optimism on Jeremiah's part in verses 4–5 (p. 582).

33. Gerhard von Rad, *Der Heilige Krieg im alten Israel* (Göttingen: Vandenhoeck & Ruprecht, 1958), 56f.

34. Wildberger, *Isaiah 1–12,* 299.

35. According to Koch (*The Prophets,* 1:116), Isaiah, in 1:10–17 (or 20?), "imitates the priestly *torah* and (ironically?) the divine rejection of the appeal made in the cult." Subsequently, in verse 16f., "Isaiah is evidently thinking of [genuine] cultic ceremonies of expiation" (ibid.). If this interpretation is correct—and I believe it is—then we have here a striking example of how the prophets challenge wrongdoing in other realms by means germane to those paradigms. For similar examples in Amos, see ibid., 51f.

36. For a discussion of the life setting of gate liturgies, especially Psalms 15 and 24, see John T. Willis, "Ethics in a Cultic Setting," in *Essays in Old Testament Ethics: J Philip Hyatt, In Memoriam,* ed. James L. Crenshaw and John T. Willis (New York: KTAV, 1974), 147–63. Willis also points to the function of such gate liturgies in upholding a lofty ethic within the Temple cultus. Isaiah's use of this form in 33:14–16 must be seen as a high tribute to cultic ethics when promoted properly.

37. Koch, *The Prophets,* 54; cf. 1:50–62.

38. Ibid., 60.

39. Ibid.

40. Ibid., 62.

41. The prophetic struggle for a holy people, transformed by the holiness of Yahweh in its midst, continues beyond the fall of Jerusalem, of course, reaching a peak in Ezekiel's vision of the new Jerusalem (Ezekiel 40–48). What has been said, however, may suffice to sketch the main thrust of the prophetic call to implement the priestly paradigm.

42. Jeremiah 8:8–9 probably offers the first indication of wise men assuming responsibility for interpreting "the law (*tôrâ*) of the LORD," traditionally the prerogative of the priests (Jer. 2:8; 18:18). Law scribes assumed an increasingly important role in postexilic times, and according to the Chronicler, "they belonged for the most part to the clerical ranks" (Joseph Blenkinsopp, *Wisdom and Law in the Old Testament: The Ordering of Life in Israel and in Early Judaism* [New York: Oxford University Press, 1983], 10). Ezra was called both a priest of the house of Aaron and a scribe skilled in the law of Moses (Ezra 7:1–6).

43. William McKane, *Prophets and Wise Men,* Studies in Biblical Theology 44 (London: SCM Press, 1965).

44. See our discussion, above, pp. 122f.

45. There has been much controversy about the degree to which wisdom elements and perspectives can be found in the prophetic proclamations (and other Old Testament literature). Amos and Isaiah have virtually been characterized as wisdom spokesmen (see, e.g., Hans Walter Wolff, *Amos the Prophet: The Man and His Background,* trans Foster R. McCurley [Philadelphia: Fortress Press, 1973]; and J. William Whedbee, *Isaiah and Wisdom* [Nashville: Abingdon Press, 1971]). On the other side, James L. Crenshaw (*Old Testament Wisdom: An Introduction* [Atlanta: John Knox Press, 1981], esp. 39–41) has issued a strong caution against distending the definition of wisdom unduly to find wisdom elements outside the wisdom books proper. Appropriate as such a warning may be, I believe that even a cautious analysis of prophetic writings, as illustrated by Johannes Lindblom ("Wisdom in the Old Testament Prophets," in *Wisdom in Israel and in the Ancient Near East* [Rowley Festschrift], Supplements to *Vetus Testamentum* III, ed. M. Noth and D. Winton Thomas [Leiden: E. J. Brill, 1960], 192–204) and Samuel Terrien ("Amos and Wisdom," in *Israel's Prophetic Heritage* [Muilenburg Festschrift], ed. Bernhard W. Anderson and Walter Harrelson [New York: Harper & Brothers, 1962], 108–15) offers solid evidence that the prophets not only combatted the sages but also shared many of their modes of communication and their ideals. For a helpful survey of these issues, see Don F. Morgan, *Wisdom in the Old Testament Traditions* (Atlanta: John Knox Press, 1981), 63–93. Morgan goes so far as to say that the "widespread use of wisdom teaching [by the prophets] may point to the possibility of a common ethic" (ibid., 90f.).

46. These two texts are treated here as complementary only with respect to their indictment of a wisdom—Egyptian or Israelite—that operates autonomously of Yahweh. As to time and setting, Isa. 31:1–3 is generally associated with the events surrounding the year 701 B.C., whereas a wide range of dates has been suggested for chapter 19; see Hans Wildberger, *Jesaja*, Biblischer Kommentar Altes Testament X/1,2 (Neukirchen-Vluyn: Neukirchener Verlag, 1978, 1988), 704–8, 1228–30.

47. The interpretation of this text is extremely difficult. Who are those claiming wisdom? To what does the "law (*tôrâ*) of Yahweh" refer? What subclass of wise is called "scribes" here? For a full and penetrating discussion, see Holladay, *Jeremiah 1,* 281–83. For our purposes it is significant to note, with Holladay, that Jeremiah is not rejecting here the priestly-scribal group as such or the written form of the law (Deuteronomy?), but their false confidence, "engendering a complacent spirit, indeed a lying spirit" (p. 283).

48. Jeremiah's words recall both the blessing of creation (Gen. 1:28) and the Abrahamic blessing (Gen. 12:2–3), now transposed to a land ("city," v. 7, must be read with a distributive meaning, including its surrounding land; thus the Greek text reads "land") where at least the latter might be

considered inapplicable. Further, Adele Berlin has shown the close resemblance of this text to Deut. 20:5–7, where those who had newly bought a house, planted a vineyard, or had become betrothed were exempted from war, probably to enjoy the blessings of the promised land before endangering that enjoyment through exposure to death in battle; see "Jeremiah 29:5–7: A Deuteronomic Allusion," *Hebrew Annual Review* 8 (1984): 3–11. In this light, Jeremiah not only exhorts the exiles to get on with life, but holds out to them the promises of the God-willed life (our familial paradigm) in the midst of exile.

49. John Bright, taking note of self-interest as the motivation appealed to by Jeremiah, nevertheless ponders (with Volz, Rudolph) whether we may not find here "a preparatory step toward that lively concern for the turning of the Gentiles to Yahweh expressed somewhat later by Second Isaiah"; see *Jeremiah: Introduction, Translation, and Notes,* Anchor Bible 21 (Garden City, N.Y.: Doubleday & Co., 1965), 211.

50. Repentance is the aim toward which the disputation speech constituted by chapter 18 eventually leads (v. 30b). In the related text, Ezek. 33:10–33, this is stated at the beginning (vs. 10f.); see Walther Zimmerli, *Ezekiel 1: A Commentary on the Book of the Prophet Ezekiel, Chapters 1–24,* trans. Ronald E. Clements, Hermeneia (Philadelphia: Fortress Press, 1979), 374.

51. This debate is summarized in Gordon H. Matties, *Ezekiel 18 and the Rhetoric of Moral Discourse,* SBL Dissertation Series 126 (Atlanta: Scholars Press, 1990), 115–25. A new understanding of the issue emerges in the course of this dissertation; see our discussion of it, below.

52. See Matties, *Ezekiel 18,* 155, 222; and Elmer A. Martens, *Motivations for the Promise of Israel's Restoration to the Land in Jeremiah and Ezekiel* (Ann Arbor, Mich.: University Microfilms, 1972).

53. Matties, *Ezekiel 18,* e.g., 196. The following paragraph attempts to summarize certain central emphases of this work.

54. "Liminal" is Matties's preferred term for the historical moment of Ezekiel 18; ibid., 147 and passim. He uses this term in a sense roughly equivalent to my "interim ethic."

55. Our contention throughout this book, namely, that the familial model of life serves as the primary ethical paradigm of the Old Testament, finds remarkable support in Matties's study of Ezekiel: "It is clear that family images are the dominant model in the Hebrew Bible for describing the origin and character of Israel" (ibid., 153). "Ezekiel is attempting to reforge that familial identity [which understood Israel's early history as a family history] in the face of the loss of a political identity." (ibid., 155). "Israel is, therefore, primarily the *bêt'āb* over which Yahweh rules" (ibid., 156; cf. 150–57).

56. Zimmerli, *Ezekiel 1,* 376. For a detailed discussion of these legal lists, see Matties, *Ezekiel 18,* 86–111.

57. Brueggemann, *The Prophetic Imagination,* 62.
58. Ibid., 68.
59. Ibid., 70.
60. See Bernhard W. Anderson, "Exodus Typology in Second Isaiah," in *Israel's Prophetic Heritage,* ed. Anderson and Harrelson, 177–95.
61. For a listing and discussion of servant passages beyond the four much discussed so-called "servant songs" (Isa. 42:1–4; 49:1–6; 50:4–9; 52:13—53:12), see Sheldon H. Blank, *Prophetic Faith in Isaiah* (Detroit: Wayne State University Press, 1967), 77–81. For Blank, as for Jewish interpreters generally, the servant throughout Second Isaiah is a personification of Israel (e.g., p. 75), although he grants that the fourth song contains "eschatological overtones" (p. 78). Christians have extended these overtones into more or less explicit messianic predictions pointing to Jesus Christ; for a full and nuanced survey of theories, see Christopher R. North, *The Suffering Servant in Deutero-Isaiah: An Historical and Critical Study* (2d ed.; London: Oxford University Press, 1969). Our interest here is not to assess in how far the servant texts of Second Isaiah may point beyond Israel, but to affirm with Blank and many others that the servant role was indeed the ethical response called for by God's new saving acts, according to Second Isaiah.
62. This agrees with our observations on Ezekiel 18, above.
63. Other texts preparing the way for Israel's prophetic mission to the nations could be cited, such as the "messianic passages" Isa. 2:2–4 (Micah 4:1–3); 9:1–7; 11:1–9.
64. Sheldon Blank (*Prophetic Faith in Isaiah*) has argued extensively that Israel as a whole was called, according to Second Isaiah, to a *prophetic* mission, a mission of bringing God's revelation (*tôrâ*) to the nations: "The Second Isaiah dramatized the prophetic role of Israel in the figure of the servant of God. . . . He equated the 'choice of Israel' with the prophet's call to service" (p. 149). For this prophetic mission, according to Blank, Jeremiah's model had been most significant (pp. 100–104).
65. Millard C. Lind has argued impressively that the Old Testament's holy war tradition has its historical paradigm in Israel's miraculous deliverance at the Sea, captured in Ex. 14:14; see his "Paradigm of Holy War in the Old Testament," *Biblical Research* 16 (1971): 16–31, reprinted in Millard C. Lind, *Monotheism, Power, Justice: Collected Old Testament Essays,* Text-Reader Series No. 3 (Elkhart, Ind.: Institute of Mennonite Studies, 1990), 182–96; cf. also his *Yahweh Is a Warrior,* 47–53. "The passage of Israel through the Reed Sea was the archetype for Israel's passage through the paralyzed sea of nations" (p. 50). This is the soil in which Second Isaiah's call to Israel to be a light to the nations has its roots, although it transcends Israel's impact on the nations in the first exodus, as we just noted.
66. This point has been demonstrated in detailed argumentation by Millard

C. Lind, "Monotheism, Power, and Justice: A Study in Isaiah 40–55," *The Catholic Biblical Quarterly* 46 (1984): 432–46; reprinted in *Monotheism, Power, Justice*, 153–67.

67. Brevard S. Childs, *Introduction to the Old Testament as Scripture* (Philadelphia: Fortress Press, 1979), 325–27.

68. Sheldon H. Blank, "The Prophet as Paradigm," in *Essays in Old Testament Ethics,* ed. Crenshaw and Willis, 111–30.

69. Ibid., 125.

70. Gerhard von Rad, *The Message of the Prophets*, trans. D. M. G. Stalker (London: SCM Press, 1968), 175–78.

71. Blank, "The Prophet as Paradigm," 124.

72. See North, *The Suffering Servant in Deutero-Isaiah.*

73. See H. H. Rowley, "The Servant of the Lord in the Light of Three Decades of Criticism," in his *The Servant of the Lord and Other Essays on the Old Testament* (London: Lutterworth Press, 1952), 33–57.

74. Blank, "The Prophet as Paradigm," 126; cf. also Blank, *Prophetic Faith in Isaiah,* 74–77, 100–104. To accept Blank's statement quoted here does not imply a limitation of the Servant to the historical Israel of Second Isaiah's time. Blank himself grants the possibility of "eschatological overtones" (see above, n. 61).

75. This placement of Jonah is meant typologically; no dating is implied, although a postexilic origin of the canonical book seems likely to me.

THE OLD TESTAMENT PARADIGMS AND THE PARADIGM OF JESUS

Introduction

Jesus is overtly designated, in the New Testament, as priest, sage, king, and prophet, but above all else, as the God-imaging human. If these terms could evoke helpful ethical paradigms in their Old Testament context, it makes sense to think that their application to Jesus may also offer a helpful key to what is ethically paradigmatic in his life and teachings. As in the Old Testament context, so also here, the focus on key terms like *sage* or *king* must not be mistaken for an attempt to isolate self-contained and self-interpreting principles. Once again, the use of key terms represents shorthand for invoking the story contexts in which these terms function and by which they continually need to be filled with content.[1] In what follows, I will develop this assumption briefly, beginning with the four subordinate paradigms in the order in which they were treated in our study of Old Testament ethics. This will issue in a discussion of kingdom ethics in relation to the Old Testament's familial paradigm. It should be remembered, however, that our goal is not to work out a multifaceted Christology, but merely to indicate, with the help of the paradigmatic roles ("offices") of Jesus, which dimensions of his ministry model ethical living for his followers. But first, we need to turn to a few methodological considerations.

Linking the Testaments

A Canonical Approach

The canonical approach takes seriously the full extent of the Christian canon, embracing both Testaments. The procedure of interfacing canonical texts with each other so as to allow them to modify and/or to advance each other's message can therefore not stop with Old Testament texts. Before these can address Christians with the ethical message of scripture, they have to be exposed to the impact of relevant New Testament texts. A full-scale effort in this direction would result in a "biblical ethics." In this volume that cannot be attempted; instead, we will ask in a more modest and sampling way what the nature of the impact of the New Testament on our Old Testament findings might be.

A first question will have to be whether the New Testament does not immediately invalidate our findings for Christians by replacing them with a set of completely different ethical expectations. Is not our extensive preoccupation with life along familial lines, for example, reversed by Jesus when he calls on his followers to hate father and mother (Luke 14:26; cf. Matt. 10:37), or when he says, in view of his waiting family members, "whoever does the will of my Father in heaven is my brother, and sister, and mother" (Matt. 12:46–50)? If such a reversal by Jesus should indeed be found with respect to our Old Testament themes, we would be forced to conclude that the latter, though perhaps of some historical value, cannot claim to address Christians with scriptural authority.

If, on the other hand, we can demonstrate that there is significant continuity between the ethical thrust of the Testaments, there still remains the question as to how much change and transformation might be effected for the Christian by the introduction of the New Testament into the discussion. We allowed Old Testament texts to supplement, balance, and check each other, so that the resultant message was different from, and more than, that of any text alone. The same procedure ought to be followed between Old and New Testament texts, in the full expectation that the Old Testament findings will be modified for the Christian in particular ways and directions. Whether the message of the New Testament should also be subject to such modification through the impact of the Old Testament upon it has been an unresolved question in Christian scripture interpretation.[2] As a working hypothesis I will assume the stance that the balance of authority weighs in favor of the New Testament where the latter speaks to an issue. I will assume further, however, that silence on, or scant treatment of, a prominent Old Testament theme by the New Testament should suggest continuity of position with the latter, rather than rejection of it.

In all this, I have assumed already that the New Testament presents an ethic normative for Christians. This ethic is rooted in the model of Jesus.[3] John Howard Yoder lists six ways in which Christian ethicists have tended to declare Jesus as irrelevant for (social) ethics.[4] The early church, according to their claims, was on its own in working out an ethic, and did so with the help of Jewish and Stoic values. In a similar way, some claim, the church today cannot expect to find its source of ethics in Jesus, but must look for it elsewhere, especially in natural law, vocation and station, or in each individual life situation. Rejecting such views, I will assume with Yoder and others that the New Testament's central ethic is to be seen in the life and teachings of Jesus. With that assumption, and due to the practical need for limitation, we will turn primarily to the Gospels with only scant reference to the remaining New Testament books.

An Ethic of Following Jesus

Just as in the case of the Old Testament, and for reasons spelled out earlier, I immediately reject three options of appropriating the Gospels' (or the New Testament's) ethic:

1. *Casuistry*. It would be conceivable that Christians might do with the Gospels what rabbinic Judaism has done with the Torah, namely, to abstract from them every negative or positive command and establish a body of laws according to Christ, rather than Moses. Christians have never been attracted to this option in theory, but in practice, the proof-texting mentality in certain circles and ages has meant that Christians have looked to individual verses for guidance in such a way as to treat them virtually as case laws.

2. *Central Principle*. The double commandment of love (Mark 12:29–31 and parallels) and the golden rule (Matt. 7:12, par. Luke 6:31) have been highlighted frequently in Protestant circles as comprehensively expressing the ethic of Jesus and as sufficient to guide his followers.

3. *Selected Texts*. In spite of the general tendency in Protestantism

to give all parts of the New Testament canon equal stature, an ethical canon within the canon has often been assumed. For radical groups like the Anabaptists and their descendants, such has been preeminently the Sermon on the Mount (Matthew 5–7). For mainline churches, such a canon has often been imported from the Old Testament in the form of the Decalogue, assumed to have been affirmed by Jesus as the Christian's central ethical guide. But a canon, in the sense of a select body of authoritative texts, can also consist of an eclectic list of passages regularly consulted on certain issues, to the neglect of other texts that also address these issues. Romans 13:1–7, for example, has often been regarded as the most authoritative and self-sufficient text regarding the Christian and the state.

To these three approaches, rejected here for reasons already discussed in the context of the Old Testament, we must add a fourth. Because the rabbinic Judaism with which Jesus stood in dialogue tended to identify ethics with the law (Torah), ethical inquiries have often begun with, or paid special attention to, those passages where Jesus makes explicit statements about the law or takes issue with particular aspects of it. Jesus' saying that he has come not to abolish but to fulfill the law (Matt. 5:17–20; cf. Luke 16:17) and the so-called antitheses in the Sermon on the Mount (e.g., Matt. 5:21–22) exemplify such foci of discussion. I suggest that these represent Jesus' affirmation of the continuity of his ethic with that of the Old Testament but do not define the positive central thrust of his ethic. They are certainly of great importance but are insufficient by themselves to take hold of the ethic of Jesus. However, this approach at least assumes a relationship between the ethic of Jesus and that of the Old Testament.

Instead of these four attempts of appropriating the ethic of Jesus, we will proceed with our Old Testament–generated paradigmatic pattern as a working hypothesis. The concept of paradigm, only rarely and fragmentarily applied to Old Testament ethics, has a long and impressive history of application to Jesus. From the *Imitatio Christi* of Thomas à Kempis (c. 1379–1471), and earlier, many Christians have received their ethical guidance by imitating Jesus. Several words of Jesus explicitly invite or suggest some form of following his example (e.g., Matt. 16:24; John 8:12). *Imitatio Christi* as the ethical way, however, leaves room for various emphases. Is one to stress Jesus' simple, wandering lifestyle, his dialectic encounters with theological opponents, his intimate relationship to the Father in prayer, or what? Generally, *imitatio* has emphasized personal lifestyle, leaving social

190

ethics to be drawn from other sources. Nevertheless, our working hypothesis can draw on a long and deeply rooted tradition of seeing Jesus as paradigmatic.

There is an equally widespread and venerable tradition of tracing the Old Testament offices, especially those of king, priest, and prophet, to Jesus. His office of sage is less frequently acknowledged in the traditional language and theology of the church, though it is given due recognition in more recent scholarly literature. This "office"-language is easily recognizable in the New Testament, of course. However, it has generally been appropriated by the church in the context of theology, rather than of ethics.[5] Thus Christ's kingship has been highlighted in the *Christus victor* motif within the doctrine of atonement. Or again, his priestly office has been identified with the self-sacrifice brought on the cross.

In recent times, however, the centrality of Jesus for social ethics has been portrayed powerfully by John Howard Yoder,[6] Marcus J. Borg,[7] and others. Yoder presents Jesus as consistently living and teaching a way of nonviolence that culminates on the cross. Jesus pursues this course against its major and repeatedly tempting alternatives, the recourse to Zealot-like violence or to Essene-like withdrawal. His is a collision course with the "powers," the God-given but fallen values and structures of society. As modern illustrations he gives, with Hendrikus Berkhof, "[t]he State, politics, class, social struggle, national interest, public opinion, accepted morality, the ideas of decency, of democracy."[8] They are necessary to life and society but have claimed the status of idols and have succeeded in making people serve them as if they were of absolute value.

By treating these powers, though they still are necessary for life, as of less than ultimate authority, Jesus incurred the full brunt of their enmity, which led to his death. But in killing him, the powers expose their own idolatrous nature, for they cannot endure functioning according to their own limited and proper definitions, short of absolute, that is, God-like, authority. In this exposing of themselves as to their idolatrous nature the powers are judged. In effecting this judgment on the powers through his life and death, Jesus, precisely through his nonviolence and suffering, becomes a major sociopolitical threat to the powers. The high priests, the Sanhedrin, the scribes and Pharisees, and Pilate did not mistake Jesus' "quietistic" ministry for a political threat; it was indeed the most powerful threat to the true aspirations of the powers they represented. The superscription on the cross (Matt. 27:37) does not point to a mistaken identity but to the recognition that Jesus could indeed pose a threat to the Roman Empire sufficient to warrant his execution.

Yoder goes on to "state the case for considering Jesus, when thus understood, to be not only relevant but also normative for a contemporary Christian social ethic."[9] Jesus calls his disciples to follow him, so that "to be a disciple is to share in that style of life of which the cross is the culmination."[10] Yoder quickly dismisses an *imitatio Christi* that extends to all kinds of dimensions of Jesus' earthly existence, like his itinerant life, his style of prayer and devotion, and so forth. Jesus, as well as the New Testament writers after him, calls his disciples to imitation in one respect only, says Yoder, namely, the shouldering of the cross. And that again does not include all manner of suffering, but only the suffering that inevitably results when one enters upon Jesus' nonviolent collision course with the powers. "The cross is not a detour or a hurdle on the way to the kingdom, nor is it even the way to the kingdom; it is the kingdom come."[11]

Taking up the cross, however, means much more to Yoder than the actual suffering borne by Christians for Christ's sake. It embraces a life of discipleship patterned on the life and teachings of Jesus. Just as Jesus' life had modeled the kingdom/rule of God in an anticipatory fashion, so the discipleship of his followers is to be a sign of God's incipient rule. But as Jesus' self-giving and nonviolent life led to his death on the cross at the hands of those representing the governing economic, political, and religious power systems, so the communal life of his followers will also inevitably find itself on a collision course with those power systems. Although not every believer will, according to Yoder, personally become a martyr, a life modeled on that of Jesus is, in principle, unacceptable to the power-based structures that still control this world. In this sense, to live a Christlike life becomes synonymous with taking up the cross.

I accept Yoder's claim that New Testament ethics is, at its center, a discipleship that orients itself on the model of Jesus, with the aim of giving to the world a sign anticipating God's intended new creation/kingdom. Although the historical assessment of the basis for Jesus' execution is a complex matter,[12] I am persuaded by Yoder's theological judgment that the cross brings into focus the deep incompatibility of an ethic modeled on Jesus with the self-serving ideologies and power structures that widely control or seek to control our world. To gain a comprehensive and nuanced grasp of the range and content of an ethic modeled on Jesus, it is necessary to explicate in some detail what taking up the cross means in Christian discipleship. What is this new life? What precisely in the life and teachings of Jesus should be seen as paradigmatic for Christian living? Our quest here is not, of course, the quest for the so-called historical Jesus, nor is it the search for the risen cosmic Christ. Paradigmatic for the ethics of those who accept the New Testament as part of the canonical Christian story is the Jesus portrayed in the composite picture emerging from that story. To discern that picture of Jesus, with emphasis on his modeling of the God-willed life, we will rely on the paradigmatic pattern traced in the ethic of the Old Testament.

The Paradigmatic Roles of Jesus

Jesus as Priest

Neither Jesus himself nor his disciples and contemporaries ever called Jesus a priest, according to the Gospels, or characterized his ministry overtly as priestly. That is not surprising. The priesthood in Judaism was hereditary and strictly defined. Although a Galilean of nonpriestly descent might well earn the claim to be a prophet or a teacher/sage, it would have been inconceivable to think of him as fulfilling a priestly role. There is no lack of texts in the New Testament, however, that characterize the ministry of Jesus by means of terms and images derived from the priestly realm. He himself is called holy (e.g., Luke 1:35; 3:22; 4:34; Acts 3:14). R. T. France says, "The principles of mediation and reconciliation with God demonstrated in the Old Testament cult find their antitype and fulfilment in Jesus, the mediator of the new covenant."[13] Usually the active priestly role and the passive role of the sacrifice are combined. Jesus had greater authority than the priests (Matt. 12:5–6).[14] He gave himself for our sins (1 Cor. 15:3; Gal. 1:4). He became our expiatory sacrifice (Rom. 3:21–26). He was an unblemished sacrificial lamb (1 Peter 1:19). He bore our sins in his body (1 Peter 2:24). His blood cleanses us from all sin (1 John 1:7), and he died as an expiation for our sins (1 John 2:2; 4:10).

The most explicit characterization of Jesus in priestly terms is found, of course, in the theology of the Epistle to the Hebrews. There Jesus' mediating role is juxtaposed extensively and typologically to that of the Jewish high priest (4:14—10:18). The author makes a virtue of Jesus' nonpriestly lineage by linking him to the higher priesthood of Melchizedek (5:6; 7:1–17). The accent falls on the new high priest's function as unique heavenly mediator between God and humanity through his atoning self-sacrifice. Such atonement becomes the basis for a life of holiness on the human plane (10:19–31; 12:14–17; 13:1–17), a life oriented toward the holiness of God revealed in Christ (e.g., 12:22–24, 29).

We must remember, in addition, that the priesthood in Israel functioned instrumentally to order the life of a people set apart, a "holy" people, around God's holy presence in its midst. The Old Testament's ethical imagination in this perspective, our priestly paradigm, called for a life zealously ordering all daily activities around God's holy presence. The ethical result would be a new life under God distinguishing and separating the holy people from the world surrounding it.

Does Jesus, according to the New Testament, uphold this ethical vision? To answer yes, one only needs to think of the centrality of his call to a restored relationship to God through repentance in view of the coming kingdom of God (e.g., Mark 1:15); his concern for true purity or holiness; his gathering of a kernel group of twelve disciples in analogy to the twelve tribes of Israel; his institution of baptism as the cleansing entrance ritual to the new covenant community; and his institution of the Lord's Supper as the sacrificial banquet around which that community should gather.[15] Clearly Jesus, according to the Gospels and other New Testament texts, upheld a model of faithful life typologically patterned on the Old Testament's priestly paradigm, to be lived out by a holy people gathered around a holy God present in its midst.

Equally clearly, Jesus did not tie this model to the specific institutions and rituals of the Old Covenant.[16] That he, and for some time his followers, continued to live within those institutions and rituals shows that these had a certain power and capacity to promote the goal sought also by Jesus and the early church. For this reason, the church could afford to slough off the superseded forms in a gradual process, rather than reject them in a radical break as inherently incompatible. As historical antecedents, they continue to clarify for Christians the essential and still valid main lines of the priestly paradigm.

Priestly terminology was extended to characterize the apostolic church. Paul addressed believers as "saints" (Rom. 1:7; 1 Cor. 1:2, etc.) and called them to sanctification and purity (1 Cor. 6:11). Peter designated them as "a royal priesthood, a holy nation" (1 Peter 2:9; cf. Ex. 19:6). The eschatological congregation will be one of "priests to our God" (Rev. 5:10). These and many related expressions, far from leading a spiritualized and shadowy afterlife, point to a tangible new reality. They describe a real people set apart for the service of God, striving zealously to be holy in ways as concrete as those outlined in Leviticus 19. What these ways include specifically will concern us below.

Jesus as Sage

Although theological attention has traditionally concentrated on Jesus' offices as king, priest, and prophet, to the neglect of that of sage, modern scholarship has clearly shown how deeply Jesus was rooted in Israel's wisdom tradition. Marcus J. Borg makes the remarkable claim that "[t]he strongest consensus element of contemporary Jesus scholarship sees Jesus as a teacher of wisdom."[17] Jesus was addressed as "Teacher," gathered disciples, taught in public places, drew on Old Testament wisdom motifs, and appealed to all to follow the narrow way leading to life rather than the broad way ending in death. Much of his teaching was couched in characteristic wisdom forms, including beatitudes, proverbs, and, above all, parables.[18]

Jesus occasionally expounded on matters of law (Torah), for Torah and the wisdom tradition had merged within intertestamental Judaism by the time of Ben Sirach. This merging had the paradoxical result that the priestly concern for holiness through separation from the nations, and the world-open, internationally oriented wisdom concern for the right way drew closer and closer to each other in their common preoccupation with purity. When Borg characterizes this situation as the quest of "traditional wisdom" for "purity/holiness," however, he seems to obscure too much the distinctiveness between the priestly and the sapiential realms that remains palpable. Much of Jesus' teaching content had its source in accumulated communal and personal experience, as had been the case in Old Testament wisdom. It derived its authority from the consent it elicited from its hearers as it found positive resonance in their experience. Would one not wake a friend and expect help when in need (Luke 11:5–10)? Could persistent pleading not move even a hardened human judge (Luke 18:1–8)? Would a shepherd not leave his flock to seek a lost sheep (Matt. 18:12–14, par. Luke 15:3–7)? Of course! said the hearers, laying themselves open to be led further by an application of such shared insights to the ways of God.

Jesus is not only the wisdom teacher "greater than Solomon" (Matt. 12:42; Luke 11:31); he is Wisdom personified. Especially in the Gospel of John, but not only there, the theme of personified Wisdom, present with God at creation and inviting in the first person, is transferred to Jesus.[19] In seeing Jesus both as a teacher of experientially accessible wisdom and as Wisdom dwelling with God and accessible only through gracious revelation, the New Testament takes up a tension present in the Old Testament already. On the one hand, the wisdom literature is marked by the optimistic confidence that communal and personal experience can sufficiently lay hold on God's designs embedded in creation to cope with the tasks of life successfully. On the other hand, the books of Job and Ecclesiastes point up the insufficiency of experiential wisdom to understand God's ways in such ultimate matters as justice, suffering, and death. "But where shall wisdom be found? . . . God understands the way to it" (Job 28:12, 23).

Paul's long discourse on wisdom and foolishness (1 Cor. 1:18—2:16) ought to be read in this light as well. When he rejects the "wisdom of the wise" or the "wisdom of the world" and holds up the "mystery" and "foolishness" of Christ and his cross, Paul not only rebukes a haughty and self-serving class of sages, but declares in true Old Testament tradition that God's ultimate ends for the world can be known only through God's self-revelation. This revelation has been granted to believers in Jesus Christ, God's personified Wisdom. To accept the revelation of his life, teachings, death, and resurrection as revealing God's wisdom for the world supersedes all understanding gained through observation and experience. Far from invalidating the latter, however, "the fourth evangelist [and the rest of the New Testament] saw in Jesus the culmination of a tradition that runs through the Wisdom Literature of the OT."[20] What the ethical content of this culmination of wisdom embraces will concern us below. At this point we note that God's will for humanity was characterized by the writers of the New Testament in terms and perspectives continuous with the Old Testament's quest for a wise life.

Jesus as King

Although Jesus could readily be called "teacher" and acclaimed as a sage, any claim to kingship was fraught with danger from two directions. In the religious realm it immediately constituted a messianic claim, and in the political realm it could only be seen as rebellion against Rome. These two interpretations of any claim to kingship merged, of course, in the popular expectation of a Messiah-king who would overthrow Roman rule to establish his messianic reign.

Amidst these dangers and hopes, however, the claim that Jesus was Messiah and king is made throughout the New Testament. The birth stories and the genealogies in Matthew (1:1–17) and Luke (3:23–38) link him firmly with the kingship of David and contrast him with earthly rulers like Herod (Matt. 2:1–18). Throughout the Synoptic Gospels, the gradual emergence of his Messiah-kingship unfolds from stage to stage. According to Mark, the demons and the sea experience and acknowledge the power of his divine messianic rule first (1:1–8:26; cf. esp. 3:11; 5:7; 4:35–41), followed more reluctantly by the disciples (8:27–10:45; cf. esp. 8:27–30). Both are enjoined by Jesus to preserve this "messianic secret," but it bursts into the open through the public oratory of blind Bartimaeus (10:46–52). It is symbolically acted out by Jesus himself in his royal entry into Jerusalem on Palm Sunday (11:1–10). A clear verbal confession to be the Messiah is elicited by the high priest from Jesus himself (14:61f.). Finally, the Roman soldiers' mocking treatment of Jesus as king, with purple robe and crown of thorns (15:16–20), and Pilate's superscription on the cross, "The King of the Jews," (15:26) unwittingly proclaim what believers know to be the truth: he is Messiah, King, and Lord of Israel and the world.

The terminology respecting Jesus' kingship is ever present and varied throughout the New Testament. Messiah, Son of Man, Son of David, and Lord are the most prominent references to Jesus in his royal role. Central to this role is his exercise of power to subject all antigodly forces and establish signs that herald the beginning kingdom/rule of God.

Every reader of the New Testament knows, however, that the royal theme receives a remarkable transformation in Jesus. He is the king born in a stable and laid in a manger (Luke 2:7). He has "nowhere to lay his head" (Matt. 8:20). He associates with the poor, sick, and needy. He takes on the role of a servant and exhorts his followers to do the same (e.g., Mark 10:42–45 and parallels; John 13:5–17). His royal entry into Jerusalem bears the marks of humility (Matt. 21:1–9). He refuses to use violence, either human or superhuman, to protect himself or to advance his cause (e.g., Matt. 26:50–54; cf. Luke 22:47–53). As a result—humanly speaking—he dies on the cross, in ultimate mockery of his royal claims. This transformation, though distinctly shaped by Jesus, is anticipated by, and deeply rooted in, the prophetic tradition of the Old Testament. This is particularly true of the humility/servant-motif (e.g., Isa. 52:13—53:12; Zech. 9:9) and the eschatological peace-motif (e.g., Isa. 2:2–4; par. Micah 4:1–3; Isa. 9:5f.; 11:9; Zech. 9:10).

Nevertheless, it would be a mistake to consider Jesus' role to be that of an anti-kingship, a rejection of all that is modeled by human kings, as is sometimes done. He is a real king, as shown by his exercise of real power to defeat the antigodly powers and to transform the world. That he does so by way of signs that, although establishing realities in the present world, proclaim the coming eschatological kingdom of God in the future belongs to God's economy of history.

Jesus as Prophet

According to all four Gospels, contemporary popular opinion held Jesus to be a prophet. In his time, that term mainly designated the classical Old Testament prophets on the one hand and the anticipated eschatological figures—especially Moses, Jeremiah, or Elijah returned—on the other.[21] When applied to Jesus, the term "prophet" was, of course, understood primarily in the latter sense, although the image of such an eschatological prophet had been shaped by that of the classical prophets. Whereas Jesus never explicitly referred to himself as a "prophet," he repeatedly claimed that status by implication (e.g., Mark 6:4; par. Matt. 13:57; Luke 4:24; John 4:44; Matt. 23:37–39, par. Luke 13:34–35; Luke 13:33).[22]

The four Evangelists (including Luke-Acts) vary greatly in the emphasis they place on Jesus' prophetic role. With the exception of Mark 12:1–12,[23] neither Mark nor Matthew shows much christological interest in this title.[24] Luke (in Acts) and especially John, show much greater interest in Jesus' prophetic role, including his identity as "the prophet like Moses" predicted in Deut. 18:15–18 (Acts 3:22; 7:37; John 6:14; 7:52; cf. also Matt. 17:3).[25]

Scholars differ with respect to the reasons for considering Jesus a prophet. David E. Aune reviews fifteen reasons offered by C. H. Dodd, discounting some of these and adding some of his own.[26] Although Jesus certainly used some prophetic speech forms,[27] Aune cautions that few of those claimed to be prophetic can be regarded as such with certainty.[28] He notes, further, the surprising absence of the Old Testament's prophetic "messenger formula" ("Thus says the Lord").[29] These observations raise doubts as to whether Jesus' prophetic role should be seen chiefly in the form of his verbal message.

Aune seems more confident in linking Jesus' predictive prophecies to his broader prophetic role.[30] Jesus' visions and miracles certainly deserve mention here, and above all, his undisputedly prophetic symbolic acts. Two outstanding examples of the latter are the Palm Sunday entry into Jerusalem (Mark 11:1–10 and parallels) and the cleansing of the Temple (Mark 11:15–19 and parallels; John 2:13–22).[31] More globally and less specifically, many scholars, and probably even more general readers of the Bible, perceive Jesus' advocacy of righteousness and justice and his sharp critique of the established authorities as his most distinctly prophetic attributes.[32]

In view of this picture, Aune's detailed analysis of the functioning of the Gospel references to Jesus' prophetic role becomes particularly important and enlightening. Aune shows that the characterization of Jesus as a prophet is widely used in the New Testament to point to the necessity of Jesus' persecution, suffering, and death, that is, to the fate characteristically associated with the prophetic role (cf. Neh. 9:26).[33] This theme is present in Mark 12:1–12, the parable of the unfaithful workers in the vineyard who persecute the owner's legitimate emissaries (the prophets) and finally kill his son (Jesus). It is a particularly significant theme in Luke's Christology,[34] introduced prominently in his account of Jesus' visit to the synagogue in Nazareth (Luke 4:16–30). There Jesus predicts the hostility awaiting him as an inevitable consequence of his prophetic role, for "no prophet is acceptable in his own country" (v. 24). His prediction is immediately borne out by the people's violent intentions. The motif that a prophet must suffer is also found in Luke 6:22–23 (par. Matt. 5:11–12); 11:47–48 (par. Matt. 23:29–31); 11:49–51 (par. Matt. 23:34–36); 13:34–35 (par. Matt. 23:37–39; cf. also Acts 7:52). It is not limited to Lukan passages and their parallels in Matthew, however. In addition to Mark 12:1–12, noted earlier, it occurs in Mark 6:4 (par. Matt. 13:57); 1 Thess. 2:15, and Rev. 16:6; 18:24. E. P. Sanders has argued forcefully that it was Jesus' cleansing of the Temple, a distinctly prophetic symbolic act, that led to his death.[35]

To the explicit association of Jesus' prophetic role with suffering and death we must add the New Testament's interpretation of Jesus in light of the Suffering Servant of Isa. 52:13—53:12, the epitome of the Old Testament's prophetic paradigm.[36] C. H. Dodd lists some twenty-five New Testament references and allusions to this text, by far the majority of which are applied to Christ.[37] The extent of the impact of the Suffering Servant on the New Testament's interpretation of Jesus and his suffering has been debated. Once considered the unquestioned model for Jesus' self-understanding of his suffering role, the extent of its impact has been disputed in recent decades.[38] The enormous significance of the Suffering Servant model for understanding Jesus has also retained its defenders, however. R. T. France, having reviewed the relevant references and allusions in detail, finds strong evidence that the interpretation of Jesus in the image of the Servant can be found in several of these.[39] He proceeds to the further conclusion that not only Jesus' specific announcements of his passion (Mark 8:31; 9:31; 10:33–34, and parallels), but also a good number of other statements concerning the inevitability of Jesus' suffering, must have had their source in the Servant image.[40] It is not my purpose to assess the extent of the impact of the Suffering Servant image. There can be little doubt, however, that this impact cannot be separated from the theme just discussed, namely, the inevitability of the suffering awaiting all prophets, including Jesus in his prophetic role.

In sum, the prophet-servant Jesus shows paradigmatically that a life of faithfulness to the prophetic calling will inevitably meet suffering, if not death. That his followers are included on this road of suffering is said or implied repeatedly, perhaps most clearly in the beatitude of Matt. 5:11–12: "Blessed are you when [people] revile you and persecute you. . . . Rejoice, . . . for so [they] persecuted the prophets who were before you." We can now finally turn to the content of the faithful prophetic life, together with that of the holy, wise, and royal life paradigmatically exemplified for his followers by Jesus himself.

The Paradigmatic Roles of Jesus and the Kingdom of God

Most interpreters agree that the center of the message and ministry of Jesus was the spoken and lived proclamation of the kingdom of God. Kingdom language (*basileia, basileō*) immediately appears to associate the content of what Jesus revealed with the royal mode of revealing it, or the royal paradigm. Jesus speaks and acts with royal authority to announce the kingdom, but also to establish it by way of sign events. Upon closer examination, however, it becomes readily evident that the other paradigmatic roles of Jesus also have as their end or target the kingdom of God. Stated briefly, the priestly role of Jesus functions to call those who believe into a priestly kingdom around the holy God as revealed in Jesus Christ. This is demonstrated clearly by the fact that the central symbol for this new community constituted by his sacrificial death, the Lord's Supper, is linked at the same time to the messianic banquet, the symbol of the eschatological kingdom (Mark 14:25 and parallels). As a sage, and also as Wisdom personified, Jesus teaches and exemplifies the narrow way of the kingdom of God as contrasted with the broad way of the world. Thus his teaching parables characteristically invite his listeners to move from what can be verified experientially to an analogous observation about the kingdom. And conversely, his teachings about citizenship in the kingdom, gathered in the Sermon on the Mount, conclude with a parable pointing to the two ways in wisdom fashion (Matt. 7:24–27). Finally, in his prophetic role, Jesus announces and exemplifies that a faithful proclamation of the kingdom leads to suffering and death. Jesus' prophetic announcement, in the synagogue of Nazareth, that the evidence of the incipient kingdom was before his hearers led to a violent response, as befitted a prophet in his hometown (Luke 4:24). And, if E. P. Sanders is right, it was Jesus' prophetic Temple cleansing act, proclaiming the end of the Temple era and the beginning of the kingdom, that was the most direct cause of his death.[41] Thus, the royal paradigm and the others as well have the realization of the kingdom as their end and goal.

Before we turn now to consider the content of Jesus' kingdom proclamation and modeling, it is necessary to emphasize that the four paradigmatic roles of Jesus sketched in this chapter, far from merely constituting methods of bringing the kingdom near, share already in the content of the kingdom. In other words, when Jesus models the new life characteristic of the kingdom through sharing in the priestly, sapiential, royal, and prophetic paradigms delineated in the Old Testament, these modes of modeling become a part of the message, and not only the way to it. The contemporary slogan that the medium is the message proves profoundly true when applied to Jesus. John Howard Yoder is right when he claims that "[t]he cross is not a detour or a hurdle on the way to the Kingdom [or even one of the ways, we might add] . . . ; it is the kingdom come."[42] But the same could be said of Jesus' call to a new holiness, Jesus' teaching and embodiment of wisdom, and Jesus' exercise of divine authority and power. The relationship of Jesus' four paradigmatic roles to the kingdom, seen in this way, parallels the relationship of the four subordinate paradigms of the Old Testament to the focal familial paradigm.

The Kingdom of God and the Familial Paradigm

Continuity of Grace

When we claim that Jesus, in his priestly, sapiential, royal, and prophetic role, proclaims and embodies the kingdom of God as the chief ethical paradigm for his followers, we already assume two things about the kingdom. First, kingdom ethics is continuous rather than discontinuous with Old Testament ethics. We reject the position that kingdom ethics substitutes something radically new for the now invalidated ethics of the Old Testament. This does not mean that the two are identical. It means even less that there is no sharp demarcation between the kingdom and the conventional ways of society; Old Testament ethics itself was already shaped by the gracious and redeeming impact of God's rule on "natural" human ways as represented by ancient Near Eastern custom and law.[43] It insists, however, that the ethics of Jesus must be understood as extending and fulfilling the Old Testament, rather than annulling it.

The second implied assumption in highlighting the kingdom as the New Testament's chief ethical paradigm is that Jesus' proclamation and enactment of the kingdom has indeed an ethical aim and relevance. Its eschatological thrust has often led interpreters to reject the notion of its ethical relevance. Some have argued that the intense expectation of the imminent kingdom left Jesus unconcerned with ongoing earthly life, apart from some tangential admonitions perhaps. Others have perceived a deep-going tension between Jesus' proclamation of the eschatological kingdom and his ethical sayings. Recent studies have shown, however, that the assumed tension between Jesus' eschatological and ethical pronouncements is a misconception; the eschatological outlook of Jesus is precisely what generates his kingdom ethics.[44]

Interpreters widely agree that kingdom living begins with repentance (Mark 1:15). It is not primarily, however, a repentance from wrong action to right action measured by some set of standards. It is not primarily a matter of human effort at all. Words like "unless you turn and become like children, you will never enter the kingdom of heaven" (Matt. 18:3), "unless one is born anew, he cannot see the kingdom of God" (John 3:3), or "whoever loses his life for my sake will find it" (Matt. 16:25) mark the gift character of the kingdom.[45] The openness to receive God's action appears as the major human prerequisite. One could also describe it, with Borg, as a new orientation of the total person toward "cosmic generosity."[46] Surprise at this possibility is involved, according to the parables of the treasure and the precious pearl, although these parables immediately proceed to show the need for human response to the surprising find (Matt. 13:44–46).

Entering the kingdom is linked, further, to the work of the Spirit, both in the life of Jesus and in the lives of his followers (Mark 1:9–15; John 3:1–5). The Spirit, or God at work in power, defeats the resisting powers of Satan. This is grace at work, opening the way into a new life. This new life has its place in a new family, the family of those who follow the invitation of the Householder (God) to be his guests. They are guests now already around his (communion) table, together with all others who care to come, and eventually they will be guests at the eschatological messianic banquet (Luke 14:15–24, par. Matt. 22:1–10).

One major task is incumbent on God's guests, albeit a task with countless variations. The invited must become inviters, the guests must turn into hosts. Hospitality, as characterized in our Old Testament discussion, is the central requirement with respect to the guest's fellow creatures.

This brief sketch of kingdom ethics could, of course, also be summarized as love of God and love of neighbor. To employ our Old Testament typology of life, land, and hospitality, however, offers two advantages. First, it opens our eyes to the continuity of Jesus' chief ethical paradigm, the kingdom, with the Old Testament's chief model, the familial paradigm. Second, it allows for developing the individual aspects of kingdom living, by linking them to acts, parables, and other words of Jesus, with a concreteness that does not usually result from a discussion of "love."[47] We will therefore move on to an interpretation of kingdom ethics in terms of life, land, and hospitality.

Life

Life, in the kingdom paradigm as in the Old Testament's familial paradigm, is not limited to an affirmation of biological existence, though it certainly includes that. It is life in family, structured by genealogy and ultimately embracing all humanity on the analogy of one vast family. "Life" here is shorthand for the tapestry unfolded in the Old Testament story and continued in that story's culminating chapter, the story of Jesus. The latter story is characteristically linked to the story of Israel, and of God's humanity, by two genealogies (Matt. 1:1–17; Luke 3:23–38). It begins with parents and a birth (Matt. 1:18–25; Luke 1–2), just as the story of humanity in Genesis. It issues into a special people around a kernel, the twelve disciples, on the analogy of the seed of Abraham called apart for the benefit of the nations (Gen. 12:3, etc.).

The horizons of "life" in the kingdom context are extended, however, and that primarily in two directions, each crossing a hitherto powerfully perceived boundary. First, although much in the kingdom's manifestation in and through Jesus acknowledges and upholds the physical-biological family structure of life,[48] the boundary of the biological family is broken open to make possible a wider understanding and experience of family; now it embraces all who "do the will of my Father in heaven" (Matt. 12:46–50 and parallels).

It is wrong, however, to see Jesus as annulling the divinely given order of the natural family by substituting the family of faith for it, even though this is frequently done. The natural family both remains basic in a literal sense[49] and also metaphorically defines the faith relationship. Only its tendencies to be self-centered, exclusive, and hostile to others is broken within the kingdom along lines foreshadowed in the story of Israel.

The second boundary crossed by "life" in the kingdom context is the boundary of physical death. This is realized through the continuity of the kingdom present and the eschatological kingdom. The centrality of life as a mark of this continuity of the kingdom is so pronounced that the Gospel of John can virtually replace the essentially Synoptic term "kingdom of God/heaven" with "eternal life" (e.g., John 3:15, 16).[50]

Someone may object that our discourse has left the subject of ethics and become an exposition of salvation. Nothing could be more appropriate than such a blurring of lines. To enter the kingdom and share in its life-giving dynamic means to become an agent of the kingdom, an imitator of its primary agent, Jesus Christ. Those who have been redeemed from demonic powers are called to battle these powers. The prisoners set free will set others free. The blind who regained sight will lead others into new vision. The unclean and outcast received at table will become hosts to others who were unacceptable. The hungry and sick who have been fed and healed will themselves meet the physical needs of others.

Land

Land, inclusive of all possession, may appear to be less obviously a mark of kingdom living. It formed a vital part of ethical living in response to God's grace in the Old Testament. The land was one of the chief gifts of grace to Israel, and its right management constituted a touchstone of Israel's faithfulness. Such a concrete anchoring of the life of faith on the map seems to many Christians to be absent from the New Testament. To worship God neither on Mount Gerizim nor in Jerusalem, but in spirit and in truth (John 4:19–24), seems the guiding statement for many Christians. "In spirit and in truth" is then interpreted as pointing either to the inwardness or the otherworldliness of the kingdom.[51]

Certain passages indeed concentrate so much on the eschatological fulfillment of the Christian's pilgrimage that they seem to negate all significant association of Christian experience with actual locations on the map (e.g., Heb. 11:13–16, 38–40). Nevertheless, we read, "Blessed are the meek [as citizens of the kingdom], for they shall inherit the land/earth" (Matt. 5:5).[52] Those who leave houses and fields for the sake of the gospel/kingdom will receive not only eternal life, but also houses and lands in this life (Mark 10:29 and parallels). I have argued elsewhere for an ongoing significant realism of Christian existence in terms of geography.[53] Gordon Zerbe claims rightly that "humanity's proper habitat in the kingdom, as in creation, is earth."[54] Analogous to the widening of the Old Testament's defined and hereditary priesthood into a priesthood of all believers rather than abolishing it, the New Testament also points to the potential sacredness (divine election for special significance) of all places. "The Land" and the Jerusalem Temple no longer define geographically where believers encounter God's presence and rule in a special way. However, God continues to use specific lands and locations on the map for special purposes, and believers continue to have a certain home right or "inheritance" in God's created world, where they experience realistically the "rest" promised to them by Jesus (Matt. 11:28).[55] They remain at the same time "strangers and exiles" on this earth, seeking the eternal "city which has foundations" (Heb. 11:13, 10), with the promise that their risen Lord has gone ahead to prepare a place for them (John 14:2f.). This presents no contradiction to the earthly realism; it continues the dual aspect of "already/not yet" that marks the theme of God's kingdom throughout.

All of this had to be said before we acknowledge that the Old

Testament's land theme can also be found less literally in the New Testament. Land meant for Israel the physical-emotional foundation for life, that is, means of production and secure home. Many words of Jesus and other New Testament texts affirm the continued significance of "land" in this sense. To pray for the kingdom involves prayer for daily bread (Matt. 6:11).[56] Walter Brueggemann sees all the kingdom antitheses (poor/rich, blind/seeing, prisoners/free, deaf/hearing, dead/raised) as comprehended in the antithesis between "landless" and "landed."[57] He draws attention to the fact that in the New Testament "the single central symbol for the promise of the gospel is land,"[58] (e.g., Heb. 11:13–16), a language that, though sometimes spiritualized, should not be loosened completely from its tangible base. Even the language of crucifixion and resurrection is, in a sense, language of exile and homecoming.[59]

As in our discussion of life, our discourse on land may appear to have moved from ethics to an exposition of salvation. And again, this is proper, for it conveys the continuity of kingdom living from its present and concrete context to its expectation of eschatological fulfillment. The Christian is at home in a sense on this earth, in particular geographical locations, but is also on the way to a waiting eternal homeland and rest. While enjoying the gift of home here and now, the believer is called to tend the land (Gen. 2:15) as God's ecologically responsible image (steward; Gen. 1:27–28). The believer, however, does not limit "land" to its material-economic dimension, as Marxism or certain forms of liberation theology do. Enjoyment and stewardship of God's gift of concrete geographical-material environment become a sign of the transcendent, eschatological dimension of possession, home, and rest.

Hospitality

Hospitality has not figured prominently in the church's traditional theological-ethical vocabulary. For Christians in general, it remains a marginal virtue, although certain monastic orders have given it greater prominence in their efforts to imitate Christ. And yet, Thomas Ogletree can call it the central metaphor for ethical living.[60] We have discussed its centrality and usefulness for Old Testament ethics earlier, in connection with the familial paradigm.

For the New Testament, John Koenig has traced in detail its ubiquity and central function as a theological motif.[61] For our purposes, it is especially "noteworthy that the images of God's kingdom that predominate overwhelmingly in Jesus' teaching are those associated with the production of food and drink or homelike refuge for God's creatures."[62]

Hospitality is, of course, a highly nuanced theme. God, as the source and owner of all good things, is the host par excellence. Jesus, like personified Wisdom in the Old Testament, extends God's invitation and welcome to all: "Come to me, all who labor and are heavy laden, and I will give you rest" (Matt. 11:28; cf. Prov. 9:5f.). In his parables, the kingdom is repeatedly presented as a banquet (Matt. 22:1–14; Luke 14:15–24) or, as in the case of the prodigal son, a homecoming marked by a feast (Luke 15:11–32). In God's kingdom, the hungry shall be satisfied (Luke 6:21).

In his earthly ministry, Jesus exemplified the kingdom's inviting openness to all. It is surely significant that his only miracle reported in all four Gospels is the feeding of the five thousand (Matt. 14:13–21; Mark 6:30–44; Luke 9:10–17; John 6:1–15). The mood of his ministry was festive, earning him sharp criticism from his opponents (Matt. 11:19, par. Luke 7:34; cf. Matt. 9:14–15).[63] Jesus' host-image was so distinctive that the disciples of Emmaus recognized him "in the breaking of the bread" (Luke 24:35). Luke, throughout Luke-Acts, accents especially the celebrative dimension of Jesus' ministry and that of his followers.[64] Jesus' host-role climaxes, of course, in the Last Supper, which in turn is linked explicitly to the eschatological messianic banquet (Matt. 26:20–29; Mark 14:17–25; Luke 22:15–20).[65]

Jesus the host, who extends God's invitation through his words, his ministry, and his disciples, cannot be understood, however, apart from Jesus the guest. As the wandering, homeless prophet, sent, but not accepted by many, he finds refuge with those who are willing to take him in. There is no room for him in the inn of David's hometown (Luke 2:1–7). Although "foxes have holes, and birds of the air have nests," he has nowhere to lay his head (Matt. 8:20; par. Luke 9:58). Loyal women minister to him (Matt. 27:55). To feed the five thousand, he accepts the loaves and the fish given to him (Mark 6:38–41 and parallels). Even the hosting of the Last Supper takes place in a borrowed hall (Mark 14:13–16 and parallels), and eventually Jesus is laid in a borrowed grave (Mark 15:42–46 and parallels). This pilgrim existence is continued by his emissaries and followers, as we see especially in Acts, but also elsewhere (Heb. 11:38–40; 1 Peter 2:11).

In his very homelessness, however, Jesus gathers around him a congregation of those who open themselves to him. Mary and Martha are paradigmatic (Luke 10:38–42), but Joseph of Arimathea belongs here too (Mark 15:42–46 and parallels), and many others. In fact, hospitality to the homeless Jesus becomes the decisive question and the gate into the kingdom.

"Behold, I stand at the door and knock; if any one hears my voice and opens the door, I will come in to him and eat with him, and he with me." (Rev. 3:20)

The parable of the last judgment portrays Christ the King separating the sheep from the goats on the basis of hospitality extended or refused (Matt. 25:31–46).

The two themes of Jesus the host and Jesus the guest do not simply run parallel courses through the New Testament; they belong inseparably to each other through a characteristic inversion. The guest who is offered hospitality turns into the host from whose blessing the hosts-turned-guests can continue to live a new life.[66] This inversion theme is introduced with Abraham already, whose three well-received guests turned out to be divine bringers of promise (Gen. 18:1–10). The writer to the Hebrews sees such an inversion of roles as an ever-present possibility: "Do not neglect to show hospitality to strangers, for thereby some have entertained angels unawares" (Heb. 13:2).

Jesus' parable of the last judgment assumes the same (Matt. 25:37–45). Throughout the earthly ministry of Jesus, we read how those who invite him become guests at God's table, so to speak. Zacchaeus is a prime example (Luke 19:1–10), but nowhere do we see this more clearly than in the raising of Lazarus, Jesus' repeated host who receives his very life at the hands of his guest (John 11:1–44). That the blessing of the host through the guest does not stop with Jesus but continues with his disciples is an ongoing theme in Acts (8:26–40; 10:23–48; 16:13–15; 16:29–34; 17:10–12; 18:7–8; 28:1–10).

Central to the message manifested by Jesus in the form of hospitality offered and accepted is the identity of those he invited and those from whom he accepted hospitality. Here lies both the good news and the offense. On behalf of God, Jesus invited all, the only advantage, if any, being that of greater need; stated in a different metaphor: "Those who are well have no need of a physician, but those who are sick," a word said at a banquet (Mark 2:17; par. Matt. 9:12). Now, a certain indiscriminateness is widely inherent in the customs of human hospitality, including those of the ancient Near East. By the time of Jesus, however, this remnant of divine intention had been heavily overlaid by careful distinctions between the worthy and the unworthy. Social status, religious purity, national origin, wealth and power, and so forth, were well systematized into rules regulating hospitality. When Jesus refused to be restrained by these rules as to whom he invited and visited, he evoked release and joy in some and deep enmity in others.[67]

We could speak at this point about justice for all, and especially for the poor and oppressed. Many ethicists do so, and they are not wrong. I have explained earlier, however, how the theme of hospitality embraces Christian responsibilities to others equally fully, while allowing the accent to fall on grace and avoiding the negative associations of justice-terminology in our language and context. We can now add the observation that the very terminology of hospitality stays closer to the language and symbolism employed by Jesus than the terminology of justice can claim. This choice of hospitality terminology sacrifices none of the earnestness surrounding justice. Hospitality after the manner of Jesus ceases to be a pleasant Sunday afternoon function and becomes a reordering force in society. It becomes also the arena of risk, battle, suffering, and martyrdom. The cross is the extent to which Jesus and God go in behalf of the invited guests.

For the followers of Jesus, the extending of hospitality remains a central way of continuing their Master's mission, of realizing the presence of the kingdom in sign form even now while they themselves are travelers on the way to their final home where the messianic banquet awaits them. The communion table remains the central and constant symbol of this guest-host role. It is also a symbol of sacrifice, of the body and blood of Jesus given on the cross. His followers are not allowed to forget that their guest-host calling is a calling to take up the cross. But beyond it and stronger is the welcoming realm of the Father who has prepared for us a table in the sight of our enemies.

Conclusion

Our last chapter may have created the impression that the ethical paradigm structure of the Old Testament has finally reached its end and purpose in Jesus. Through his fourfold office, he has definitively proclaimed and modeled the God-intended life, the life of the kingdom, as foreshadowed by the Old Testament's ideal of life under God, our familial paradigm. Having served its purpose as scaffolding for the erection of the higher ethic of Jesus—so it may seem—the Old Testament's ethical structure can now be dismantled. Such a reading of our final chapter would entirely mistake the nature of narrative-canonical ethics.

A narrative-canonical approach assumes that the story itself, extending through both Testaments, is the ethic. It makes its impact on those who accept it as canon, in its totality. It shapes those who accept it as their story into characters increasingly conforming to its understanding of the God-intended life. This result could be achieved, and often is, especially in the lives of "simple" Bible-reading Christians—through immersion in the texts of the story, that is, through persistent Bible reading.

In such reading, the last chapter of the story, with Jesus as its main character, will naturally claim a certain finality, as in it the direction and purpose of the earlier chapters are revealed. On the other hand, these earlier chapters become as little superfluous to the story as the early chapters of a novel can be dispensed with once the final stages have been reached. Just so, to use another image, the final years of a person's life will certainly interpret retrospectively much that has gone before, but we would surely not assume that the earlier years of life had value only as preparation for this final stretch. The story line of a novel is one; the life of a person is one; the canonical story of God with humanity must also be read and experienced in its unity.

To ask whether Old Testament ethics can be abandoned once Jesus has manifested its climax is to ask whether salvation from Egypt, from political-economic oppression, is no longer God's will once salvation has been extended, through Jesus, to embrace the defeat of cosmic powers. It is to ask whether land is no longer to be tended responsibly once we know that an eternal home has been prepared for us. It is to ask whether father and mother should no longer be maintained in dignity once we know that we have new fathers and mothers and brothers and sisters from among those who do the will of God. To truncate God's story like this, though frequently done in the church, was certainly not the gospel of Jesus.

Instead, we have tried to discern a structure of paradigms that can be helpful in two ways. First, it can function to recognize and focus the various formally distinct ethical components and concerns embedded in the Old Testament story. Second, it can link those elements with the ethical thrusts of the New Testament story because the same paradigmatic structure is also inherent in that part of the canon. In other words, our attempt has been to help Christians lay a firmer and more comprehensive hold on the ethical components of their canonical story, to the end that this story might become more effective in shaping individual and communal Christian life.

Notes

1. Cf. also George W. Stroup's well-stated warning against isolating Jesus' titles (*The Promise of Narrative Theology: Recovering the Gospel in the Church* [Atlanta: John Knox Press, 1981], 161–64).
2. A listing of the vast literature on this subject cannot be attempted here. A collection of classical essays is available in Claus Westermann, ed., *Essays on Old Testament Hermeneutics,* trans. James Luther Mays (Atlanta: John Knox Press, 1979). An assessment of several options of relating the Testaments to each other in terms of their relative authority is offered by D. L. Baker, *Two Testaments: One Bible* (Downers Grove, Ill.: InterVarsity Press, 1976). My own plea for a fair hearing of the Old Testament, in view of my own denomination's tendency to consider it to have been superseded by the New Testament in all matters, can be found in Waldemar Janzen, "A Canonical Rethinking of Anabaptist-Mennonite New Testament Orientation," in *The Church as Theological Community: Essays in Honour of David Schroeder,* ed. Harry Huebner (Winnipeg: CMBC Publications, 1990), 90–112.
3. The emphasis on an ethic of imitation of Jesus in this section naturally leads us to the Gospel materials. It is not my intention at all, however, to imply a contrast between this ethic and the ethical teaching of Paul. On the contrary, Victor Paul Furnish has shown that imitation of Christ, with special emphasis on his servanthood and suffering, is extremely important in the ethic of Paul, even though certain accents are set differently than in the Gospels; see *Theology and Ethics in Paul* (Nashville: Abingdon Press, 1968), 217–24.
4. John Howard Yoder, *The Politics of Jesus* (Grand Rapids: Wm. B. Eerdmans, 1972), 15–19.
5. John Howard Yoder, *Preface to Theology, Christology and Theological Method* (printed course notes; Elkhart, Ind.: Associated Mennonite Biblical Seminaries Co-op Bookstore, 1981), 167. Yoder himself encourages the use of these "offices" of Christ in the context of ethics, but—as do so many—considers only those of priest, prophet, and king, omitting that of sage. In a more recent publication, however, which Yoder coauthored, all four offices, including that of sage, are employed in structuring an ethic of peace based on the fourfold model of Jesus; see Douglas Gwyn, George Hunsinger, Eugene F. Roop, and John Howard Yoder, *A Declaration on Peace* (Scottdale, Pa.: Herald Press, 1991).

6. Yoder, *The Politics of Jesus.* The following characterization of Jesus by Yoder is based on the general thrust of this work.

7. Marcus J. Borg, *Jesus: A New Vision: Spirit, Culture, and the Life of Discipleship* (San Francisco: Harper & Row, 1987).

8. Yoder, *The Politics of Jesus,* 145, quoting Hendrikus Berkhof, *Christ and the Powers* (Scottdale, Pa.: Herald Press, 1962), 25.

9. Yoder, *The Politics of Jesus,* 25.

10. Ibid., 45.

11. Ibid., 61.

12. For a review of hypotheses on this question, see E. P. Sanders, *Jesus and Judaism* (Philadelphia: Fortress Press, 1985), 23–58. Sanders's own position is that Jesus incurred the wrath of the authorities because he announced prophetically the end of the Temple, in the course of his proclamation of the imminence of the kingdom of God (cf. esp. pp. 71–76). Central in this announcement was the prophetic symbolic act of cleansing the Temple (Mark 11:15–19 and parallels).

13. R. T. France, *Jesus and the Old Testament: His Application of Old Testament Passages to Himself and His Mission* (Grand Rapids: Baker Book House, 1982), 47. See also Frank J. Matera, "Christ, Death of," *Anchor Bible Dictionary,* ed. David Noel Freedman (New York: Doubleday & Co., 1992), 1:923–25.

14. Some consider this passage to be the basis of the high priest typology developed in Hebrews; see France, *Jesus and the Old Testament,* 47.

15. Both the continued emphasis in the New Testament on holiness and its transformation are helpfully discussed in Paul S. Minear, "Holy People, Holy Land, Holy City: The Genesis and Genius of Christian Attitudes," *Interpretation* 37, no. 1 (January 1983): 18–31. In his words: "Holiness thus becomes an essential constituent of the new creation, the new age . . . the dawning kingdom" (p. 23; see scripture references there).

16. Minear points to at least two aspects of holiness in the Christian context: (1) Holiness (and defilement) resides in people, not in things. (2) Both holiness and defilement have their source in the human heart (ibid., 23, 24). See also esp. Mark 7:1–23 and parallels.

17. Marcus J. Borg, "Jesus, Teaching of, C. Jesus as Teacher of 'Wisdom,' " *Anchor Bible Dictionary,* ed. David Noel Freedman (New York: Doubleday & Co., 1992), 3:806.

18. See the exhaustive listing of wisdom sayings in Rudolf Bultmann, *History of the Synoptic Tradition,* trans. John Marsh (rev. ed.; New York: Harper & Row, 1976), 69–108, 166–205, and the more recent discussion by Borg, "Jesus, Teaching of," 806f., and *Jesus: A New Vision,* 97–99.

19. See Raymond E. Brown, *The Gospel According to John,* Anchor Bible, (Garden City, N.Y.: Doubleday & Co., 1966), 1:124.

20. Ibid., 122. Marcus Borg's sharp antithesis ("Jesus, Teaching of," 806f., and *Jesus: A New Vision,* 97–99) between "conventional wisdom," based

on a view of the universe as governed by reward and punishment, and Jesus' subversive "alternative wisdom," based on a universe characterized by "cosmic generosity," is well taken if the former refers to a self-reliant exercise of autonomous human intellect. That this course was a hazard for Old Testament wisdom already is evidenced by Job's three friends. On the other hand, von Rad has shown that a recognition of its limits was an important aspect of the proper exercise of the Old Testament's proverbial wisdom; see Gerhard von Rad, "Limits of Wisdom," in *Wisdom in Israel,* trans. James D. Martin (London: SCM Press, 1972), 97–110. Similarly, Bernard Brandon Scott's attempt to distinguish the innovative, subversive individual wisdom "voice" of the historical Jesus from the communal "voice" of traditional wisdom often superimposed on Jesus' voice by the evangelists seems to me to stretch the innovative dimension of Jesus too far into discontinuity with the Israelite-Jewish tradition. See "Jesus as Sage: An Innovative Voice in Common Wisdom," in *The Sage in Israel and the Ancient Near East,* ed. John G. Gammie and Leo G. Perdue (Winona Lake, Ind.: Eisenbrauns, 1990), 339–415.

21. David E. Aune, *Prophecy in Early Christianity and the Ancient Mediterranean World* (Grand Rapids: Wm. B. Eerdmans Publishing Co., 1983), 153–54. I am indebted to Aune's work for much of the material in this section. Cf. also David Hill, *New Testament Prophecy* (Atlanta: John Knox Press, 1979), 50–58.

22. Aune, *Prophecy,* 156f.; Hill, *New Testament Prophecy,* 57f.

23. A pre-Marcan passage, according to Aune, *Prophecy,* 158.

24. Ibid., 154.

25. Ibid., 154–56. The references to a Moses *redivivus* in the Acts passages are implicit. Because Luke does not depict Jesus in these terms in his Gospel, Aune posits reliance on older traditions in Acts. David Hill (*New Testament Prophecy,* 54) sees considerable attention to the Moses theme in the Gospel of Matthew, too.

26. Aune, *Prophecy,* 160–69, referring to C. H. Dodd, "Jesus as Teacher and Prophet," in *Mysterium Christi,* ed. G. K. A. Bell and Adolf Deissmann (New York: Longmans, Green & Co., 1930), 53–66.

27. Aune, *Prophecy,* 163–69; Bultmann, *History of the Synoptic Tradition,* 108–30.

28. Aune, *Prophecy,* 163–69, 187.

29. Ibid., 171.

30. Ibid., 171–88.

31. For the meaning of this crucial prophetic act, see the discussion in Sanders, *Jesus and Judaism,* 61–71; cf. also Borg, *Jesus: A New Vision,* 173ff.

32. Ibid., 157–61; Borg, "Jesus, Teaching of," 809f.; Gwyn et al., *A Declaration on Peace,* 27–32.

33. Aune, *Prophecy,* 155–59, and further literature there. The motif of the violent fate of the prophets was widespread also in early Judaism (pp. 157, 159); cf. also Hill, *New Testament Prophecy,* 61f.

34. Aune, *Prophecy,* 155, 157, 158f. Some of the relevant Lukan passages (see below) come from Q and thus have parallels in Matthew. However, "Luke not only emphasizes the prophetic status of Jesus as a positive christological title far more than the other evangelists, but he also understands Jesus' prophetic role in terms of the motif of the violent fate of the prophets" (pp. 158f.). Though not part of our canonical investigation, we note parenthetically that Aune (pp. 156f.) considers this perspective to be also the one held by the historical Jesus.

35. Sanders, *Jesus and Judaism,* 61–76.

36. See our discussion of suffering as the central aspect of an emerging prophetic paradigm, above, pp. 172–76.

37. C. H. Dodd, *According to the Scriptures: The Sub-Structure of New Testament Theology* (London: Collins, Fontana Books, 1965), 92–96.

38. For a summary of this discussion, see France, *Jesus and the Old Testament,* 110–13.

39. Ibid., 114–25.

40. Ibid., 125–27. "Yet there is a strong consensus of opinion that the major, if not the only, Old Testament source of these predictions [of Jesus' own suffering] was Isaiah 53" (p. 127).

41. Sanders, *Jesus and Judaism,* 61–76.

42. Yoder, *The Politics of Jesus,* 61.

43. Borg's antithesis between the ethics of Jesus and "conventional wisdom" falls short by not distinguishing sufficiently between the latter and the manifestation of God in pre-Christian Israel; cf. Borg, "Jesus, Teaching of," 808–10; and *Jesus: A New Vision,* 97–124.

44. Bruce Chilton and J. J. H. McDonald, *Jesus and the Ethics of the Kingdom* (Grand Rapids: Wm. B. Eerdmans Publishing Co., 1987); Ben Wiebe, "Messianic Ethics: Response to the Kingdom of God," *Interpretation* 45, no. 1 (January 1991): 29–42. Cf. also Dennis C. Duling, "Kingdom of God, Kingdom of Heaven," in *Anchor Bible Dictionary,* vol. 4, ed. David Noel Freedman (New York: Doubleday & Co., 1992), 63.

45. Chilton and McDonald, *Jesus and the Ethics of the Kingdom,* 80ff.

46. Borg, "Jesus, Teaching of," 808; *Jesus: A New Vision,* 100–103.

47. We assume here that the content of the concept "kingdom of God" could be structured in different ways. To place it under the headings of life, land, and hospitality is not to claim that there is an exegetical necessity to do so. These categories do, however, offer a hold on the many and sometimes elusive texts and genres pertaining to the kingdom that is both comprehensive and deeply rooted in the ethic of the Old Testament. It protects the kingdom of God from being misapprehended through

extrascriptural categories, such as existentialist, purely sociopolitical, or abstractly theological notions.

48. Chilton and McDonald (*Jesus and the Ethics of the Kingdom,* 61f.) emphasize the manifestation of the kingdom's power to bring healing, a clear indication of the inclusion of biological wholeness in Jesus' extension of God's rule.

49. Thus the Gospels present Jesus as affirming the marriage relationship (Matt. 5:27–32; 19:3–9) and expressing concern for parents (Matt. 15:1–9; John 19:25–27). He and his disciples assumed naturally that the gospel would be preached to and treasured within family units (Matt. 10:13; Luke 19:9; John 4:53; Acts 10:2; 11:14; 16:31f.; 18:8; 1 Cor. 16:15; 2 Tim. 1:5; 1:16). Statements of Jesus about "hating" father and mother (e.g., Luke 14:26), and so forth, must be seen as hyperbolic emphases on loyalty to God, in line with his advice to pluck out one's eye or cut off one's hand (Matt. 5:29f.).

50. Duling, "Kingdom of God, Kingdom of Heaven," 60: "For the believer to 'see' or 'enter' the Kingdom of God is to have eternal life."

51. The insignificance of land theology in the New Testament seems to be borne out in the extensive study of the theme by W. D. Davies, *The Gospel and the Land: Early Christianity and Jewish Territorial Doctrine* (Berkeley, Calif.: University of California Press, 1974). Although appreciating many aspects of this work, I have to disagree with Davies's central conclusion; see my article, "Land. B. New Testament," *Anchor Bible Dictionary,* ed. David Noel Freedman (New York: Doubleday & Co., 1992), 4:150–53. For Walter Brueggemann's appreciative but critical response to Davies, see his *The Land: Place as Gift, Promise, and Challenge in Biblical Faith,* Overtures to Biblical Theology 1 (Philadelphia: Fortress Press, 1977), 170ff.

52. Hebrew *'eres.* Whether we translate "land," in keeping with certain Israelite-Jewish expectations of restored Israelite possession of Palestine, or "earth," in view of the universalism of messianic expectations, *'eres* means the surface of this globe and not an inward or otherworldly locus of Christian reality.

53. Waldemar Janzen, "Geography of Faith: A Christian Perspective on the Meaning of Places," *Studies in Religion/Sciences Religieuses* 3, no. 2 (1973): 166–82; reprinted in Janzen, *Still in the Image: Essays in Biblical Theology and Anthropology* (Newton, Kans.: Faith & Life Press, 1982), 137–57.

54. Gordon Zerbe, "The Kingdom of God and Stewardship of Creation," in *The Environment and the Christian: What Does the New Testament Say About the Environment?* ed. Calvin B. DeWitt (Grand Rapids: Baker Book House, 1991), 82.

55. Cf. W. Janzen, "Geography of Faith"; Paul Tournier, *A Place for You* (New York: Harper & Row, 1968). In the Old Testament, an under-

standing of the sacredness of place based on specific experiences of God's presence is anticipated in Ex. 20:24.

56. This petition has also been interpreted as a request for the "bread of tomorrow," meaning the eschatological banquet. In view of the continuity between the kingdom's present and eschatological nature, I hold this to be quite compatible with a literal request for bread.

57. Brueggemann, *The Land,* esp. 172.

58. Ibid., 179.

59. Ibid., 180–83.

60. Thomas W. Ogletree, *Hospitality to the Stranger: Dimensions of Moral Understanding* (Philadelphia: Fortress Press, 1985), 1: "This volume is informed not so much by a single conception of morality as by an over-arching metaphor: to be moral is to be hospitable to the stranger."

61. John Koenig, *New Testament Hospitality: Partnership with Strangers as Promise and Mission,* Overtures to Biblical Theology 17 (Philadelphia: Fortress Press, 1985); cf. also John Koenig's "Hospitality," in *Anchor Bible Dictionary,* ed. David Noel Freedman (New York: Doubleday & Co., 1992), 3:299–301.

62. Koenig, *New Testament Hospitality,* 27, and scripture references there.

63. Koenig discusses the celebrative mood of Jesus' ministry; ibid., 26ff.

64. Koenig, "Hospitality," 301. One is reminded of the emphasis on festive common meals that characterizes the worship of God in Deuteronomy.

65. See also Koenig, *New Testament Hospitality,* 38–42, 117–19.

66. For further discussion of hospitality as partnership, see ibid., 7–10.

67. "Part of the offence [of ignoring strictly drawn religious convention] was the joyous freedom of Jesus' table practice" (Chilton and McDonald, *Jesus and the Ethics of the Kingdom,* 96; cf. also 96–99). Similarly Borg, *Jesus: A New Vision,* 101.

SCRIPTURE INDEX

217

SCRIPTURE INDEX

222

AUTHOR INDEX

AUTHOR INDEX

SUBJECT INDEX

SUBJECT INDEX

canon/canonical, 1, 6n.1, 21n.3, 29–30, 32, 34, 39–40, 47n.5, 4748n.9, 52n.33, 65, 72, 77, 78, 82n.23, 89, 99, 114, 125, 128, 143–44, 146, 170, 176, 179n.8, 186n.75, 190, 210–11, 214n.34; authority of, 3–4, 47n.5, 188–89, 211n.2

Christ. *See* Jesus

Christianity, early, 48n.9, 95, 194

Christology, 187, 198, 199

Chronicler/Chronicler's History, 143, 144, 179n.10, 182n.42

clans, 10, 41, 43, 53n.42, 61, 67, 82n.14, 98, 104n.33, 105n.42, 106, 111, 117. *See also* family *and* tribes

clean and unclean, 63, 88, 107, 113, 121, 161, 204

"Constantinian fall" of the church, 142

covenant, 2, 13, 60, 63, 66, 69, 76, 77, 87, 92, 95, 96, 97, 99, 100, 103n.29, 105n.42, 108, 114, 138, 152, 159, 194. *See also* legal codes/series; Covenant Code

Covenant Code. *See* legal codes/series

Cozbi, 108

criticism: canonical, 3, 4, 47n.9, 81n.7, 144, 188–89, 210, 214n.34; feminist, 51nn.29, 31, 33; form, 30, 91–92, 102n.19; historical/traditio-historical, 3, 30, 49n.17, 102n.19, 103n.23; literary, 30, 81n.7, 103n.23, 179n.8; text, 22n.10

cross, 13, 191–92, 196, 197, 201, 209

crucifixion, 206

cultus. *See* priests and cultus

Cyrus, 146, 172

Daniel, 52n.37

dating (of texts), 39

David, 7, 8, 9, 14–15, 15–17, 20, 22n. 10, 23n.11, 23n.13–24n.16, 24nn.18–19; 35, 39, 44, 45, 49n.18, 50n.26, 120, 131, 141, 142, 144–45, 146, 148, 152–54, 157, 160, 164, 170, 180n.13, 181n.27, 197, 207; adopted son of God, 144; court history of, 139n.63

Davidic kingship/kingship line, 35, 45, 145, 148, 152–54, 160, 163, 179n.10, 181nn.27–28, 197

Davidic/messianic theology, 145, 146, 152–54, 160, 179n.10, 185nn.61, 63;

196–97, 203, 209, 215n.52. *See also* Jesus *and* Messiah *and* New Jerusalem

Day of Atonement, 113

Day of the Lord/Yahweh, 113, 154

death penalty, 37, 57; laws pertaining to, 63

Decalogue, 1, 2, 3, 46n.4, 58, 59, 60, 61, 62, 64, 66, 67, 69, 75, 77–78, 80, 81n.7, 82nn.21, 23; 85n.68, 87–105, 106, 108, 111, 112, 114, 128, 133n.11, 136n.38, 178, 190; addresses, 97, 104n.33–37; and comprehensive coverage, 89–92, 95; and familial paradigm, 96–99; centrality of, 90–92, 99–100; content of, 92–96; eighth commandment (stealing), 98, 99; first commandment, 69, 83n.40, 89, 100n.4; fourth commandment, 97–98; God-directed commands of, 90; motive clauses in, 91, 97, 99, 104n.38–105n.39, 114; neighbor-directed commands of, 90, 104n.33; ninth commandment (witness), 98–99; parents commandment, 60, 67, 90, 91, 98, 102n.20, 105n.39; Sabbath commandment, 91, 93, 97, 102n.20, 106; sampling content of, 89, 92, 95; second commandment, 89, 97, seventh commandment (adultery), 98, 103n.27; sixth commandment (killing), 98, 103n.28; tenth commandment (neighbor's property), 99, 104n.35

Deuteronomic Code. *See* legal codes/series

Deuteronomic theology, 113, 133n.11, 173, 180n.12, 181n.32

Deuteronomistic History/Historian/ School, 24n.22, 51n.28, 71, 132n.5, 141, 143, 144, 145, 146, 150, 151, 152, 179n.10, 180n.13, 181n.27

Egypt/Egyptians, 18, 33, 35, 37, 38, 39, 45, 48n.14, 57, 60, 61, 65, 67, 68, 70, 81n.12, 83n.38, 109, 110, 112, 114, 115, 116, 117, 125–26, 129, 143, 150, 151, 154, 165, 170, 172, 174, 210

Eleazar, 13

Elijah, 19, 20, 25n.25, 156, 173, 198

Elimelech, 33–34, 38, 40, 41, 42, 44

Elisha, 173

Elohim. *See* God/Yahweh; as Elohim

Emmaus, 207

229

SUBJECT INDEX

Peor, 12; Baal of, 12

Persia, 172

Peter, 194

Pharaoh(s), 7, 9, 70, 124, 145, 152, 154, 159, 179n.2

Pharisees, 191

Philistines, 24n.16

Philo, 22n.8

philosophy, Greek, 123

Phinehas, 2, 12–14, 20, 21n.6, 22n.7–8, 26, 107–08, 109, 118

Pilate, 191

Priestly Code. *See* legal codes/series

priestly paradigm, 3, 12–14, 19, 75, 76, 78, 86n.70, 88, 92–93, 100n.1, 106–18, 121, 131, 132n.1–135n.25, 140, 141, 154, 163, 164, 166, 178, 182n.41, 194, 201

Priestly (P) source, 21n.6, 48n.13

Priestly theology and writing style, 113, 134n.22

priests and cultus, 12–14, 17, 22n.7, 82n.14, 106–18, 120–21, 133n.9–10, 135n.25, 140, 149, 155, 158, 164, 165, 168, 181n.28, 182nn.35, 42; 183n.47, 205; and Jesus, 176, 187, 191, 193–95, 200, 202, 211n.5; and prophecy, 160–63, 173; gate liturgies, 161–62, 182n.36; high priests, 191, 193, 197, 212n.14; resemblance to magic, 133–34n.15. *See also* legal codes / series; Priestly Code *and* Levites *and* Levitical preaching

promised land. *See* Canaan

prophetic literature, 62, 101n.12, 183n.45

prophetic paradigm, 3, 12, 17–19, 75, 78, 86n.70, 88, 121, 154–176, 181n.30–186n.75, 178, 199, 201

prophets/prophecy, 1, 17–19, 20, 24n.20, 27, 41, 52n.36, 65–66, 76, 78, 82n.14, 101n.12, 122, 131, 135n.25, 140, 143, 144, 149, 154–176, 179n.2, 185n.64, 193, 197, 198, 199, 200, 214n.33; and holiness, 160–63; and Jesus, 173, 176, 187, 195, 198–200, 201, 202, 211n.5, 212n.12, 213n.31, 214n.34; and king-ship, 156–60, 179n.10; and priests, 160–63, 182n.41; and suffering, 155, 199–200, 201, 214nn.36, 40; and the good life, 166–69; and wisdom, 164–65, 183n.45; authority of, 76, 173; false,

173; judgment speeches, 25n.24; non-Israelite, 173; of hope, 169–73; oracles, 24n.16, 25n.25–26, 79, 176, 178; pre-exilic, 170; "prophetic counterculture," 141; relationship to Israel, 173–76; temptations of, 176

Protestantism, 189–90

proverb (genre), 65, 72, 78, 79, 100n.1, 120, 123, 125, 126, 130, 167, 168, 195

psalmody, 144

Psalter, 144

Quelle (Q) source, 214n.34

rabbinic scholarship, 22n.8, 46n.4, 58–59, 72, 189, 190

Rachel, 35, 39, 45, 50n.26

rape, 127

Re, 33

reason, 71, 80n.6

Rechabites, 143

redemption, 39

reductionism, 20, 29–30, 46n.5, 55–56, 63, 85n.64, 150, 178, 189

Reed Sea, 185n.65

resurrection, 196, 206

Roman Empire, 192, 196–97

Romanticism, 91–92

royal paradigm, 3, 12, 15–17, 18–19, 33, 75, 76, 78, 86n.70, 88, 100n.1, 121, 129–30, 136n.41, 140–54, 157, 160, 163, 164, 166, 178n.1–181n.29, 178, 200, 201

Ruth, 7, 33–35, 38, 39, 40, 41, 43, 44, 45, 49n.18, 50nn.20, 22, 26; 52nn.33, 35; 55–56

Sabbath, 58, 90, 91, 95, 97–98, 104n.33, 104n.35, 106, 113, 116, 117, 128, 132n.2; and creation, 132n.2

sabbath years, 113, 116

Samaria, 158

Samuel, 24nn.16, 22; 142, 143, 151

sanctuaries, Israelite, 2, 13, 88, 98, 106, 111, 162, 163; accessibility of God in, 133n.14; contamination/violation of, 21n.5–6, 108. *See also* tabernacle/tent

Sanhedrin, 191

sapiential paradigm. *See* wisdom paradigm

Sarah, 7, 32

234

SUBJECT INDEX